Between
Lives

Between Lives

An Artist and Her World

❧

DOROTHEA TANNING

W. W. Norton & Company   New York • London

For information about permission to reproduce selections from this book, write to
Permissions, W. W. Norton & Company, Inc.,
500 Fifth Avenue, New York, NY 10110

The text of this book is composed in New Baskerville,
with the display set in New Baskerville Italic
Composition by Tom Ernst
Manufacturing by the Maple-Vail Book Manufacturing Group
Book design by Dana Sloan
Production manager: Leelo Märjamaa-Reintal

Library of Congress Cataloging-in-Publication Data

Tanning, Dorothea, 1910–
Between lives : an artist and her world / by Dorothea Tanning.
p. cm.
Expands on: Birthday, 1986.
Includes index.
ISBN 0-393-05040-8
1. Tanning, Dorothea, 1910– 2. Artists—United States—Biography.
3. Ernst, Max, 1891–1976. 4. Artist couples—Biography. 5. Tanning, Dorothea,
1910—Friends and associates. I. Tanning, Dorothea, 1910–Birthday. II. Title.

N6537.T36 A2 2001
709'.02—dc21
[B]   2001024006

W. W. Norton & Company, Inc., 500 Fifth Avenue, New York, N.Y. 10110
www.wwnorton.com

W. W. Norton & Company Ltd., Castle House, 75/76 Wells Street, London W1T 3QT

1 2 3 4 5 6 7 8 9 0

Contents

We, at times, too young for what is old,
and too old for what has never been.

—RILKE

Preface

The sixteen years since I wrote some of my recollections in *Birthday* have produced not only their share of events and people but an almost obsessive need to remember more and more of my past life. The present book is, then, an amalgamation of that earlier record and the additional years of living while listening to memory's voice—by turns antic, troubling, above all insisting to be heard. I have also come to realize that my earlier decision to severely limit the cast of characters was more perverse than honest, for, as everyone knows, we are the product not only of our own choices but of the sounds, sights, and especially the people we have encountered along the way. To accept this concept one must accept chance; the people are not always the most luminous. But whoever they are, they have marked a life.

Of those first bronze greats nearly all are gone now, survived by a few widows, dry and full of touched-up memories to feed the host of historians picking through the powder of vanished identities in search of secrets—

7

and the steamier the better—to polish off and serve up as biography. I vowed not to be such a name-dropper. Surely something could be told of what happened without naming names. But it was a cruel vow: private to the point of irritation; even, as I realized, unfair to the reader, who deserves to be allowed to identify a few ghosts (some of whom are still among the living). More and more of them jogged my memory until it seemed sometimes in the middle of the night they were all ganging up on me, demanding to know why they had been left out. "You knew me, too. You worked with me, you played with me, you laughed with me, you cried on my shoulder. . . ."

It was true. For every named person there are dozens who equally mark one's years. So how is it decided which names belong? How remarkable must their owners be, how renowned? Is there a gauge of some sort that measures a name's resonance, its impermeability, and, above all, its worth? Is this a category where my Ronnie or old Charlie Brewer does not fit? Or is their existence only in the events that memory has stored up for me, incandescent little flashes lighting the corners of solitary dailiness? Yes, those faraway beings are fireflies, you might say, each one a bit of phosphorus, a life that brushed mine and caused me, in its glow, to exist. And now they sit on memory's windowsill with little regard for chronology. Just as on wakeful nights a train of thought is not a train at all but a motley of rolling stock in total and unpredictable disorder, jumping track, asleep in barns, or speeding backward, yes, always backward. So that the thought of vain, deluded

Aunt Till, my mother's sister, who considered herself too good for any of the men she knew, follows, in my runaway train, the short film of an overturned kayak in the Housatonic river rapids that swept my sandals away (I never saw again my handsome partner in lederhosen with edelweiss-embroidered suspenders, who grabbed at the reeds, thus tipping our bark so charmingly) and my arrival barefoot in Grand Central Station that evening. Or follows the bracing picture of Louis Aragon (surrealism's celebrated bad boy, seventy-something by that time) racing my teenage niece to the end of the pool in Seillans, France. How not to share, for instance, the exquisite vision of Clare Booth Luce and her unawareness of why she was in Venice on that day of triumphant art? Are everyone's drowsy souvenirs as vagrant, even frivolous and kaleidoscopic? Yet, great or small, they anchor this account of a life and deserve their place in its unspooling. Thus, though my story follows its own undeviating course, it is relieved—sedately or horrifically—by these intrusions: whirling flecks and lucent gems orbiting the days and years, adding their colors to an unpredictable picture.

I like to think of it as a garden, planted in 1910 and, like any garden, always changing. There are expansions and diminishments as well as replacements, prunings, additions. One person's garden, one person's life. So far.

—*Dorothea Tanning*
November 2000

Between Lives

CHAPTER ONE

Headlong

IT IS A STORY you tell lying down, when all the storms have rumbled off elsewhere, the fires abated, the musicians packed up, tents blown away like milkweed, the earth turns—maybe. The story is in the place where you are. The room, unverifiable, is no more than its motes. Silence is soft and asks for nothing save the steady sequence. It is all like water slapping the sides of your boat and you both awash in memories, his own early ones a tapestry of Catholic childhood in Cologne. And mine?

There in the intimacy of two beings, supine, were my disembodied voice and his listening ears, as we felt our present selves melt away during the telling. But what could I tell, what was there in my childhood to compare with storybook Rhineland and little Max Ernst in his nightie looking for the railroad tracks and falling in with a procession of fanatics who called him baby Jesus? His father, a devout Catholic and a weekend painter, was impressed, even exalted; so that, carried away, he then painted his boy as the Christ Child, thus incidentally compromising his own chances for heaven. (He was later to participate in the excommunication from the Holy Roman Catholic Church of that same son. Part of this solemn ceremony consisted in spitting three times on Max's name—so Max told me.)

How could Galesburg, Illinois, in the 1910s to '20s, a place where you sat on the davenport and waited to grow up, compare with Cologne: its mighty cathedral shedding stained-glass lambencies that fell about children's shoulders like jeweled capes, turning them into princes and poets? My early memories surfaced, wavered through time, riled the stream—bloated forgotten fantasies rising in murky fluids. But almost always the wrong ones. I fished for vital statistics; even decisive events eluded me like soap in the bathwater. I was born, yes, and ran fast but never away. When I was seven I drew a figure with leaves for hair. Was I a tiny surrealist? Are all children surrealists, visually? Maybe surrealist painters were children with years, playing with the irrational. Maybe they knew that antic imagination is fun.

Somewhat later, aged eleven, it seemed important to share my élan. One of the ways to bring enrichment to other minds is to set up a lending library, which I did in our abandoned chicken house. The library was stocked with my own and my sisters' books, and these the neighbor children were invited to borrow and thus to read. Of course it took only two or so months to completely wipe me (and my poor sisters) out of books. Had I enriched some little minds?

Then and gradually, under the same blanket sky as Max's, I strove and fended and believed that my star was as free as anyone's on earth. Later I was hung about with intricate hips and shoulders and round arms and breasts as diffidently worn as the ones in those museum pictures beside which little white cards inform the visitor: *erotic* (male derma does not seem to rate this qualification). That was me, who rather liked it all, not recognizing the barriers reserved for headlong females and tiny stars. That was me, high flier, skimming forbidden ground, keeping an eye out for snares. No name, no face, but alive behind every man-made facade, a condition only, but invincible in its raw supremacy. To ignore, I said. Keep flying. Steer clear of signals, roadblocks, towers. I was tempered steel, and, after all, if there were no need to overcome obstacles one would become insignificant. So now, wise or foolish, I have landed.

To this beloved face I cannot accuse. He is mine and I am his and hindrance is elsewhere. Here I confide my tangly self, the oceanography of lost heartbeats and submerged hopes dredged up from the dimmest deeps, brushed and cleaned of their barnacles, offering its details to Max, who says, as always, "And then what."

Would he possibly want to hear about my mother, whose most distinguishing trait was simply her motherness? Could he want to know that this patient, single-minded being loved life instinctively as filtered through her children (three)—the loyalty to and pride in her husband being innate and foregone? How could a tiny artist grow into a big one without that quilt of maternal love with its pattern of solace for hurts, its curving comfort, cloud-soft, its consolation for having to exist, its sweet smell? The mother-goddess (the term would have embarrassed her), doctor and protector, hovered over us in the full conviction that we were worth the trouble; not listening to Uncle Ed, for example, who scoffed that I was a dwarf (he had a daughter of his own, my age, almost twice my size), for she knew I would grow up. She did not, however, plan on my going away so soon. It must have pained her, though she read my letters, the others said, with total seriousness. For, all too sure of my own convictions, I would write, when away from home, preachy letters to the family (sometimes, I am sorry to say, accompanied by an urgent request for money; my father obliged, but sparingly, hoping that when I became blackly discouraged I would come back to where I belonged), telling them how to think, to change their false values for real ones, to live more meaningful lives, to extend their horizons, and so on. How embarrassed they must have been, these gentle people, confronted with the growing proof of oddness in the family, and hoping they could keep it covered up— after all, I was not dangerous. But still, wondering: where did they go wrong?

My father, a model husband and parent, was at the same time mostly absent, forever immersed in old tomes of history and geography, conveniently distanced from domestic details. Understandably, for his was a household of women, including those who didn't already live there.

They would show up with faithful regularity and wardrobe trunk for long stays, strengthening thereby the feminine hold on the place. His hosting of my mother's relatives must have been daunting, though I think there was enough of the rooster in him to keep full control of his flock. As for us, the inhabitants, there was always an aunt or cousin once removed (alas, not far enough) crowding us out of our rooms while their incessant chatter drove my father to his third-floor den. As for me, now aged twelve, I felt a blessed neutrality in his company, the man from a far country (Sweden).

Now the water is still and I see the shape of a summer day in 1922. Outside the Orpheum Theatre in Galesburg everything glares, so that the street and shops seem to be simmering in a desert hallucination, a mirage without the sand in it. My father and I are out together in the blistering afternoon to see a cowboy movie. No one else would go. Cowboys! Family scorn, unanimous, sends my father on his way, if he really insists on it. But I'll go. In my white shoes and organdy dress. Downtown heat flings up a shimmery veil from the pavement bubbles and our heels indent its black tar like miniature horseshoes. My father wears a panama hat and buys two tickets at the window, one for him and a half one for me. And I remember my sister that morning:

"Who wants to see Tom Mix!"

And indeed who does? Certainly not my father, who is there for the horse, Tony, not for the rider. Horse-crazy, my father. Tom Mix is nothing to me either. I might as well have stayed up in my tree fork where nailed to the big branch in front of my seat is a box with key and tin lid, for secret formulas, plans, messages.

I begin to regret . . . but in the dark someone smiles at me from the screen: Lord Churlton. Blue moonlight shows me a careless leg encased in close breeches and sensuously cuffed boot. It swings over a windowsill. In a trice it has been followed by arms, torso, and head, all under plumed velvet hat, lace collar, doublet, gloves, rapier, and great hints of fine linen on pulsing muscles. Two cruel black eyes burn into mine.

And while my father thrills to the clever Tony, I am lusting after Lord Churlton, the villain. Never mind the secret formulas in the tree box. There is a time for everything. And you, Churlton, don't bother with that simpering lady wiggling her careful curls and swelling her bosom. Leave her to Tom Mix and come to me. I am waiting. Are you really a villain? What is a villain? O passionate Lord Churlton!

I tried to draw him that evening. Not in his ruffled shirt and velvet redingote or yet as Adam, but standing in a doorway and wearing red-striped pajamas. As the fabric and tanned cheeks had to be colored, out came my box of watercolors, two rows of tiny round pans of faintly colored cement (it tinted rather than colored) accompanied by a brush resembling a glue applicator. The likeness was poor, but then, who could do justice to Lord Churlton? I dreamed of his coming to Galesburg, even as I knew that he would not. . . .

"And then what?" Max cuts in.

My father's name was Andrew (or Andreas, back in Sweden) Peter George Thaning. To keep the pronunciation he changed the spelling. A rag of old-world pride made him try to interest his children in the "family book," a compendium of names with titles, professions, deaths, births, and marriages—the usual. He was self-exiled, a dropout, a runaway from home and country at age seventeen, and it was now all he had left, his precious book about faraway people become as legendary as King Arthur's Round Table, the big comfortable house back there now become a castle, the grain fields an enchanted wood, the river an endless ribbon of ice upon which a little boy skates home fast with the breath of wolves on his neck.

He had become a fervent American and even went off to the Spanish-American War—with a hometown fellow Swede, Carl Sandburg, American poet. Through the years, Carl Sandburg would call on us when he visited Galesburg. One day—I must have been fifteen—my father showed Carl my drawings, saying proudly:

"We will send her to art school when the time comes "

"Oh, no. Don't do that. Not art school. They will stifle her talent and originality."

How could my father not heed the great poet friend? In contrast, one of his two cardboard concepts, nobility, was not a quality but a class, to which he had been told that he belonged—a shaky position to maintain in Galesburg. Harder to accept, even, than the neighbors' egalitarian views was what the doctor said about his heart condition and to listen to my mother deplore his hiking, running, swimming. "Lying in that lake for hours!" Because the other cardboard concept was physical splendor. And strenuous sports never end for those who aren't going to die anyway. . . .

He admired Hitler as a glorifier of sports. We listened to the news from remote stadiums: Olympic records being broken as crowds went wild. We listened to the funny new rhythm of marching feet that got mixed up like static in our radio, stronger and stronger.

Then Hitler started killing people. And that is what really killed my father. Shattered by deception, his heart stopped beating about the time Hitler was marching up the Champs-Elysées.

"And then?" says Max, wanting nothing left out.

Oh, Max, what's the use?

Once in a while, from Chicago, or New York, or wherever, I had to go back there, touch the place, believe it was there and that it had something to do with me. But only a hopeless romantic could like getting off a train at our town, could think that stepping down onto the platform of Galesburg's depot was part of an adventure worth living, something to be savored and treasured like the dear persons who had remained there. Of course you identify with it, if you have been there when you and it were very small, before you went away.

But, again, how could my student days compare with Max's university capers around raging bonfires on the banks of the Rhine, where philosophical parlance blended

so strenuously with Lorelei sirens? Could I imagine there
was anything amusing about my buying a pair of satin slippers one size too small because it was the only pair in
town, and about the indescribable agony of wearing them
to the prom? The bright remarks I had prepared for the
ears of hard-to-get boys burned to ashes in what seemed a
direct electrical contact with my feet, irretrievable victims
of vanity.

Max listens gravely. "How awful," he says. "And what
then?"

If there was anything at all that troubled my certain
destiny as a painter, it was the Galesburg Public Library,
looming, massive symbol of pure choice. Imagine a wide
gray stone building of vaguely classical design and chunky
proportions. It sat in the very center of town, in a modest
island of grass surrounded by barberry bushes. On the
next corner the post office and, a few blocks away, the college that tried to teach me something, anything.

For like all nice girls I went to college. Two things
dominated the academic life there. One was sports events
such as football where on cold November Saturdays we sat
on wet bleachers in raccoon coats, screaming ourselves
hoarse at the mass of bodies tangling in the mud of the
quadrangle. The other distraction involved secret societies
with names in Greek letters. Each of these was a kind of
mini Ku Klux Klan to which you might experience the
bliss of being invited as a member. Blackballed hopefuls
could always join up with a humbler one, though the same
rituals prevailed in all of them: spooky candlelit seances,

condemnations, punishments, unspeakable initiation tortures. Most curious of all, you were supposed to *want* this amalgam of S and M, all benevolently condoned by the institution that was preparing your mind for the future.

To the chagrin of my parents, and unlike most of the girls there, I did not select a fellow undergraduate to marry as had been hoped. I had other plans, not well received at home. In fact, for Mother's friends, the very mention of *artist* was synonymous with *bohemian*. Art school is not a *school*. The girl is all turned around. College will straighten her out, will soften harsh lines, will calm the wayward, spinning colors, the oddness, the fever. How needless my parents' worries about the bohemian life I was headed for. They would have solidly approved, poor things, of the big-city art world, a kind of club based on good contacts, correct behavior, and a certain tactical chic involving doing the right thing at the right time.

Every time I passed the Galesburg Public Library I would see myself hidden in the stacks, making the kinds of discoveries that were not likely to be made at my college. This had already happened, in fact. For at age sixteen I was employed there, part-time it is true, but the employment provided a certain illusion of independence and even included a vacation—mine, that took the form of a rented cabin at Lake Bracken, a sprawling and appropriately named country club. My earned money would pay for two weeks.

Alone. Self-consciously, uncompromisingly alone. No to sisters. No to friends. No to boys. No, no. Instead, the

clean ritual of laying out paper, pencils, crayons, watercolors, the usual stuff, on the deal (ah, the simple word!)
table. Something would happen, had to happen. It filled
me up and down, back to front, and my head said that it
would spill out cornucopiately onto paper or canvas. This
two-week evasion, bought with the ugly money I had
earned drably, would produce flowers or monsters—I
didn't care which, for they would be mine. Sometimes I
stared for hours at the very white paper.

Beyond the screens of the porch, mosquitoes and lake
danced and rippled, respectively, under moon and sun
(for there was a moon, I had calculated with that), and
inside the musty little cabin four camp beds sagged, all
empty and uncovered but one; the pallid cushions, pancake-flat, exhausted, unable to sit up straight; the deal
table. I had dragged it to the screened porch, such a reasonable place for a worktable in July. Reasonable, too, to
go to bed early after an interminable day, for this would
certainly bring on tomorrow, a better event in all its glow
and promise. Sweaters and raincoat covered my blankets
at night, for it was cool and often rained.

There were visits, just three. My sisters came out and
looked at me baffled, hurt. They brought a pecan pie
that sat on the drainboard, wrapped in its checkered
towel. Another time, wearing fluffy afternoon dresses,
three more or less buddies came visiting, girls who had
thought I was one of them until this. Their violent unsatisfied curiosity floated around the afternoon cabin in a positively miasmal drift, a heady effluvium that mingled with

the reek of crushed verdure and lake water. Unabashed questions did not even linger unuttered but seeped into the vapid conversation on the porch, heavy as gases and as hard to wave away.

Once a boy came, ah, *he* would have made sense for them—came dragging his tennis racket and his courtly (courting) manners; looked a lot at the empty cots and then back, in clumsy longing, at this weirdo trying to tell him a little something and failing utterly. Because that was not it, and he had to be got rid of, sweetly, no fuss.

After that there were the long solitary days, the ungodly silence into which dipped the rain's whisper, far-away boaters' banter sounding surprisingly near (that voice, was it someone I knew perhaps?), an evening bird lighting on the roof, hopping on it. Cats could be counted on to fight up there, too, and numerous twigs to snap at night.

There was no fear, no boredom; only the leaden concavity where fullness failed to appear. Because failure was the shape of two weeks at Lake Bracken and the thought grew and spawned a crystal answer that froze into a certainty: lakes are made to drown in.

Among my duties at the library was a weekly reading of the stacks, according to the then-prevalent classification, the Dewey decimal system. The trouble was, once I had got back among the shelves, it was hard to find me, and the head librarian, a resolute, imposing woman, wearing pince-nez that trembled on her nose when she walked, would sometimes flush me out herself, in a perfect towering rage. Standard-bearer of morality according to her lights, she had instituted an ingenious method of marking with a small red cross under the catalogue number any book that she considered immoral, unfit for minors. Thus I had no difficulty in finding the best books.

Erewhon, Leaves of Grass, Salammbô, The Scarlet Letter, The Red Lily, Down There—and Poe, Coleridge, De Quincy, Walpole . . . those spell-binding revelations, those delicious hymns to decadence, dozens and dozens of them, getting all mixed up with the others on the shelves of that corrupt stony structure, with its American flag and the names of great men incised around its entablature. Several of these hallowed names were also on the books with red crosses. Over the years, the library became my haven, its treasures slyly challenging the voice of "art," in the tug-of-war for my ambitions, its sirens singing and crying by turns, its weight crushing my fatuous certitudes forever.

As the days became nights and the months years, my soul detached itself with reckless finality from that warm and comfortable quotidian. It watched gravely from a distance as the body went about its vain gestural procedures. It waited with patience while the big trunk, sporting brass corners and five latches, got secretly packed. Goodbye, Galesburg. Goodbye, Anatole France. Goodbye, Public Library. I will "visit" friends in Chicago.

Now the trunk can be sent for, openly. My letter—"It's in my room," and "Just take it down to the depot"—was read aloud like a death knell by two shocked parents. Their grief: a warm luxury that I could not but treasure, because I was alive.

Thirty-five years later the Galesburg Public Library burned to the ground, its 200,000 volumes feeding the sky-high flames while the town's water supply sputtered out and my sisters watched with tear-stained faces. Thank God I wasn't there.

Not that I never went back. At first, needing pretexts such as holidays and Mother's birthday, I went often. (One of these cost me my job in Chicago. But more on that later.) Thus, I am remembering Mother's colors: jade green, American Beauty red, peacock blue, old rose. While she sews them into her lazy-daisy quilt I am on the Chicago train to Galesburg. Last gasp of memory here: we are four, we are going down to the homecoming football game. I have not the faintest interest in football. My pretty friend is thrilled The two boys are happy medical students with medicine bottles of government alcohol, 140-proof— something extravagant like that. We are at the water cooler in the swinging train, where you slip out cone-shaped paper cups and fill them with ice water at a minia-ture spigot. Fire sears the throat at the jaunty tilting of the little bottle and there is a scratch of laughter to mask the first time. (For God's sake do not cough.)

How the train speeds through the stupid landscape! How screamingly funny it all is at the dance! My future medico clings to me as I to him. We are in stitches. When you have four feet you can keep standing up. I have his two besides my own, he has my two. Not only we do not fall, we manage the slides, the turns, the sudden rhythms. Each held fast to the other and my eyes were mostly closed, not to see the mile-high waves I felt around our slanting floor. I was probably happy the way people have always been happy on the dance floor. The mirror ball sends its chips of light circling the universe, nobody watches you, nobody cares, the musicians are all Olympian benevolence in their smart pink tuxedos, gods smiling down into your half-open mouths, providing gently pagan rhythms that coax you into wanton concupiscence and make you forget that tomorrow is Sunday and church where the stained-glass windows are jade green, American Beauty red, peacock blue, and old rose.

Now after two years a sudden desire sends you back, just a short visit, your valise stuffed with handcarved notions wrapped up in a tender woolly image of the separate little person you once were.

Separate you still are. And you think you know everyone, that they know you and that you will somehow amaze them. But the town has grown, though this may not be at first evident in stepping off the train. In fact it appears to have shrunk. There is a lot of hollow wind in the depot, blowing dead train tickets and gum wrappers across the floor, but there are no people except an old man with a broom who stops sweeping to stare at you when you ask about taxis. The coffee shop? He doesn't remember.

A car drives up and delivers your sister, who hugs you and takes you away from there. Sitting beside her, half listening, you are quite lost. It is the wrong town.

Can this be Main Street, so queerly empty to the eye, so drab and quiet? Itching with ghosts in the crisscross gusts that slice past empty store windows and that separate the dust on the inside from the dust in the street. A parking lot gapes where once you tried on gloves at a mahogany counter or bought a hat for too much money. What happened to Lescher's soda fountain, and the Alcazar, smoky macho haven where my father, being a male, could buy his Sunday cigar? Where is the big bank window where shaky paper currency from all over the world was displayed on a panel, with a United States one-dollar bill in the middle and the legend: *Good old American dollar, always remains the same*?

The big trees, lofty Sherwood Forest trees, where are they, our proud Galesburg trees? They leaned together in long ogival files that made tents of the streets, gallerias with leaves for glass. Where are the trees? The town is dense and fat, cubic, a smoke stain on the land; and now you are not a part of it at all but only a speck among many unknown specks that you see as in a culture, starkly, darting around oblivious of your mixed feelings. It is simpler that way, you tell yourself, another place altogether, bottled and corked and labeled, an elixir gone dry.

"But you wouldn't know."

Max: "I think I do. The place you had to leave. Everybody has one."

*   *   *

Chicago, clanging, blowing and steaming with glut,
wind, lust. Here—this is 1934—I meet my first eccentrics.
They float through antic evenings to the sound of jazz
and the tinkling of glasses containing icy drinks. The
drinks are made of dubious alcohols, this being a
holdover from recent Prohibition. There are thousands of
icy drinks and I feel more and more certain of an exceptional destiny—so much is waiting for me.

There in Chicago (it was on the way to Paris, was it
not?) the imperative was to find a job at once. This mate-
rialized in the form of a restaurant dining room where I
wore a colonial dress and greeted the diners. The place
was called, that's right, the Colonial Room. I lost no time
in telling my college pals, some of whom as fresh gradu-
ates with no big plans to marry immediately, joined me, to
work as waitresses. The owner liked to hire college girls,
believing them to be a cut above the professional types in
matters of manners and morals. For instance, we were
strictly (and, I would think, mysteriously) enjoined not to
frequent—that is, to date—any coworker in the restaurant, on pain of losing your jobs.

Sometime later, the owner brought in an "efficiency
expert." This stocky, middle-aged man darted around the
place all day, watching us girls in the exercise of serving
food to the diners. At the end of the dinner hour he
would closet himself with the boss to report on us. Still, all
in all, he seemed friendly enough.

Quite enough, as a matter of fact, for about the fourth or fifth day he invited some of us up to his room in a hotel, where he taught us how to French kiss. He took us, one by one, into the bathroom and pushed his tongue into our mouths. Not one of the first, I waited my turn until finally he pulled me in and French-kissed me. That was it. No sliding hands under my dress, no fondling. He may have spent more time with one or two of the others, though no one complained afterward. But from that time on, you could say that we of the Colonial Room had gained a certain efficiency not anticipated by our boss.

Another kind of efficiency held sway in the art school I was attending in the afternoons, three to five, between the lunch and dinner hour. This place was called the Chicago Academy of Art. It occupied a floor in a commercial building and had all the marks, smells, and sounds of "art": turpentine, gessoed canvas, varnish, that sort of thing, and in the drawing class, the velvet sigh of twenty-some charcoals on paper—music to my ears. I signed up.

For three weeks I drew from a live human being who stood or sat in glorious nudity on the model stand. But the teacher, a local artist much appreciated on the Chicago art scene, did not seem to find me at all promising. He would swing by, on his inspection around the class, without any comment on my drawing save a sad shake of the head. It seemed I was not drawing in the prevailing mode of the day, which followed Picasso's lead in squashing the figure down to the proportions found in African tribal art: chunky and totemic with powerful tor-

sos, short, bent legs, and savage faces. Aside from hopeless me, drawing what I saw, all the students were merci-
lessly squashing down their figures, the charcoal dust
flying, the drawings ever blacker. I had seen reproduc-
tions of Picassos, other ones, that I admired (Blue period).
And if he later squashed his figures down, I assumed he
had his reasons. But I didn't see why the rest of us should
do the same thing. Moreover, the ambiance I had hoped
to find in the Chicago Academy of Art did not material-
ize. Concentrated and matter-of-fact in their pursuit of
technical mastery, a skill that leaves little time or inclina-
tion for ideas, my fellow students bore the air of purgator-
ial candidates for an imminent heaven of advertising art.
As it became clear, commercial art was the specialty of the
place. Thus the three weeks.

My goals lay hidden like hibernating bears. I had a
room and share-bath at 619 Rush Street. It was a tall old
house run by kind, drab Mrs. Reisinger, who always
appeared to have just escaped some terrible fate, like, say,
the reappearance of an unwanted husband. But she had a
restaurant on the main floor called the Colonial Tea
Shoppe and most of us roomers were her customers. She
had, as well, a weakness for art and artists, and one or two
of the others, permanently out of pocket, ate on the tab.
Her pet was a stalwart, youngish painter of magazine illustrations of adventure subjects. They were mostly violent
scenes of rearing horses, clouds of dust, and, what really
called forth my admiration, smoking guns whose explosions were *visible*, all in glorious black, white, and grays

and destined for *Collier's* or *The Saturday Evening Post*. But, in spite of their skillful panache and Mrs. Reisinger's staunch, late-evening pep talks, they were never accepted.

The Colonial Room was also an abode and especially my means of support. So for the time being, art existed only in the great hushed rooms of the Chicago Art Institute. This was my academy, the place where adventure really began.

Adventure? Relationships? That depends on what one understands as an adventure. Or a relationship. There were, at least, some near misses. Such as one summer evening and a date with a Chicago gangster. He had been a regular eater at the restaurant, turning up at dinnertime on Fridays. After a glance at the menu he would read his paper and appear not to notice where he was. But he was clearly a gangster: squarely built, not tall (they never are), with a big face straight down from brow to chin, a line for a mouth (which they always have) and big sparkly cufflinks peeking out from his pinstripe sleeves. Yet there was an unfinished look about him, as though the sculptor had been called to the phone and had forgotten to finish the job. To think that this was all in the Colonial Room, with me in a colonial pannier and fichu, hugging menus, beadily surveyed by the Efficiency Expert as well as the gangster!

Because, one Friday evening, while I led the man to a table, he muttered his invitation: would I care to join him later that evening? Should I hesitate, think that over? He was so offhand, so direct, so weary, too. It made me feel daring and worldly. . . . "Yes."

Leaving the house and its cozy events, I joined my gangster ("Call me Max," he told me) and his chauffeur. We drove a long way, through streets and suburbs, while I babbled the usual banalities, my date listening rather absently. We wound up in a cocktail lounge where he appeared to be well known. The place, I decided, was a mob hangout. Maybe he owned it. In fact, he was called away almost at once and parked me on a bar stool without a word. The barman told me to have something. I wasn't sure. Yes, he said, I was supposed to have something while I waited. Two Alexanders later I was feeling dizzy and began wondering what I should do about it. Were those drinks spiked with something? But that was not it. For just then the barman leaned forward to tell me that Max (yes, really) wouldn't be back and that there was a taxi outside that would take me home. Angry and humiliated, I climbed in. Fortunately, the driver was kind, for I had no idea where we were: it wasn't at all the city I knew. Coming in that evening, 619 Rush looked very good to me, and I had a deep sleep. By the way, the next day's paper gave full report: my date had been gunned down in a shootout only a block away from the bar.

Not long after, having lost my job at the Colonial Room (an infraction of attendance: Mother's birthday being the same as George Washington's, I had disobeyed the order to stay on duty on the holiday. What else could I do? Washington may be our country's father but she was my mother, and on her birthday, an event organized by my father, we would all stand outside in the snow and watch him shoot skyrockets—fireworks—into the night sky), I answered an ad, portfolio under my arm, for advertising illustration. The work sounded especially promising.

It was exhilarating, at first sight, and just where I thought I belonged: three or four artists not entirely visible but bent and intent behind big drawing boards in a large office space. The directors—there were two of them, a man and a woman—were affable but businesslike as they led me to a smaller room where they asked me to pose for a photo.

"But . . ." I began.

"No, no," they both laughed, "it's just routine. We have to record our artists."

They showed me a screen behind which I was to take off my clothes. Should I? Well, if this is the way things are done in Chicago . . . So I obliged. Then I was stood before a dingy backdrop .

"Can't yo u smile? Put your hand on your hip. Relax."

When, after dressing again, I picked up the portfolio, the man had disappeared. The portfolio stayed unopened. I was told by his partner, "We will call you and see the work then." Of course that was all.

So if you ever happen on the photo of a cute girl standing in the buff, with an uncertain smile and an uncertain hand on an uncertain hip, that would be me. Only after I left did I realize I'd been had. Walking down Michigan Avenue, flushed with hindsight like the true fool from Galesburg that I was, only then did I understand what it was all about. Then, after a while, perking up, I consoled myself: we are less likely to make mistakes once we have learned how easy it is to do it. But I still wonder, now and then, about those artists, if they were artists, and oh . . . what was on those drawing boards? And I like to think that, soon after—their game being so easily detectable for anyone inclined to detect—unmasked and pursued, the culprits scuttled their archive and fled.

Surely, city life has *some* grace, surely this can't last forever. Indeed, it did not. For one evening brought me into an awesome lamp-lit room lined to the ceiling on all four sides with books and presided over by a pair of gentle owls about five feet two inches high. They were man and wife, he a compiler of modern verse, both of them makers of it. Oscar Williams, poet. His *Little Treasury* still seems so appropriately titled, quite one with the earnest bespectacled face, bird-bright, behind thick lenses.

As for his poetess, Gene Derwood her name, she personified everything I had not known in Galesburg. Intensity streamed from her very crossed eyes. Her Joan of Arc bangs, her small piquant features in their paper pallor, her dark brown cape—somehow I always see her as a sepia vision: brown hair, eyes, cape, perhaps the book she held—all formed in iron of unquestionable authenticity that achieved my total devotion. In a group discussion later, one of those rambunctious arguments that spring up among showoffs, I had only to see her stand up in her magic cape and, in her dovelike voice, object— "Fellow, fellow!"—to know that I had found a milieu.

How did they come here? How had the books, floor to

ceiling, door to window, flown into these shelves, clinging
there close, close together, congregating on this softly
glowing shoal in their long flight from where to where?

The whole scene struck me as a kind of tableau vivant
that was to be gazed at, taken in quickly before the curtain
fell. How long had they been here? Not long, surely. The
talk always referred to New York, the only place, the end of
any voyage. Yes.

They planned, daily, the thousand-mile trip, with stops
for sleep and sandwiches. Carefully. For money was the
stumbling block, the element that kept their ailing jalopy
in the garage instead of on the highway, eastbound. By
and by we planned the trip together, except that their two
wistful faces were grave when I admitted that I was as out
of pocket as they. Oh, I would pay my part. I would manage that. And so the date was set.

It did not seem remarkable to me that I was packing
my trunk again, this time for New York. Had I not, at age
seven, decided I would live in Paris? And was not New
York on the way? The whole procedure of packing, the
choosing and rejecting, the meaningless fidelity to perfectly useless objects, the rash discarding of probably use-
ful ones, sloughed off like the familiar keys, corridor,
room, faucets, India prints I was leaving forever, all was as
natural as graduation from some school or other.

Then, two days before departure, I had a phone call.
The car was still in the garage, prostrate. It was too old,
diagnosed the doctor-mechanic. It would require a heart

transplant, a chassis replacement, a set of four new shoes. Our adventure was indefinitely postponed.

Have you ever unpacked a trunk—the one you had been filling up for weeks with your earthly possessions— before it has gone anywhere? The very possibility of such an about-face was unthinkable. Tucked into every object in the trunk was a piece of my continuity and my decision, so that should it all be removed, thrown out, turned back into abandoned drawers and empty closet, I myself would be so turned back, scattered, hopelessly dispersed, like a routed army, with nothing left but to surrender. Even unpacking a suitcase is a melancholy business, all too well known to present-day voyagers whose flights are airily canceled at leering last minutes.

Picture, then, the would-be New Yorker on her haunches before the trunk that holds her life's accumulation, everything from the portfolio of drawings on the bottom to a box of watercolors, Uncle Bob's cigar case stuffed with rolled-up stockings, snapshot album, leather notebook, insignificant trash of all kinds without which the traveler would be a shadowless, no-dimensional wraith. It is clear to her that a voyage has to be undertaken.

"You are going on a journey," says the fortune-teller. Oh, you are right.

At the bus station on the scheduled day of departure I buy a one-way ticket for New York, and after rocking and lurching, asleep and awake, through the September countryside and faceless towns for an inordinate number of hours, I am disgorged with the dreadful trunk at New York's Greyhound station down on Eighth Avenue.

"To Greenwich Village," I order the taxi driver.

"But where?"

"Just go there. I'll tell you when to stop."

At the first ROOM FOR RENT sign we pull up. I go in, take a look, pay five dollars to the landlady, who gives me a key to the room (a minute windowed closet), the driver brings up my trunk, *on his back,* and in five minutes the door is closed and I am a New Yorker.

That evening my notebook is out of the trunk. My pencil is poised just as if that taxi had simply brought me from around the corner where I had been waiting.

> *Red sign, yellow cab, blue door*
> *A photo black and white but not*
> *Really: colors are trembling*
> *Around the edges before night*
> *Falls. A daylight night*
> *Blue-green and the taillights*
> *Red.*
> *Red on blue and green.*
> *There are dogs, dog-color*
> *Men with guns, man-color*
> *All the colors of virus, fleshly.*
>
> *I go in because it is there*
> *Purple evening playing a card*
> *Pumpkin-red fortune, mauve shadow*

In the rooming house
Red sign purple cab blue boar
Brown dog
Cigarette glows orange. A boar hunt
Cannot be regarded.
There is no color in it.

If this was not much of a poem it at least had a rag of willfulness, the color scheme was aggressive, and that gave me pause. It was clear to me that I should be an artist in an artist's studio where such tendencies would surely contribute toward self-realization.

And Max, with his "And then what?"

A few lines for a few years. A line a year—is it worth more? Because some years leave no stamp at all on the mind. They are like a mere series of dots marking something foggy, dim, breathless, up in the air. Put a few dots after a word and you have a year's worth of unanswered questions, to say nothing of audacities, plights, and errors in abundance.

The fact is, one doesn't care too much about remembering them. The draggy odd jobs (not odd enough), the squandered evenings, the obsessed boyfriends, the relationships; the return to home base for breath; the sometimes perfidious girls with whom I shared rooms, apartments, confidences.

One of these, not perfidious at all, except perhaps in

the eyes of my parents had they known, once got me out of the family bosom by an urgent letter about a job, a little ploy we had dreamed up together. Of course the job was ninety-five percent invention, but in New York and in her brownstone apartment on Fifty-eighth Street, everything was possible.

We shared rent and curry powder sandwiches, took Hindu dancing, read the *Bhagavad Gita* and Emily Dickinson, impartially. We wore grass skirts at an appliance convention dinner, serving pink and yellow nourishment on beds of banana leaves to boisterous salesmen, for which service we collected five dollars upon leaving at one in the morning. My sidekick found this mirthful; I was dispirited. We supered at the Metropolitan Opera: *La Traviata, Orfeo.* My mother, informed, was in heaven. Music! She didn't know that her daughter, arriving at the theater at precisely ten to nine in the evening, put on a gunny-sack costume (sweaty smell) and found her place on stage marked by a chalk number (fourteen, I can still see it). The curtain rose. Music. I was one of about thirty sinners, agonizing in hell. I waved my arms for ten minutes while contralto Kirsten Thorberg, her sturdy legs encased in Roman talaria—they were very close to my face—descended, singing. When the curtain fell at the end of this aria, the condemned were herded out to climb the same little iron staircase, remove the gunny sacks, dress, and leave the theater, taking their two dollars at the stage door, where a man with a big cigar distributed the sad bills to us, the brave and talented supers.

Her name was Ronnie and she was the happiest person I have ever known. That her paintings—for she was an "easel painter"—were piled up in the spare room instead of hanging in art museums cast only the palest shadow on her unbelievably sunny outlook. Never having lived anywhere else, she still loved New York with a steady passion that sent her, propelled her, hurled her into every event called public. A city block could be a miracle; a concert, an exhibition, a ballet was always sublime.

And things happened so fast for Ronnie: a new exhibition by Calder, *Stanley* Calder, said poor Ronnie, having no time for refinements of language; her target was Art, always and forever. Her indifference to exactitude was so insidious that at times it was as if I shared it. Though appalled by the specter of mental sloth, I felt saved by my antennae of observation, which seemed, for the time, to sit in for sturdier activities. Therefore, it was Ronnie's *serrugated* knife that wouldn't cut; later, on an infamous day, bombs were dropped suddenly on *Bar* Harbor; and there was always her poor brother, who had been *circumscribed* when he was a tiny baby. He had gone on to disappoint his parents' hopes that he would become a rabbi; had instead gone into clutter and was at present, number two drag queen, whispered to be in thrall to drag queen number one, both of them currently packing them in at a downtown venue. Ronnie sighed. She had given him up as a date for me, and the matter was closed. For Ronnie, guileless as a strawberry, the world was like that, unsurprising. The years brought her hippies, rock stars, junkies, punks; she loved them all. The "scene," she called it, not expecting that it would lose a bit of its luster without her. For, arriving in Paris, France, years later for an exhibition of her pictures, she dropped dead—I believe of happiness—on the day of the opening.

Besides, datewise, I was already involved, when not drawing and painting on modest-sized canvas boards that could be carried to ad agencies and the like, in an off-and-on association with a man I believed to be a promising writer. What else could you be with a name like Homer? A published article in *Harper's Magazine* had consecrated him in my eyes. He had also what is called a drinking problem. I didn't know that this is a category into which some people perfectly fit, for life.

Mostly, I was not concerned with anything except addresses of ad agencies and those who decorated my days, I perhaps decorating theirs. Busy with projects and pursuits and pipe dreams somehow like my own, they were intense, confident, and unfazed by worldly reticence in the face of their exuberant audacity. A rendezvous with John Cage (who would change America's music forever) and his wife, Xenia, in the Metropolitan Museum of Art— our first meeting: someone said, "Where shall we go first?" And John, "Well, I want to see a *famous* painting." Whereupon I remarked, emphatically, "But *all* the pictures here are famous!" (Poor Dorothea.) Perhaps he treasured me for my naïveté, for we were fast friends over the years, with many afternoons at chess and evenings telling stories. Actually, at story times it was hard to say

who told the most beguiling—or hilarious—ones, John or
Merce Cunningham, John's friend and collaborator, in
himself a whole new shape of dance. Both of them, along
with innovators from film and painting and just plain fantasy: Leo Lerman, chronicler of them all, in burnoose and
fez behind his table piled with pastries; Johnny Nicholson,
who started a restaurant where décor was delirious and
important and copied all over town to this day; Peter
Lindamood, whose little brownstone apartment held, along
with an unbelievable quantity of schlock, the sacred chair
that Garbo had sat in, barred by a velvet rope. Peter and I
cavorted in Central Park one morning at sunrise for Maya
Deren making an avant-garde film, which I never saw.
Perhaps it was never finished.

A brief crush on an art critic who was also a commie
brought me, necessarily, a flirt with the Party. But the Party
so drained his small store of passion that there was nothing left over for me. After three months of meetings,
where I was taken into the fold (albeit gingerly), and a few
mirthless dates with my anguished boyfriend, I gave up.

These were the years when most New York art galleries
were huddled in the comparatively narrow confines of
Fifty-seventh Street between Third and Sixth Avenues. If
you walked along Fifty-seventh Street from Fifth Avenue to
Lexington, up one side and down the other, you were
rewarded by an exciting, though spotty, exhibition of
European pictures, with a timid sprinkle of American ones
hanging in between. What was remarkably happy about
such a promenade was that more than half of the great

ground-floor spaces on this very handsome street were so occupied. And though many other galleries were tucked away on cozy upstairs floors, it was the big gallery windows that provided the topics of comment when, in the evening, two embryo artists stepped out to "take the air." This we did quite regularly, in all but the foulest weather, bundled up against the wind that blew from around the corner on Fifth. Every second window was ablaze with French impressionist paintings in curly antiqued frames or German expressionist ones in gold frames. The American pictures sported low-keyed baguettes.

Magical Fifty-seventh Street was, in fact, our academy. It was where everything worth looking at came and went, only to make way for the next masterpiece. Blithely penniless, we could walk into any one of its carpeted, paneled, museumlike interiors, stand before the pictures or sculptures, and discuss them undisturbed. We had strong opinions, but kept our voices down—a custom in art galleries (and one well suited to our opinions).

Here and there among the "greats" nestled a few staid shops selling English hunting scenes, or Meissen cabbages in porcelain, which we ridiculed happily. There was a shop of *curiosités* (their word), its immense window crammed with those dusty, brown, ill-lit objects that passed for primitive art. One snowy day we, the same two stars of the future art world, lingered there, wanting, as one always does, to spot something "good." Indeed, in we went, and in no time at all had bought a little brown statue. We then changed our course back toward Third

Avenue, where, under the roaring elevated, a delighted merchant bought it for a nice markup. Then we changed direction again and headed for a good restaurant. *On fait ce qu'on peut.*

Occasionally we would swing around for a few blocks on Fifth Avenue. Here the displays of garments, so close, geographically, to the ineffable visions around the corner and yet so far, cosmically, unleashed our sneers. The giddy inanity of mannequins in their fashionable outfits, their unawareness of their silly selves, like the swaggerer who doesn't know there's a donkey tail pinned on his back, turned our snickers into hoots of scorn that echoed in the late-evening street as we staggered back to our fourth floor well pleased with ourselves and the evening.

One such day in 1937 or 1938, after closing time, we edged into one of our favorite galleries (was it Paul Rosenberg's?), where there was already a little crowd of nobodies like us sitting on the floor before a large Picasso painting called *Guernica.*

We listened as a gaunt, intense young man with an enormous Nietzschean mustache, sitting opposite us, talked about the picture. It was not his accent, which I couldn't place, that held me, but the controlled emotion in his voice, at once gentle and ignited, that illumined the painting with a sustained flash of new light. I believe he talked about intentions and fury and tenderness and the suffering of the Spanish people. He would point out a strategic line and follow it into battle as it clashed on the far side of the picture with spiky chaos. He did not, during the entire evening, smile. It was as if he could not. Only afterward was I told the man's name: Arshile Gorky.

At times, someone appears who sees all. Gorky was one of these. Agonizingly, he saw everything that was being done in painting, and that had already been done. He admired certain faraway artists' works with evident passion, and, like a dye you swallow before the X-ray, it showed up in his own pictures. It stained them with the dreams of his idols until, in his last five or six years, and emerging from the spell as from anesthesia, he found his own way, solitary and sovereign. Proving, lest we forget, that it isn't always "the early work" that defines an artist's worth.

Meeting rarely, we were never more than polite acquaintances, our conversation mainly unspoken. After all, for him, I was Max's wife. Later still, and far away in France, I was to hear the terrible tale of Arshile Gorky's appallingly cruel last days. First, the colon cancer, grimmest of nature's strikes fallen upon him, the hapless human. Then the accident: Julien Levy is at the wheel, a fact so outlandish-seeming for me; Julien, born to watch and to listen, certainly not to drive cars. I see him as in an old film clip stepping out into the Burbank studio commotion, not really there, not really anywhere, yet for the purpose of some movie easing into the driver's seat, smiling as the stage machinery pulls the car away. . . . Only his passenger, Gorky, will learn that it's for real: the car crash, our world's ugliest humiliation, and the final despair of this lonely and broken genius who takes his life away. No amount of blame or gnashing of teeth can change the procession of events. For a moment, I see them all—busy, twisted images ending in amnesia, along with countless smashed desires, vain pursuits, and immense hours crowded with question.

A rare moment, that day in the Paul Rosenberg Gallery with the voice of Arshile Gorky, as I in my structure-proof life move on, not too dashed about washing out stockings at night so they can be worn again next day, not too vexed about propping my never-larger-than-twenty-inch canvas on a chair for want of an easel, not even maddened by flimsy friendships based on circumstance.

Because in 1936 I look in on the Fantastic Art, Dada, and Surrealism exhibition at New York's Museum of Modern Art. Of course there have been intimations: the great Armory Show of 1913 (too soon for me); books, albums and catalogues from Paris; magazines, too, and enigmatic pamphlets; surrealist shows at the Julien Levy Gallery (lots of financial flops here, I learned afterward).

But here, here in the museum, is the real explosion, rocking me on my run-over heels. Here is the infinitely faceted world I must have been waiting for. Here is the limitless expanse of POSSIBILITY, a possibility having only incidentally to do with painting on surfaces. Here, gathered inside an innocent concrete building, are signposts so imperious, so laden, so seductive, and, yes, so perverse that, like the insidious revelations of the Galesburg Public Library, they would possess me utterly. From that day "aberrance" was for me a meaningless three syllables, and "deviate" another three, synonymous with the glorious minorities. My own drawings, technically timid scraps of old obsessions, stayed underground.

There was a day in July 1939 when I boarded a ship (the *Nieuw Amsterdam*) bound for France, last lap of that life-long itinerary that had begun in Chicago. My pockets were full of letters of introduction to artists (and not much else), Tanguy, Max Ernst—"Oh no!" "Oh, but yes"—and Picasso, too.

Of course, no one is at home. No Parisians are ever at home in August, if they can help it. Somnambulist concierges (they frown before you open your mouth, anticipating what?) shake their heads: "He is in the country." They stare at me, doubtless wondering at this bizarre American who chooses to ring doorbells in August. An especially doomed August—a city paralyzed by anxiety, breathing painfully before the imminence of war. With a big lump in my throat I wander the wide deserted avenues, the gardens, the museums. I knock on mute doors, I get lost in the labyrinthine streets. I am hungry at the wrong times.

Back in my room, at loose ends, baffled and feeling insubstantial, I sit with my sketchbook, drawing Paris from the window. I draw the clouds that are so patently French, draw the roofs, the vanishing streets, the houses' patinas and their patience, draw them urgently as a spy would use a special camera, would hide behind a curtain just as I am lurking in my hotel room, to snap something fleeting, some evidence of heartbeat, a perhaps sad secret.

Outside there is nothing simple, not one person I know or a friend of a friend. There is only a firm resolve planted like a tree in my determined future: to come back. My artists? They too will come back some day, say the French clouds, the deserted cafés, the grisaille streets.

Soon the war is there like a train on time. My American embassy says go home. The telegram from my father says go to Stockholm to Uncle Hugo. In order to do this there is only the (disrupted) train service—across Belgium, across Germany, with queer stops and queerer changes of trains, my steamer trunk that had planned to stay somehow keeping up, not quite missing connections. Burly Hitler Youth kept me company in the stifling compartments. Oh, I had quite an entourage in those hot smelly trains where there were no breaks for day and night, needless to say nothing to eat, just the smell of other people's oranges; and big bold boys in short khaki pants, their knees, their terrible iron knees . . . their insistent baiting that got through to me in spite of scrambled words:

"You Americans, you think you have an air force. Your pilots, ha! We will take care of them [laughter], the Reich will show them, our Luftwaffe will bring them down like flies, and so on and on

I smile and smile. After all, I am in Germany and these boastful boys with strong blond hair on their steely thighs already know (how?) that my country will enter the war.

Paris had withdrawn from me, spurned my embrace, turned her face to the wall. Those thirty-two days studded with failure had blasted open my eyes and my mind. Germany was a train ride complete with grotesques. By the time I reached kindly Stockholm I had rubbed elbows with enough collective madness to know it would never matter what I might think of what was happening. So the voyage had not been for nothing. Something had been achieved after all. Never again would the sound of political harangue embarrass my other-tuned ears. Never again would I sit burning with embarrassment at meetings in which I did not belong. Never again would I confuse heckling with heroics. Those dreams were not mine.

Besides, had I not already begun on something else, something lifelong, with a stop at that dada-surrealism show three years before? So by the time surrealism would come to New York in the guise of exotic human beings, some time later, I would be ready for it, ready with my pictures, ready with my thirty birthdays, ready for this story to begin, to go on, to begin again.

It was now goodbye France, hello Sweden. At Uncle Hugo's place outside Stockholm a yellow-haired girl in starched blue and white, with sumptuously upholstered bones, with perfect bare feet, and with whom I cannot exchange one word, brings my breakfast tray at nine: the usual things with, in addition, a generous plate of herring. At eleven another breakfast in the dining room, attended by Uncle Hugo, who gives us the news: Poland is now divided like a pie, Soviets and Nazis at a tea party. Oh, when I get back! I can hardly wait. What will they say now, Jerry and Greg and Joan and the others I had met back there in the Party? (Of course if you are carrying a torch—clenching a fist—for a way of life, for a way to govern, you will always have something to say, and they did. But this time it was lame, lame.) I thought hard.

To calm my turmoil I painted Aunt Hannah in oils. She took this as seriously as if I were a commissioned artist and insisted on dressing in silk and wearing her pearls. These demanded my most strenuous effort—think of it! —one pearl after another, and another, all evenly matched, *of course.*

Dry leaves were falling, skidding across the frosty grass. Winter was racing toward Stockholm; Nazi mines were planted in the North Sea.

"Stay, stay," begged my cousins. But all I wanted now was to get home, if the war would let me. From Gothenburg, on the *Gripsholm,* it took ten days. Mines in the Atlantic Ocean, fatalism among the valiant crew of the *Gripsholm,* who could only drown their daring in aquavit; giddy optimism among certain youthful passengers in second class, reading Waugh's *Vile Bodies,* and laughing off their fears.

* * *

It did not take long for daily deeds, and needs, to take over, however, once I was safely on the dock in New York. After a while, and in spite of agonizing news from those places I had so recently known, it was as if I had not been in Paris at all.

When not bent over the drawing board (ads for Macy's—girls, girls, girls, in bathing suits, girls in dresses, then girls in fur hats or Ophelias drowning in a new cologne; a page of fake jewels, a page of handbags . . . handbags!), I sometimes scavenged for bargains in places like Klein's, a cut-rate clothing store on New York's Union Square, treasured at the time by indigent girls and women, treasured for its heaven-provided bargains for the young and urban hopeful. A five-dollar dress in which to seduce the future," a little black dress" is what they were saying that year, and in Klein's it was like winning the lottery, because, lo, there it was! Tried on in a small, balefully bright room, the eerie green paint made liquid by a looking-glass wall. In this tank of waving, contorting, neon-lit swimmers, the mirrors coarsely reflected bodies of the not quite poverty-stricken. Here a tumult of women dropped their skirts and slips on the floor, clutched their handbags between their knees or between their teeth. They discovered their sad flesh to each other, who did not care, while grabbing the object of their choice—choice, that kernel of glory in the pit of despair. They were ready to overlook the limp collar, lipstick smear, missing belt, broken zipper, opened seams, ripped lining, all signs of wear by the frail, beautiful models who had preceded us. We pulled and twisted the hapless garments over our heads or feet first and, for some, up to the bulging girdle where most often they wouldn't go any farther without their adversaries' relentless determination to be in them. If there was no one looking, a quick tug defied the recalcitrant opening, and a small dry protest of tearing rayon imitated pain.

Contortions justified by perfect choice, looking neither right nor left, oblivious, intent, we shared the mirrors in the frenzy of frivolous hope. At nightfall these five-dollar rags would be transformed into raiment. And seen from across the people and the shaded lights, barely outlined in the chiaroscuro hour, the dark envelope would be chosen for the second time in one day, this time along with the life inside it—surely such efforts could not fail to bring their reward.

It must be noted that in 1941, marriage to Homer S. bandaged my tumultuous off-and-on period *à deux*. Stubborn or innocent, or both, I had thought this last resort would save something. Of course, it did nothing of the kind. Marriage has never *saved* anything except, perhaps, face. By May it was clear: there was nothing left to save but a rag of existence with this man copiously educated in academic institutions, his fancy brain hopelessly addled, I am sorry to say, by alcohol. Because of his hitting the bottle so avidly, even his lucid moments were not lucid anymore. It was sad to see him dragging his unnamable chagrin across town and country, a shell-less snail leaving a track of pale gray tears.

Soon your artist was again gainfully occupied with advertising art and getting around, instead of glooming over a gigantic mistake. A half year of solitude in my Fifty-eighth Street apartment was spent at the easel when not grinding out those fashion illustrations of which, at the time, one had to be horribly ashamed—that is, if one had the crust to pretend to be a "serious" artist. Those months were not, however, without a series of amazing events.

The Macy's art director for whom I worked had seen my paintings and later, visiting the Julien Levy Gallery, happened to talk to Julien himself, telling him he should have a look at my work. He called one day and in spite of my stammering reply that I had only a couple of things ("That's all right—I'll look at the two and a half"), made an appointment, came, saw, paced the room, and said, "From now on you're in my gallery. When you have enough we will show them." Then, before leaving, he added, "The first thing is for you to meet some people. Next time I have a cocktail party I'll call you." Oh yes! But weeks, months dragged by, winter came and went. Of course, I mused sadly, it was too good to be true. Until one spring day and the phone: "I'm having a party. Can you come?"

1942. One of those May afternoons as only New York May afternoons can be. An apartment in Chelsea, all dark wood and those wonderful slatted shutters peculiar to old

New York windows. A Recamier sofa, an iron sleigh bed breathing Paris, a Hans Bellmer (surrealist artist) doll, Duchamp's assemblage *Fresh Widow*, and scattered everywhere objects, pictures, books, and more pictures. Indeed, coming in for the first time I was so overwhelmed that it was hard for me to register Julien's easy introductions to—as I remember them—Yves Tanguy, Max Ernst, Kurt Seligman, Bob Motherwell with beauteous wife, Maria, Max Ernst, Consuelo Saint-Exupéry, Peggy Guggenheim, Max Ernst, Max Ernst. It was, then, Julien Levy who did it all—not deliberately, he didn't believe in plans—who nonchalantly launched my art and found me a life companion. This on the strength of two finished works! One of them, *Birthday*, mentioned earlier—

"But that's when I came in," muses Max.

"Yes," I answer. "That's where you came in."

And even though it may be the middle of the night we lean, Max and I, over our shared past, so recent, so green, and, yes, so simply a prologue; peering with a kind of careful wonder at our first days, first events, first people, our brash leaps, miraculous escapes. We examine the long chain and all its details like the wonderful spine of some perfectly preserved skeleton, an extinct species never to be seen again.

CHAPTER TWO

Before and Always

THE PRISM OF events flashes and turns, coloring each day like paint on a canvas. Great days or failed ones, a leap, a bound, a stumble, a gulp of patience to survive the wait; all are dropped beans on the forest path leading back to the beginning. The moments immediatcly preceding our first gaze weren't really more decisive than, say, a day twenty years before when he was perhaps composing with glee and with Tzara a dada manifesto, while I in my eleven-year-old optimism was trying on a bra which, receiving nothing, was as wrinkled as a fallen parachute on the breast of the earth.

So the beginning is an impossible phantom, meaning less as that dot on my drawing, in a class perspective lesson, the spot in the middle of the paper whcre all lines—roads?—came together at a place called Infinity. Only, supposing out of curiosity you tried to go there, you'd never make it. The spot would have gone, would have streaked ahead, and you would have to start all over again. It was a trick not only of the eye but of fate itself, for the point was neither beginning nor end, just a stupid black dot that would retreat endlessly.

Now on this diagram of my own devising, the lines, instead of converging, open to reveal a middle distance where we contend, Max and I, with all kinds of ardent ferment: headlong risks crowned with quiet victories; prickly defeats relieved by entrancing vistas. We blend our lives as easily as the colors in our pictures, we scoff at perspectives which are, after all, so false: the endless stairs, the unscalable walls, even the doors I had painted, half open like Venus's flytraps, irresistible snares inviting me in. Yes, I had painted them as if doing so would liberate me from a doom of perspective, the beckoning nowhere that had dogged my errant life so far.

Poised, for a while behind brownstone and glass, listening to traffic and knocking radiators. What day is this? Is it the tomorrow announced yesterday? The fires, the slaughters, the economy, the coups. Discussions with the Russians. Never terminated, there will always be enough of them for the day after. You watch, you consider, you give them your attention, a kind of praying like an answer to the muezzin's call with a rug flop. Yes, watching the world on TV is an urgent gravity, our prayer. We spin the dial instead of lighting a candle. Listening, watching, we mark time.

At first there was only that one picture, a self-portrait. It was a modest canvas by present-day standards. But it filled the place as if it had always been there. For one thing it *was* the room.

I had been struck, one day, by a fascinating array of doors—hall, kitchen, bathroom, studio—crowded together, soliciting my attention with their antic planes, light, shadows, imminent openings and shuttings. From there it was an easy leap to a dream of countless doors. Oh, there was perspective, trapped in my own room! Perhaps in a way it was a talisman for the things that were happening, an iteration of quiet event, line densities wrought in a crystal paperweight of time where nothing was expected to appear except the finished canvas and, later, a few snowflakes, for the season was Christmas, 1942, and Max was my Christmas present.

It was snowing hard when he rang the doorbell. Choosing pictures for a show to be called Thirty Women (later Thirty-one Women), he was a willing emissary to the studios of a bouquet of pretty young painters who, besides being pretty, which they couldn't help, were also very serious about being artists.

"Please come in," I smiled, trying to say it as if to just anyone. He hesitated, stamping his feet on the doormat. "Oh, don't mind the wet," I added. "There are no rugs here."

There wasn't much furniture either, or anything to justify the six rooms, front to back. We moved to the studio, a lively place in any case, and there on an easel was the portrait, not quite finished. He looked while I tried not to. At last,

"What do you call it?" he asked.

"I really haven't a title." (I really didn't.)

"Then you can call it *Birthday*." Just like that.

Something else draws his attention then, a chess pho-

tograph pinned over my drawing board. "Ah, you play
chess!" He lifts the phrase like a question and then sets it
down as fact, so that my yes is no more than an echo of
some distant past exchange. "Then let's have a game,"
pause, "that is, if you have time."

We play. It has grown dark, stopped snowing. Utter
silence pervades this room. My queen has been checked
twice and is in very bad posture. Finally I lose. What else
could I do under the circumstances? All thoughts of
defense, counterattack, and general strategy are crowded
off the chessboard and I see only the room with two
pieces in it, my space challenged, my face burning.

There is something voluptuous, close to the bone,
about chess. "Your game is promising. I could come back
tomorrow, give you some pointers. . . ." So the next day
and the next saw us playing frantic chess (save when I was
bent over my drawing board, doing advertising illustration). Thin laminae of an old husk, decorum, kept me sitting in the prim chair instead of starred on the bed. Until
a week went by and he came to stay.

That we were both painters did not strike me at the
time as anything but the happiest of coincidences. In fact,
so unbelievable it was, so touched with a kind of graceful
humor, that, weighing the imponderables, I told myself,
yes, if it lasts three weeks it is still all right.

It took only a few hours for him to move in. There was
no discussion. It was as if he had found a house. Yes, I think
I was his house. He lived in me, he decorated me, he
watched over me. From one hour to the next my plain,

echoing floor-through was packed like a series of boxes so that our voices, when all the moving and hefting was done, stayed close to us as indeed they had wanted to from the beginning. I watched, in an agreeable state of mild vertigo. It was above all so natural and right, I thought; the long wait on the station platform was rewarded by the arrival of the train, as one knew it would be, sooner or later. In no time at all, the last picture found a place by the door and the last mask was hung over my desk.

He brought everything he had. A glory of objects and pictures expanding my rooms, making other worlds out of my walls. And as if that were not enough, the Hopi idols, Northwest Coast wolf mask, New Guinea shields. There was a totem pole that just touched the ceiling. A little dog named Kachina came with him and sat trembling under the Eskimo potlatch (a big wooden bear that was a bowl for seal oil) standing between the two front windows. Over a door a Papuan paddle, on the desk a carved horn spoon, totem-handled. "Such an abundance!" I said.

"But this was the very first piece." Max held up the spoon and told its story.

It was all about an antique shop on Third Avenue, often passed by Max, who lived nearby. One day he pulled up short. There, amid a great jumble of objects, lay the Haida spoon, the four figures of its black bone totem staring, from iridescent abalone eyes, their superb refusal of the surrounding bric-a-brac. Max went in. From the back of the shop stepped a small, shiny man, soft-spoken but politely adamant about the spoon.

"Oh, I couldn't sell it separately, it is part of the set."

"What set?"

"But don't you see? It is a collection of spoons."

A second look confirmed the shopman's remarkable words. In the window, laid out in marching order, were spoons in silver, cloisonné, wood, ivory; Georgian spoons, Roman spoons, a baby spoon. . . . There ensued an argument like a tug-of-war for the goat-horn beauty (the shop-keeper thought it was seal tusk), and Max found himself talking of the great and wonderful art of the so-called primitives—British Columbian, Alaskan, Indian, Mayan, pre-Columbian—while the other listened in utter fascination, putting in a question now and then. Did those mysterious people still create such things? Alas, no, that life was disappearing fast.

In the end he sold the spoon. The buyer, leaving his phone number, said, "And I have friends who are also interested. Let me know if you get something else." It didn't take long. The next day Max answered the phone. "I'll be right over." A magnificent Eskimo mask had appeared in the shop overnight.

It was the beginning of an almost electrical streaking to Third Avenue. While the shopman's Georgian silver rather quickly disappeared from view, he obtained, to delight the hearts of Max and his friends, ever more astonishing examples of ever rarer tribal art. Along with Max, friends Breton, Seligman, Matta, Tanguy, and Masson led the way for their new American friends. The supply seemed inexhaustible until a sleepy museum of

American tribal art, with sleepy direction and hopelessly
messy archives, so chockablock with dusty artifacts that
circulation had hitherto been difficult, began to wonder,
like a man who suddenly notices his receding hairline,
how and when so much had vanished and where it had
got to. But, like money-laundering, it was all a mystery
and our merchant only the last in a long line of receivers.
Such was the tale.

Handsome. A dusty label on the top shelf where useless
words are stored just in case. A word of tired approval to
describe something: a gift, perhaps a gesture, a "handsome" solution. But not Max. It was disturbing as an
adjective, for I did not want it, could not bear the idea of
category. When he came along his looks were so tangled
in my mind and eyes with all the other things about him,
with all my dreaming over his paintings before I finally
met him, and perhaps above all with his strangeness, his
not fitting the trim, thick-necked ideal of male physical
splendor so prevalent among us, that, completely aside
from the erotic matter of our coming together, I took him
to my heart without one backward glance.

No girl can bear not to be the beautiful one in a bedroom situation. She must be the prize—a Daphne who
will turn into a tree if the pursuer is not careful. She
must be a little hard to get. But then when we undressed
and I saw at last what I had thought to shun, a physical
being all harmony, all smiles, all petal and lean muscle,

and all for me, then it was too late, my dry little considerations were laid aside, and I happily dropped with beads
and clothes the layers of vanity my clumsy worldliness
had hitherto ordained. His narrow body, further emaci-
ated by concentration-camp nonfare, was, in its economy,
more like those of boys diving off the bank at the swimming hole than the curvy excrescences of Michelangelo's
cherubic boys.

He answered all phone calls. One evening we actually
found ourselves at famous Helena Rubinstein's apartment, where the well-known face presided over a card
table (of high stakes?) while, across the big room, someone was playing the piano. I leaned on it (gracefully, I
thought). And the next day the talented performer
phoned. Max answered: "Dis is de butler. Nobody home."

If he ventured outside of me, he knew he had not to
lock the door. At these rare times we wrote letters, daily.
They brought a different charm into the house, they
mocked the opaque background of absence. They said
things we never said out loud. How deprived are all the
letterless lives today, how sad the phone, the fax, the e-
mail. In his letters there was no place for revelation of
past trials, no hint of his giant share of struggles, persecu-
tions, narrow escapes; no condemnation of circumstance.
As I was to learn over the ensuing years, Max Ernst was as
unembittered as he was undaunted. The pure inner core
of him would continue to mock the ironies while recognizing their tackinesses and their poisons. He would
paint. He would always paint. With his hands, flowers of

hands with their big fans of bones inside, strong as strong, and square. To be placed on a hip, or in repose or in pockets, as he stood one day, looking over my shoulder at the drawing.

"Do you like doing that?"

Under my pen dipped in India ink lay the white Strathmore three-ply illustration board, peopled by girls and women. They were fully dressed. And the dresses and suits and coats would be bought at Macy's. Or perhaps it was beachwear. Or perfume, trailing little clouds of scent, evanescent pen lines, palely shadowed. I put down my brush in a kind of freeze.

"No, of course not. No, I hate it."

"Then why do you do it?"

Silently, to myself, good God. I was embarrassed, oh worse. All this trivial activity simply revealed my fathomless insignificance and pointed a finger: how can anyone, doing *that*, pretend to be an artist? How can a true artist so stoop? I agreed, I agreed. Writhing. But he was still there with his idle question, and answer must be made somehow. So I said,

"You don't understand."

"Please. You are the painter of *Birthday*. You can't stop now."

"I'm not stopping."

"Yes. That stuff there on the drawing board. That's stopping."

"It's provisional. Temporary. In the meantime . . ."

"There is no meantime." He said this with great gentleness, not as a pronouncement or even chidingly, but as pointing to something that was already our common care. Where was I?

"I have to make a living." (Weak.) There was a short pause. Then:

"Ecoute," I heard him say. "I have always earned my living by my painting. I think I can do it for two."

If these words had been recorded on the spot and if I had played them back a thousand times over the years, I could not remember them better than I do now. This was his proposal, not on one knee but standing in the waning afternoon light between me and the picture, like a collage figure pasted on this absurd back room of East Fifty-eighth street. There wasn't much space. Before I knew it, we were hugging each other, a momentous, solemn hug, a desperate hug where we might have been two castaways on a raft, as New York swam around us, two insignificant motes in the universe that we would, from then on, inhabit together.

Stunned and happy, I went to the phone to call my agent. "I quit." It was so simple. (Years later, meeting at some gallery opening, this nice man, in love with advertising, looked at me sadly, saying, "When I think what you could have become!")

That picture! Days later I was showing it to a would-be collector, a man I had met once at an office party. A sort of business-political analyst, he was the boss of my then boyfriend. I did not know that he collected art. Now here he was, in his three-piece suit, sparkling white shirt, and quiet tie, here in the afternoon light of my fourth-floor walk-up. Max stood, hand on hip, in the doorway. He listened pleasantly until the visitor asked the price.

"The picture is not for sale," said Max. A modest silence, as his words sank into two brains. The visitor then said:

"But I think Dorothea should decide." And looking at me, he added, "Don't you want to see your portrait hanging in the Oval Office?"

Those were his exact words. My ears did not deceive me. Or did they? What oval office? Were there several oval offices? Was his own office oval? Or was it just a term for something? That this man, perhaps about forty-five years old and unknown to the public, actually entertained the belief that he would someday be the president of the United States of America was so outlandish that one had to ignore it like a blunder—a sneeze, a stumble. Indeed, its slapstick absurdity almost marred the momentous tone of that afternoon which, for me, was nothing less than historic—my history—for I saw my life ending and another one, also mine, beginning. Yet the man's question gives pause, for it is surely an example of that fundamental given in the American consciousness, confidence in the democracy with which a father can lean over the cradle of his newborn infant and say, just as in the fairy tales, "Someday you will be the president." (Though today he may prefer to add "of the corporation," for who in their right mind would want to be *the* president any more?)

A brief moment of rapid phrases, high tension, a

pause. I hesitated—was I dreaming? Because Max was say-ing quite distinctly:

"I love Dorothea. I want to spend the rest of my life with her. The picture is part of that life."

To this the collector had no reply. Nor did I. As for Max, my visitor's oval office provided him with another of his droll stories.

What festooned our bower with extravagant blooms was the ongoing surrealist adventure. Twenty years old for him, still new for me. A Paris blaze, its sparks had now fallen on New York to provide a little alchemical warfare.

It can safely be said here that during this last century our way of seeing the world was profoundly changed by contact with surrealism. There are many who believe it is still alive as a means of inquiry and discovery. Few, how-ever, realize that what we truly have inherited and made our own is dada, the nihilistic movement that preceded surrealism by seven years. Its genesis took place in the Cabaret Voltaire in Zurich, Switzerland. Here were gath-ered several wild and woolly young iconoclasts filled with despair over World War I and fed up with bourgeois (aes-thetic) values. I can imagine them, after a few drinks, in their mock-seriousness, spoiling for scandal, inventing their defiantly meaningless attitude towards art, one of them (Tristan Tzara, I'm told) closing his eyes and put-ting his finger on the dictionary, on the word "dada." The name stuck. Marcel Duchamp, who had already scandalized the New York art world at the 1913 Armory Show with his *Nude Descending a Staircase* became, of course, its leading member and paved the way for countless subsequent artists hoping, with their *ideas* (not much else) to *épater la bourgeoisie.*

But at the time it did not take long for Dada to reach Paris from Zurich and for poet André Breton to see it as the linchpin on which to hang his surrealism—a milder form of challenge and far more suited to poetry and painting. It packed enough of the enigmatic to keep minds and pens occupied indefinitely and, meanwhile, could be enjoyed by all (contrary to its immediate ancestor, which, proudly, having no connection to anything, has a way—I guess for that reason—of enraging people to this day).

Perhaps in anticipation of its shock value, or that wonderful vibration that phenomena send across the world, surrealism was heralded in New York by *View,* a magazine of new writing and pictures started by the young Charles Henri Ford.

It is hard now when the word "surreal" is used for the merest incongruity to realize what a bomb it was at that time. And to see surrealism incarnate, in the persons of André Breton and friends, arrive in 1940, after having been quite literally and almost single-handedly saved from chaos and worse by the intrepid Varian Fry at the helm of the International Rescue Committee in Marseille, was a big event for all of us. For these stragglers called intellectuals it was a reprieve. They had waited, forlorn as orphans, to be taken from Marseille, via Spain, to open-armed America, a place that would care for their beautiful brains and offer them its own treasure: a brand-new way of life.

That way of life, ours, was variously lived and appreciated by the refugee population. Some stayed on to embrace it totally after the war. Others were simply perched here as on a desert atoll, longing to get home. Consuelo Saint-Exupéry was happy enough among us, a volatile Carmen, originally from San Salvador but belonging to Paris, and wife to "Tonio," Antoine de Saint-Exupéry. Her dalliance with fellow refugees while he ranged the skies did not in the least affect the bonds, defined by tempestuous quarrels and long periods apart, that kept them in a shared state of excitement, agony, and bliss while he, daredevil "Saint-Ex," flew his crate without navigational tools, as one knows from the stories and from his own books.

Scene: New York, on a winter evening in 1943. Because it is wartime, the blinds are closed as Tonio drifts in with the snow on Sutton Place, where his Consuelo is waiting out the war. We are there with her, to admire him, and to listen avidly to news of the front. His quietude is like the falling snow that tamps everything down to deepest silence. The talk tarries behind drawn curtains and Max and Tonio play chess in the lamplight. It may have been his last chess game, for we heard the news some time later: flying his reconnaissance plane over the Mediterranean, flirting with German U-boats as Icarus flirted with the sun, he dips and swings once too often, and is heard from no more.

Surrealists in New York! They were welcomed everywhere. The doors of penthouse and brownstone alike
were open to them, just as in old centuries the motleyed
pantaloon was a must at boring princely parties. Ship-
wrecked surrealism. For some it was stimulation, excitement. For others, simply amusing. For yet others, absurd
and "controversial"—a favorite word of the era meaning
undesirable. For me it brought a kind of relief to see my
aberrant pictures find not only tolerance but enthusiasm
among these seminal exotics whom I had admired for so
many reasons.

To think of those early New York evenings—this is
1943—is to think of games presided over by *le surréalisme
même*: André Breton. The Game of Truth, the Blindfold
Game, the Game of Murder, whatever the game, he led
the proceedings in a manner always solemn and resolute.

Under Breton's aegis we plunged with a positively
juvenile fervor into these games, which seemed so necessary to him. Had it something to do with his attention to
the work of Sigmund Freud? Scratching around in the
psyche? Wanting, perhaps, to make some further contri-
bution to vital knowledge? (He did.)

He detested music but made an exception—ironic,
surely—for Offenbach, the only notes he could listen to
without actual distress. Yet, when he read a poem his voice
was as permeated with tremolo as an opera aria. I pondered
this. Was it stained with musical feeling? Unconsciously? A
heady thought.

Speaking only in French, this singular man was careful

not to learn even three words of English for fear of dulling the edge of his own exquisite writing instrument. He was perhaps not at all convinced of proto-Indo-European roots having anything to do with French. As for English, it was simply preposterous, a doughty menace to his best possession. Wonderful it was to think of him tip-toeing around his precious language-bed, administering antibiotics to keep the Americanisms at bay. If the air was rich in stop consonants, it was also poor in fricatives, and he secretly assured his patient that it would not be long before they were home again.

Seeing André freshly divorced, his friends were forever trying to find him a girl. One evening someone brought a pretty redhead. In vain. "I am a businesswoman," she said, dryly (this makes Max laugh). "I don't drink, I don't smoke, and I don't make love." Unequivocal. Translated for André, who smiled.

He was a wizard at silent laughter. With his mouth tightly closed, his face crinkled, and his soft upper body began to shake rhythmically as if he had been wound up. This was his laugh. It seemed to say: I really don't want to laugh, but I'm laughing anyway. His ritual manner, his large impassive face masking what worlds of desperate revolt, his love of the occult, his intransigence, oh, all those things combined to present to my eyes the true man from elsewhere. For me no fantasist's created being from outer space could ever compare with this subtle amalgam of human sorcery.

And what of his friends? His relations with Max Ernst

were a tangle of thrusts and jabs and polite smiles, of Max's grinning defiance and Breton's trembling retaliation, which took the form of frequent banishments followed by partial reconciliations.

I witnessed a sample of these at a New York party, one of my first evenings with Max and his friends. Suddenly everyone stopped talking, and listened as Breton, facing Max, said for all to hear:

"*Je n'écrirai jamais plus un mot sur vous!*" ("I'll never write another word about you!") And Max:

"*Je m'en fous.*" A strong expression, translating to, let us say, "I couldn't care less."

Something terrible is going on, I thought, as Breton raised one hand in a gesture to the room, his voice rising and full of disbelief:

"*Il s'en fout! Il s'en fout!*"

All this time I stood there, understanding little, and aware of myself as no more than an object blown in off the street, something or someone so extraneous and out of place that the entire absurdity of my presence there was concentrated for me in the silk flower I wore in my hair. My irrésistible gesture, pinning on a flower at seven-thirty, showed me up, at ten, as a rank outsider. It did not, however, prevent Max from grasping my hand and pulling me with him from the room a few minutes later.

Nor did their quarrel last forever. By the time we came to Paris, six years later, all was forgotten, at least on the surface. Yet, across the years their heroic struggle deepened, with each time the spasm lasting a little longer until, one sudden day, there was nothing left to be banished from. Arp was gone, if he had ever been there; Aragon, Tzara, Eluard had long since fallen out of favor and into more dubious company involving cards. Tanguy and Duchamp were already American, thus remote if indulgent; Miró, in Spain, deeply locked in his own universe. As for Picasso, he and surrealism were stale friends, even though he had once played its games.

Breton's answer to the truth-game question "Have you any friends?" was "*Non, mon ami.*" As Max said, when interviewed after Breton's death, no doubt he was conscious of the beauty of this confession of absolute solitude. Friends or not friends, the dichotomy prevailed, translated into *le groupe surréaliste.*

Intellectually, they flew close to the flame. Instinctively they were far from knowing the perverse appetites they so admired and glorified, feeling rather little of fire in their loins but much of the imaginative luster. For most of them woman was a delicious mystery. These surrealist men loved to kiss her hand; they did not back her into a corner as a "macho" fellow would have done and as some women might have liked. Of course they had their share of adventures, but they tended to prefer marriage and fidelity, endowing the simple ancient concepts with a kind of luminosity, as if they had invented the former and resuscitated the latter. Given their fundamental rejection of the actual irrespirable world, procreation was considered sloppy, even though a few of them had actually, albeit ruefully, become fathers. As for emulating the fantasies of Sade's personae,

they didn't even try. The games presided over by Breton
flirted with daring but only in words. He threaded a swarm
of projects: an ephemeris they named *VVV* (paid for by
Bernard Reis, an avid collector of modern rare books, surrealism's New York host for succulent dinners prepared by
wife Becky and, later, involved in some unsavory trial about
an inheritance), an exhibition, First Papers of Surrealism,
book display, store windows, manifestos. Even the tirades
were courtly and *belles* as to *lettres.*

Although he never wrote about my work, I was not too
concerned. I seemed to detect extenuating circumstances:
his strained relationship with Max, mostly. Very likely, in
Breton's mind I was *dependent,* in every sense of the word,
on my mate. Though he had reproduced *Birthday* in *VVV,*
his New York magazine venture (three issues), well, I was
Max's woman and Max was his friend and collaborator.
His own wife, also a painter, was not comfortable when
this happened. *"Alors—tu aime les pieds nus maintenant?"*
(Her words, reported to me by Max, translate to "So—you
like bare feet now?") All so unsurreal, I thought, and
somehow dispiriting.

I had noted with some consternation that the place of
women among these iconoclasts was not different from
what it was among the population in general, including
the bourgeoisie. Also—was I wrong?—being uneasy about
prefaces in the first place, I really didn't want one. It
seemed to me that the prefaces Breton wrote at that time
were usually feverish and exaggerated in relation to the
artist in question. Another reason, a small detail maybe: I

spoke almost no French during the years when we were with him. You can imagine what I must have looked like: mute before this great personage for whom communication was either spoken or written.

It was all this ambivalence and contradiction that fascinated me. *Les surréalistes.* Although their ardor for the untried swam in an intellectual decoction of theory, their philosophical inquiry leaned indeed toward eroticism, a powerful (but, as far as I could see, cerebral only) magnet along with revolt. How strong the words of, say, Lautréamont must have echoed in their souls—*"cache-toi, guerre"*—like hot sun and wave fury that turns sharp rocks into yielding stones, round and soft. Only it was they who softened under the words. Doesn't understanding preclude violence?

I never heard them discuss the rights of either men or women. They knew, as anyone should, that a woman is profoundly distanced from a man and, moreover, quite possibly as well or better equipped to confront slippery enigmas, even to find the answers that had so far eluded him.

Woman? All they knew for sure was that they desired her. *Désir,* a gigantic five-letter word. The millions of words they lavished on her were not diagrams for her degradation. They were disguised hymns to her mystery. I don't believe that even in the most romantic moments of literary history have writing men so adored the idea of woman.

New York had no sidewalk cafés for them. Did wild ideas spurt less freely indoors? Was theirs an unease among the soft lamps, the freeform ashtrays, the foam sofa cushions of New York apartments? After the war they went back to where they came from, leaving the key on the door. Many others have used it since, but no one has brought in any new furniture

Among my new friends the language was French, everyone having lived in Paris at some time or other. And ever since my own aborted stay there I had been determined that French should also be mine. When I met Max, I had already been taking some intensive French lessons from a fat old lady in my street named Madame Hélène Dupont. As it happened, she wasn't French at all but Russian, with, I realized later, a strong Russian accent that rendered her speech something like baby talk. Also, she was never completely dressed, but enfolded in some kind of a kimono or wrapper that, although held tightly with brooches and pins, was not quite effective in containing her very distinct odor. Just the same I persisted; the lessons were cheap and I was in a hurry. One day Max came to pick me up for lunch after my lesson and noted her engraved card on the letter box. It said: *Mme Hélène Dupont, Présidente de la Pensée Française.* This became one of his favorite stories.

For those who hung around art in those days, Fifty-seventh Street opened its doors and its minds, beginning with Julien Levy's gallery, known as surrealism's showcase since 1932. He had brought, mostly from France, where radical changes were happening in art and ideas, a stunning series of visual explosions whose seismic vibrations were felt here in studio lofts and galleries all over town and as far away as California. By the time the Museum of Modern Art got around to mounting its exhibition Fantastic Art, Dada, and Surrealism in 1936, Julien's gallery had given New York four years of surrealist shocks like the Dalí exhibition I walked in on one day in 1941 to find Dalí and his wife occupying the place like an invading army. Julien told me later that his first two Dalí exhibitions did not sell even one picture. (He would say things like this with consummate irony but very offhandedly as if expecting you to know that such is the art dealer's life.)

Before saying that Julien was sophisticated, you would have to define his kind of sophistication. Was he an Ulrich, Musil's sardonic, jaded young aesthete, or Proust's Swann, or even Dorian Gray without the portrait? Fantasies that would have made him laugh. Yet, his persona was a magnet for adjectives. They swarmed around him, clung to his profile (lovely to draw), hair (shiny and black), silhouette (slim, *gracile*), the ensemble suave, debonair, elusive, without any one trait pinning him down. When Walter Pater said, "Art is life seen through a temperament," he was surely anticipating Julien Levy. His gaze was just not quite sad. He had been everywhere. He had, perhaps, done everything. He not only signed me on as one of the artists of his "stable," but, in so doing, brought me into a whole new world, the one I had been waiting for.

My first exhibition in the Julien Levy Gallery occurred in the fall of 1944. Imagine a house on Fifty-seventh Street, its second floor reached by a tiny elevator. Imagine two handsome rooms with a pretty secretary to match. Here, it seemed, people irresistibly came—to look, to listen, to wonder, but, alas, rarely to buy. In looking back, one sees the confusion. It was all so unfamiliar, unnerving, even confrontational as might be said today. These were not pictures to fill the spot over the sofa. And Julien Levy, well, he was not your familiar art dealer either. He was helpful, he was patient, he would tell his visitor about surrealism; and when the elevator door closed would turn, spread his hands wide, palms up, in bafflement at the visitor's—incomprehension? timidity? obtuseness? But the next minute, exasperation forgotten, would see him telling something funny, maybe about a certain artist who gave his very rich collector a *prix d'ami* (friend's price), a figure somewhat higher than the gallery's price tag.

My own show there (three pictures sold) rated me another one in January of 1948—his last, as I recall, before closing the gallery. But before going, he "placed" me with another gallery, which turned me loose before we got around to an exhibition because I was "difficult to get along with." I had been writing the gallery infuriated letters about such things as changing the titles of my pictures when they sent them to other shows. One of these, for instance, was called *The New Look*. It was a little portrait (full-length) of myself except that my skin was black instead of white. They called it *The Black Rose*. Why, why? Ah, but "the new look" was passé, didn't I know? (This had been a fashion craze from Paris—Dior).

If the Julien Levy Gallery was a center of the surrealist

excitement, probably the most deeply excited person there was Julien himself. Having brought dada and surrealism back from Paris like trophies, he took his real reward in finding more of the same signs at home: Arshile Gorky with the sadness of the world permanently upon him; Joseph Cornell, quiet and intense; the brothers Berman, Eugene and Leonid (not quite surrealists—they were called "magic-realists"); and many more, all under Julien's wing, on Julien's walls, in Julien's pantheon of treasured artists alongside the already famous.

Certain crepuscular afternoons in Julien's apartment above the gallery provided sustained late-day magic along with the dry martinis. It is an appropriate term, magic, perfectly describing the glow that pervaded the sepia tint of the room and fell on the painted and unpainted people who moved in and out of it. Artists all in their way; the sounds they made, murmurous and furry like the big hat on Lotte Lenya. Under it, her face a blur of sooty eyes and red mouth, she talked in that dark voice she had, while waving a right hand laden with rings, cocktail glass, and cigarette holder. The accent. Not the name of a country, it spelled otherness, it hinted of a world where amazing things happened as naturally as the familiar scene outside Julien Levy's long windows.

A blue afternoon lies upon a crimson one and produces a mauve hour. In this room were the performing arts "in person"—opera, theater, dance, with, especially, music for everyone: Purcell on the hi-fi, Vittorio Rieti, Darius Milhaud, Virgil Thomson, Sylvia Marlowe, Alexey

Haieff in attendance. Virgil pronounced impeccable asides from his soft throne of a chair, seeming to orchestrate sounds and voices; Sylvia's, voice, for example, quick and firm as were, I knew later, her fingers on the harpsichord. Virgil and I both dined one evening at Sylvia's, where I looked forward to a pleasant evening of chit-chat. But Virgil had to get away to hear a cello recital and, moreover, insisted that I should go with him. "Go," said Sylvia. But I was loath to spend two hours listening to a musician I hadn't even heard of. Virgil was adamant, even pleading. "Please, Dorothea, someone has to be with me. You see, I tend to go to sleep and need an elbow jab when that happens." How could I refuse it, put that way? On the way over to the theater he filled me in. ". . . a talented boy. I didn't review his other recital, so I'm going to do it this time." We settled into our seats, fifth row on the aisle. We applauded the talented boy's appearance. Then, as predicted, it happened: the fellow had scarcely time to tune his instrument before Virgil was peacefully sleeping. But as instructed, I only punched him when he began to snore, which he did a number of times during the program. Each time he would pick up brightly, look at me, incredulous—"Was I snoring?" and fix his eyes straight at the stage for two or three minutes before the next nap. Incidentally, this kept me, too, wide awake. From the theater we got separate taxis, for him to his desk at the *New York Herald Tribune*, and for me to my apartment. Though I do not read newspaper reviews, I was curious enough to buy next morning's rag, to see what Virgil could possibly say. There it was, a long and laudatory column of print, the elucidation surely of Virgil's dreams of beautiful music infused by the "talented boy" and assisted by the printed program.

At Julien's there were, of course, painters to talk to; some mentioned earlier, like Eugene Berman, who had seen my first pictures. He led me to Balanchine across the room. "She is just the artist you need for the sleepwalker sets. Costumes too," he told him. These were the days when ballets had "scenery," and George Balanchine was as keen on it as anyone else.

A momentous meeting, for it began a collaboration that literally swept me off my feet. Because, studying my maquette one day (this was October 1945, and we were in my studio, on East Fifty-eighth street), George Balanchine, in a burst of creative fervor, cried, "Yes! Like this!" And to demonstrate, he swept me up in the air, a one-hundred-and-fifteen-pound lump, my embarrassment adding another hundred pounds. Oh, how to be light and supple, how not to be a dead weight on his famous spine that normally took on thistle-light girls, trained to make themselves so. Of course, it only lasted a moment. He put me down gently as he talked with our composer, Vittorio Rieti. The ballet, *The Night Shadow,* was presented by Les Ballets Russes de Monte Carlo in the old Metropolitan Opera House in March 1946, under the leadership of George Denham (I've forgotten his real Russian name). *The Night Shadow* had the distinction of participating in the last season ever of the company and of the old opera house. A later collaboration with Balanchine was *Bayou,* a work danced to music by Virgil Thomson and presented by the New York City Ballet at City Center. Two more ballets, one with the same company, were needed to bring home to me my basic distaste for collaboration: *Will o' the Wisp,* and another, much later, in London, *The Witch.* Of this one my most vivid memory is the earth-shaking event of taking a bow on the stage of Covent Garden! Thus, two great opera house stages had held me—for the time it takes to skip a heartbeat.

What I knew all the time, however, was that I did not belong in this milieu. Collaboration was not for me. By 1951 it was time to move on. So much had happened and was happening on my various papers and canvases—where I was bringing more and more of what I needed to paint the statement that was my imperative; more audacities, more demands, above all more challenges to make, gauntlets to throw down—that there was no place for anything else (except my eternal notebooks, without which I would be as bereft as a swimmer without water). And always the rocklike purpose hidden like an underwater current throughout the shows, the games, the luminous evenings of New York or star-ridden ones of Sedona, Arizona, and sweeping me, thoughtfully, through these years of self-discovery, encouraged by Max.

Sometimes, at Julien's, there was Joseph Cornell. Gaunt, pearl-pale, and surprised, he usually sat just a little apart, as I did. And, actually leaning to me, he spoke chaste, cobwebby things about *my* drawings (he called them "feés"), and wanted to see more. Had I something in a drawer, some drawing, a feé that he could incorporate into a box? Indeed, how I have regretted that I did not, or thought so!

Cornell's reserve and his feathery presence were often, and devotedly, watched over by Gypsy Rose Lee, Broadway dazzler and artist's darling. She it was who organized screenings of his collage films in her Edwardian-styled Sixty-third Street house. And she it was who first bought Joseph's astonishing boxes (by the way, she was my first collector, of a tiny painting called *Children's Games*), who inspired other ones, and who had a secure place in his pantheon of glittering, ineffable women, raised by him, I sometimes think, to that stratospheric realm inhabited by angels, who, as everyone knows, are sexless.

His was like the courtly love of the thirteenth-century troubadors: the relation of lover to adored lady as a pure passion, ennobling, ever unfulfilled and ever innocent. In this respect, Joseph Cornell was a modern Dante, with his deep religious feeling and physical abstinence. Consummate romantic in an intoxicatingly worldly world, he came frequently to town as from some remote monastic commune that remained unknown to all but a few. If you won his confidence you were invited to meet the two people who shared and shaped his daily life: his mother and his adored brother, Robert, a spastic invalid for whom Joseph's every creation was a present. Robert's smile, Robert's delight, Robert's approval, stemming from a valid, undamaged intellect, were what Joe sought as ardently as most artists seek renown. His friendship with Marcel Duchamp is legendary. From Duchamp he learned the value of pure choice. "I choose, therefore it is." A pair of eyes looks at a pile of detritus. A hand reaches out, takes an object from the pile. The object is thus beatified.

An afternoon in winter, weary-gray and windy. We are five to drive to Utopia Parkway, in Flushing, Queens. There a small white frame house holds Joseph Cornell, brother Robert, and their mother. She has baked a cake and there is a plateful of oatmeal cookies. They are set out on a lacy tablecloth, and here we all have tea. We are talking so compulsively that there is not one word to remember. Mrs. Cornell is silent and shy. Joseph sits dreaming, perhaps wondering why we are here. Occasionally, he will interpret a phrase of Robert's. Only after tea does he invite us to visit the icy garage, at the back of the house, where the boxes are kept.

Shelves to the ceiling hold works in progress as well as finished boxes, waiting for their release by their creator. To this Santa's workshop, moreover, only the "ladies"— three, in this case—are welcome. Max and another friend of something's, being males, are left in the parlor. But I come back to the warm house carrying treasure: a white palace among bare trees and mirror sky like the world outside; an unbelievable gift from an unbelievable friend, all in a box and all mine. Later years, when my home was in Arizona, saw us corresponding in innocent (his) dreamy letters filling equivocal (mine), dreamy needs. I wanted a document picture of a sailing vessel, he sent a little book about the sinking of the *Mary Deare*. He wanted more "feés." I tried to decorate my letters his way.

Others who in the following years knew him better than I have given fuller accounts of this artist. I only knew him as a friend. We trusted each other: kindred artists with much in common. I was the kind of feminine romantic whose romanticism feeds on random, obscure or forgotten texts and pictures that abound in musty books and documents. Like Cornell. We were alone in our landscape, I thought at the time.

A summer Long Island, in a place called Great River, grows out of that winter. At the bottom of a long green lawn, wicketed for croquet, is Long Island Sound, slapping sluggish water against the sides of a small rowboat, a *bateau ivre* that waits vainly for the lift and dip of oars and voices. Vainly, because the rented house, one of those soulless houses responsible to nothing more substantial than the renters' relief at getting away from the city heat, but intended to provide summer fun for Muriel and Julien Levy with friends Max Ernst and Dorothea Tanning, turns out to be a prison, surrounded as it is by armies of bloodthirsty mosquitoes. They wait for us outside the screens. We, plucky divers, plunge from time to time into the garden (sown and nurtured by Max when the lease was signed in May) to pull up a tiny carrot or lettuce. Otherwise, we are screened and safe in the big verandah. We gaze sometimes at the forlorn croquet mallets outside while playing chess. (Julien was dead serious about chess, and as we didn't play with a clock, a single brain-cudgeling *parti* with him

could last for days. He had also delved deep into the eso-
teric sciences from Buddhism to Blavatsky and knew how to
read the tarot. So on rainy days before the chess there was
your fortune to attend to, with Julien telling the cards as a
special favor, solemnly, respectfully, perhaps direly—and
only if he thought you could take it.) Or we might be making chess pieces and chess pictures that come back to town,
where they figure in Julien's winter exhibition, The Imagery
of Chess.

There, one evening (January 5, 1945), in the Julien Levy
Gallery a small invited public watched seven chessboards
manned by seven intrepid players: Julien himself;
Frederick Kiesler, avant-garde architect and dreamer; Alfred
Barr, the director of the Museum of Modern Art; Xanti

Schawinsky, chess whiz; Vittorio Rieti, composer dear to Balanchine; Max Ernst; and me, Dorothea, all of us braced to take on blindfolded chess master George Koltanowski. Marcel Duchamp called out the moves. (For the record: everyone lost except Kiesler, who managed a draw.)

CHAPTER THREE

Flight

REELING WITH the sudden spectrum of choices fanning
out before us, and moving through the city's magnitudes
as in a spectral prologue played to the hilt; more absorbed
than ever with the process of painting, as if from now
on each work would mark its moment indelibly—for time
did not so much pass as turn around us rather savagely,
prompting rash, defiant spurts and somersaults, the kind
of dynamic that wants only brambles and smoke to evoke
Dionysius—waiting for a sort of peace to calm us in our
strenuous elation, and not too sure of our next move, we
played and painted with equal verve. The back room was
still my studio, now solely devoted to painting, those ada a
dim memory. Max had found a cold-water flat (a curious
name, for though it had no heat the water was hot and by
filling the bathtub with hot water one could warm the
flat—a little) around the corner, on Second Avenue.

In May 1943, we fled the city to summer in a place
vaunted by Etiemble, one of Max's fellow refugees. It
was Sedona, Arizona, far from Long Island, far from

Connecticut, far from anything either of us had ever known.

In fact, its landscape of wild fantasy could not be classified and forgotten when summer was over. Less than three years later we were back to stay, my recent bout with encephalitis, a scary virus, demanding a long period of recovery. What better place to get well than Sedona?

We would go back to that place of crystal air and red rocks that reared under pure blue. We would leave the city, its docked warships, its tsetse fly if he was still around, its bellowing nurse, its cold, wet streets, its improbable fire sirens, taxicabs, ambulances, and knives. This time we would take everything: rolls of canvas, stretchers, paints. And the totem pole, the potlatch bowl, the kachina dolls, the pictures. We would build a little house.

Why, we said, do artists remain in cities? Must they chum with collectors, attend openings, witness name-droppings in Upper East and West Side pastures (Atossa, daughter of Cyrus, wife of Darius and mother of Xerxes, was a follower of Sappho) in order to make good pictures, good objects, good anything? No, we will do it the other way.

It was February 1946. Before the illness I had finished designing the costumes for Balanchine's ballet. Alas, I would not see the result, for we left New York a month before the premiere. A flurry of telegrams received in the remote "guest ranch" that hid me was even a special sort of delight, uninvolved as I was with temperamental ballet dancers and large numbers of people.

In leaving New York we had secured my apartment by lending it to Marcel and Teeny Duchamp; willing it to them, really, for when the next lease came around, "my cousin," Teeny, signed it. One of the droll results of this was that for a time there were four names on our brass letterbox down in the little entrance vestibule: Matisse (Teeny was still Mrs. Pierre Matisse), Ernst, Duchamp, Tanning. (When this amusing fact is reported—in books, the press—the last of the four names is omitted. After all, why not? In reports of this kind it is luster that is required, not accuracy.)

So many events, so many people, so much to leave behind. Yet, Sedona is the other way. And there begin some incomparable years. We build the house—of wood, for there is no water for concrete; we chase away the cattle from our five tomato plants; we haul ice twenty miles from Cottonwood. We fill our kerosene lamps to read by; we stand our ground in sudden confrontations with scorpions, centipedes, tarantulas, black widows, and, in the broom closet, a snake. The snake is a simple garter snake but, discovered by Max, renders him ashen. And when I, who had in childhood learned to coexist amiably with these creatures, pick it up and carry it outdoors, Max's admiration is total: Dorothea can not only paint, she can charm snakes! Who, in my place, would disabuse him, who would say, "It's harmless"?

When electricity finally blooms, an explosion of brash white light, we are exultant and thoughtful, while our phonograph plays Stravinsky, on 78-rpm's, very loud. The sounds roll out, widen and crash against the crimson rocks. We feel certain of our fate.

The place is not a town nor even a village. A general store dispenses beer, canned beans, and cattle feed, and there are lovelorn tunes in the jukebox ("That Old Black Magic"). Hear the twangy jokes of cowhands. "Hi, Max!" they say, sizing us up, taking us in, giving us the benefit of the doubt. "You here to paint scenes?" Down the road is the post office, exactly eight by eight, Coke dispenser outside. Miraculously, letters sometimes arrive. . . .

All packages were irresistible to Max, rectangular surprises, wrapped and tied to be torn open and laid bare. We have come down the canyon from Flagstaff and the weekly visit to the supermarket, liquor shop, and Penney's, with a stop at the post office, which yields a package from France. Back in our would-be driveway, we unload the heavy cartons from the car, surprises all; even the laundry, brought into the kitchen with the wine and groceries and immediately stripped by strong hands of its flimsy pink paper wrapping, the string broken or pulled aside to reveal the same old towels, shirts, socks. . . . Every time. As he walks away from the stupid sheets, their faded colors, their trailing string, he just as quickly forgets his momentary disappointment. The laundry has not laid bare even one new miracle. But there are avocados and the book from France, from Paul. Open it. Astonishingly its title reads *Huit Poèmes Visibles* ("Eight Visible Poems"), by Max Ernst and Paul Eluard. The day has, after all, delivered its surprise.

At times a word seen, *Sheetrock*, and there he is, building the house, saying those words: two-by-four, Sheetrock, Sheetrock. What it was for I've forgotten, only that it was necessary to him in his concentration on the raising of a work; the house. So that thinking of temporality and circumstance, I found myself imagining him elsewhere, in places he might be occupying at this instant: great halls, libraries, a lofty studio and not the shed of the Sedona Lumber Company, where he now stood choosing from among the warped and knotty two-by-fours, the green lumber of wartime, fiberboard, the big nails. Yes, this was here and it was now. Max would build our house and there would be doors and windows that opened and closed; there, finally, he could sit in one of our two chairs (it was called at the time a "captain's chair") like a captain of the tight unshifting little house, open a book and read as if nothing had happened, as if nothing had been squandered, nothing taken away. He would have simply bridged the time and the space halfway across the world where perhaps some other book in some other language had once opened before him, opened the dialogue. So that Sheetrock was some meaningless word, absurd, inappropriate, even though it breaks my heart to remember his voice saying it.

We made constant and iridescent plans, clean sprays of froth, because like surf they dissolved into airy shapes impressed on our hopes, unrealizable scenarios of an impossible future, *Future*, the word he couldn't even hear without deep embarrassment and a weary disdain. Alas, it was my word.

We are all supposed to be looking into the future while keeping an eye on the present, are we not? Out here the telescope has been turned around and I see only the past, the immediate one back there, shared and tantalizing, leaking into a present which bulges clownishly, unfunny and perilous. It is here to be negotiated, to penetrate on tiptoe and not too blindly, thus to avoid great pain. And the future? Yes, Max was right. It is an awful word.

He talks about a world I haven't known, where the tragedies have, in his telling, a way of wearing their masks inside out and where the most comical events do the same. Ludicrous situations, doomed group projects, explosions and fizzles like dropped stitches; artists, poets; the women, numerous, often beautiful and always at least eccentric if not unhinged.

His stories of these crazies, which I must say he told with a certain relish, made me long to be mad, too. Oh, I want to be wild, I would moan. No. No. Yes, just a little crazy . . . God forbid. No. I've had enough of that. His tone was all at once serious and alarmed. But I wanted, ah, how deeply, that superb indifference to reason, to the *a fortiori* and the therefore. It was an insouciance that was never to be mine. It was a tragedy that I, foolish woman, would be spared. Knowing this, he kept me near.

Faraway events, even the smallest ones, change color in the telling. They all seemed so close there in the wide-open nights of Arizona, far from their penumbral absurdities and confusions, their blur. While our walls improvised home, the spaces around our table and our bed were hung with the web of our stories, a long strand of shimmering beads strung with knots and areas of time and place in between each one, often as not concerned with events of which we were not even a part. I could make him laugh. He could make me sad with words as candid as tapestry, an extravagant weaving of color that seemed to leap from his pictures into those narratives and asides that played jokes on my credulity without, I am certain, ever telling a lie; and that will mostly vanish with me, a listener whose recall is far from total. Already pale, they shift in and out of focus, clinging to my suddenly opaque mind like dried mummy linen to an indistinct silhouette that, grasped, is only powdered nothingness where someday dedicated diggers will hack away in vain for some clue to his aura.

à Dorothéa, Reine des Neiges Love Max

CHAPTER FOUR

❧

An Artist
Remembers

OUR FATE WAS mixed up with exigency, an exigency utterly personal and inflexible, a demand addressed to ourselves *to go on from there*. Max, having at the outset made some covenant with himself—or perhaps not; a covenant might have been superfluous to his chemistry, a mere foreign element that would not be absorbed into the heaven and hell of his inquiring imagination— plunged again and again. Down where breathing is not possible for any but a *Blind Swimmer*, a title he gave to several pictures, and a program for an artist who would rather drown than tread water, tread water.

He was as isolated as an unnamed island, unnamed because too far away from any other landmass, out of bounds. Determined that there shall be no unknown quantities, some intrepid bunglers try to pop him onto their maps. Wasn't he one of the surrealist chain that surfaced after those ugly explosions of 1914–18, or was it before? Something about dada. The twenties. The twenties? But everything was so jolly then. Surely we know all the islands. Surely they all have names. Surely it's all made up, a trick, a fabrication about him and his inappropriate myth. Uncomfortable all that about his being a bird.

But there was that quick way of turning the head, and, indeed, the regard from even one blue eye would have been unnerving enough. And there was his whistling, something he did only when alone or, wonderfully, with me. It was his song. "*Comprenez, mon amie,*" this to me from the great Breton himself, "*qu'il est un oiseau, féroce. Soyez avertie.*" Translation: "Understand, my friend, that he is a bird. A cruel one. So, be warned."

In love, loving nature best. It was what he had counted on. There wasn't any question of betrayal with so much bounty. Everything stayed on for him, even after hours, after days and windy years blowing the leaves apart to reveal a hundred thousand birds under spells. Stones, girls, flowers, birds, all under spells.

He was amazed by what had been attempted on him in 1914, when first his glittering youth was slammed into the scratchy soldier suit and sent into the soup of mud and blood; there on vague lost battlefronts he strove, perhaps hoping not to aim, not to fire. Certainly not to kill. So that release came, hard-won, in the form of a shell that exploded in his face. He wandered for days through wastelands and towns, wanting to rejoin his regiment, for then he might find care for the wounds. "My whole face seemed to be floating." At last, at some field headquarters, he was sutured and bandaged.

But he was still their soldier, sound in mind and limb,

equipped to do their bidding. At one point, commissioned
to bring food back to the troops at the front, he rode with
the treasure on slow-moving trains until one evening the
train halted suddenly at a station—which was it?—some
beleaguered place crowded with refugees, limping, moil-
ing human wreckage gazing at him and his Santa Claus
sack, their great stares almost unseeing and without hatred
(for you need energy to hate). There in the station he
opens the big sack and distributes the goodies. "It was like
a party. The stares came alive, turned to lively glances, the
children stopped crying, everybody laughed and sang and
ate. It was fine, fine. I got rid of the load."

"But then you were in big trouble."

"Yes. Only, you see, the war ended five days later."

Time after time, bemused, ironic, secure, wanting
nothing, he watched his own shadow as it fled and wandered, like that first time, as it traced what was to become
the pattern of his life. Cynical he was, but if you said it you
were wrong. Reading and breathing and drawing he had
taken measures and had weighed theories thrown out like
apples for hungry schoolboys. He never said, "I believe."

How did he see himself? A beautiful boy beloved by
women? Then a beautiful man loved by women? It must
have been at least a small delight for him to meet the tender talking eyes, swimming with invitation. All kinds. All
his life, everywhere. To see in them the glitter of admiration, question, longing. It must have made them more
beautiful, even those who were not. (How different from
breathless Don Juan, who endlessly pursued his cheap

idea of the perfect woman, the perfect love. Poor Don Juan, without imagination, was, even Molière said it, "a vulgar rogue, expert in lovemaking, quibbling, and crime." There is no parallel here, not only because of centuries but because out of his own chemistry Max Ernst drew the magic formula for making women what he wanted and what they wanted to be: symbols of grace.

This is what they must have seen, too, looking into his eyes. *La nudité de la femme est plus sage que l'enseignement du philosophe*—woman's nudity is wiser than the philosopher's teachings. Max's words.

How did he stay so blessed, so easy? How can you keep your aura and your distance in the face of constant menace, blind immensity, familiar, with always a war to provide them? I will never know any more about that day in 1940 when the police came to his house in Saint-Martin-d'Ardèche, came for him with handcuffs. For he was still a German. Their enemy. I will never know what he said. Did he say anything? He could have laughed. For it was an event he was ready for, had known before: his unfitness for the rules and his dada words out of tune. So was he to know it again and again, the long hilarious convulsion of being out of place in a derisive happening where as always and despite the exertions of the artist the rules and rapacities see eye to eye and speak the same language. Was there trauma? Not his, surely. I see them as evenly matched: the man, the sequential environments, all obdurate. Each time, stepping over the current misunderstanding as one steps over the rubbish in the streets of the world, he saw only his own shadow stretching before him, pointing the way.

Yet there were his wives. What of them? German, French, American, each time there must have been a decision of some kind. To be sure, it has to do with love. A sweet mirage, beckoning, leaning toward enrichment or toward perpetual adventure or toward discovery *à deux*. And surely, above all, the conviction that it can't go wrong this time.

So first, as a demobbed soldier at the end of war, he becomes the husband of Louise and father of Jimmy. The artist, ex-student, and ex-soldier is transformed into a family man, and it is like being suddenly crowned king when you had simply been out skating, say. Being a king is no laughing matter, for a king must be responsible and kingly. A complicated and demanding role.

Did he fit the design? I cannot know. For it was not one of the stories for my ears but was perhaps from another tapestry—its threads too knotted and elusive to spin out into the colored web of days and years that followed: Paris days and years populated and presided over by those outrageous shaggy monsters of nonconformism who called themselves dadaists and later surrealists, who, upon seeing him arrive with his box of miracle, stepped back to make way and a place for him to play another kind of role no less royal for being made of impossible ragtag revolt (for like all princes they dreamed of changing the world).

Half playing, half desperate, surrealists haunted flea

markets and junk heaps for the materials of their statement. Rich in leisure if poor in pocket, they knew the
power of the transforming process. Even the poets wrought
stunning objects made of words entwined with the city's
refuse. Inspired by artists of war-demolished Germany
(Arp and Schwitters and Hannah Hoch in the 1920s) and
the collages and reliefs of the already magisterial Picasso,
they saw art as oracular statement made of the unexpected. They called it dada. A wrapped-in-bandage violin
(Maurice Henry), a pair of Siamese-joined shoes (Meret
Oppenheim), Duchamp's surprises, Man Ray—the list is
long. Found objects. Irony answers the baneful. Such was
the air in which Max Ernst breathed. To them he added
his own icons and his detachment.

A borrowed passport from friend Paul Eluard had
brought him across the frontier. Germany to France.
Soon he had a new name, Jean Paris, for the boss of the
factory where he painted—elephants upon bracelets, *les
articles de Paris*. How is this done? Oh, easy. He shows me,
very fast. Yes, so fast that before long his coworkers had
become his enemies. He was absurd, a foreign trouble-
maker, the dirty *boche*. Besides, the boss was soon to
abscond with all of their unpaid salaries.

By this time it didn't really matter. Down the sweaty
stairs and into the street, where his lungs swell with free
foggy Paris air. Windows are on fire from the sun setting
down at the end of the avenue. Rivulets from recent rain
made iridescent by thoughtful dogs on and off leashes
slide in between the cobblestones. Picture the café, plac-

arded with names of beverages nobody wants. Byrrh, for instance. A word everywhere seen, a something to drink. Yet in all the years, all the cafés, I never heard anyone order it.

At a table no bigger than a serving plate, its checked cloth clamped against the breeze, he orders wine; watches absently as the glass gets a quick swipe of the waiter's grayish napkin and the pale yellow stuff is dumped into it with that circular twist of the bottle so dear to stylish waiters. O accordions! O palmists, O necromancers! Up and down the street. The flea market festers near, swollen with refuse.

Soon he will walk back to Paul's, walk all the way, for Paul lives in a suburb. He stays with Paul, and Gala, Paul's wife, grinds her feral gaze into his eyes. So that finally Paul says, "Take her." Paul is like that, share and share alike.

Adventures *à trois* had by then hopelessly smudged the memory of *à deux*. There were excursions: to the Tyrol or Honfleur, it was all the same. Paris environs in playful seasons, and the Americans, too, who skimmed the cream and drank wine from giddy stemware in places they had acquired for songs, always named Le Vieux Moulin: abandoned mills that no longer turned; abject, crumbling heaps of damp stone and wood, rescued from oblivion, resuscitated with plaster and concrete and fitted with inside toilets and refrigerators brought over at some cost and great effort from the States, and only if you knew someone in the diplomatic service.

These were expatriates, an expatriate being someone who never forgets for one instant that he is one. Some of them were still around in my time. When discussing international events, which they did with passion, they invariably said "we" in reference to what American politics were up to. I found this incongruous coming from people who were as earnestly playing at being French as Marie Antoinette played at tending sheep. Hedonists named Daphne and Nancy and Caresse, devotedly cared for by dirt-cheap housekeepers named Delphine and Ninette and Chantal, did not lack for indigent artists and poets to decorate their weekends made of plenty of *luxe* and *volupté, sans* the *calme.*

He went everywhere with Paul and Paul's wife. It lasted long months during which time the burning cigarette eyes ground against him, not with him, while he made hundreds of drawings of them—did he know why?—because at last the eyes were exorcised. Not, however, before he was desperate to be free. "Why? What happened?" I ask. "She didn't want me to paint" is all he will say.

Paul too had had enough, and, dipping his elegant fingers into the paternal coffer—just enough, not more— he embarked for Saigon. A month later Papa wired, "I pardon you. Come home at once." Exchange of telegrams: Paul, Max, Max, Paul. "Bring me my wife and I'll come back." "With pleasure." The jaded lovers then embarked too, and it was a simple matter to deliver the eyes to their mate, no hard feelings, and to wave them farewell as he stayed on to absorb alone the heady east-west concoction that was Indochina.

Stepping onto the gangplank of a derelict Russian steamer for the return to France a month later, he began a voyage unmatched in farce if not in pure chaos. The boat was a "crate," and as if in concern for harmony, its passengers and crew might have been vying for honors in eccentricity of a particularly obtuse kind, paying little heed to the creakings and rumblings of their bark, seemingly prepared to risk all for the joyous hope of someday docking in Marseille.

Officialdom by now may have consecrated the Swiss doctor professor of anthropology, funded on that pseudo-safari by a foundation or two, who was at the time returning to his peers. But in truth he was little more than a scamp who, just before sailing, had bribed the guardian of some jungle temple to look the other way while he made off with a large sacred snake. Why did a Swiss doctor-professor want a Buddhist snake? Back in Switzerland he would triumphantly present his find to the local zoo, after its ocean voyage in a wicker trunk. Meanwhile, the deck swarmed with club members: an Association of Bereft Fiancées, banded together in pilgrimage and in a common loss: their intended grooms, French soldiers all, had perished in the Franco-Indochinese War.

On the lower deck, the prim closed door of debauched Mademoiselle Yvonne, a missionary, who lost no time in turning her cabin into a cozy opium den, frequented mainly by members of the crew. Soon something quite unexpected happened.

A few hours out of Saigon, the boat was ascream with terrified virgins (Max's words for them), several of whom had seen the hapless snake slither out of its hamper onto their deck. General confusion, high-pitched virago voices of wrath and terror. An hour-long search did not turn up the creature; the ladies trembled and fumed. But the unprincipled doctor-professor later learned that his dearly paid prize had gone back to its temple, by escape down a toilet and an easy swim across the bay.

Vengeful oriental gods? Malicious western polter-geists? Whatever the spirits, whatever the reasons, for three days the boat was flung against the water with sick-ening fury. In the Red Sea she stopped, her engines gasp-ing for coal. Days of white suns went by in a delirium of bursting heat until, like all the other hallucinations, a res-cue ship hove in sight and was, unbelievably, not painted on the horizon at all but a real ship with real coal to spare. The old boat moved forward once more, its passen-gers waking to their destinies, emerging from the void.

Like most of the others, the lighthouse keeper was going home. Every day he paced the narrow deck, haggard though without apparent pain. He seemed not to have the power of speech. An occasional whispered *oui* or *non*. It was soon known that for fifteen years he had kept a lighthouse and, now retired, was returning to Marseille with his sav-ings, there to buy a little house and to tend a little garden. Such was the nature of his dearest wish. Until, soon after

passing the straits at Singapore, he was discovered by a cop-
per-haired person listed as a stenographer.

"What kept you in Saigon?" Max had asked her one
day as she stood intent before the posted passenger list.

"My work."

"Commercial something?"

"Yes. Import-export."

She had her place changed to a table for two in the
dining room, just her and the lighthouse keeper.

"What kept you in that lighthouse?" she asked him.

"It was a trust. You see . . ." he murmured. He told her
all. Soon they were leaning together, hand in hand, gazing
at the pewter ocean, hands under the table in the swelter-
ing dining room, hand in hand late at night on the deck.
And thus a romance grew bold on board, how nice. In the
souks of Colombo, he bought her large precious stones.

On the dock at last in Marseille, everyone came alive:
porters tussled with trunks, and people behind the barriers
screamed exaggerated greetings. A figure detached itself
from the bustle on the quay, moving faster than the others,
running in fact, arms aloft, turning and running back in
zigzags through the crowds. It was the lighthouse keeper.

"I almost didn't recognize him," says Max, "he talked so
fast: 'Where is she, where did she go . . . I can't understand,
have you seen her, have you seen. . . ' I couldn't do anything for him. What was there to do? She had vanished."

As the man stood there in shock holding his head, he
visibly diminished, as incorporeal as a transparent lighthouse window giving onto an infinitely rolling sea.

He turned then to a station guard and politely asked the directions to Les Offices Maritimes. His money gone, he would of course sign up again, another lighthouse. What else is there? And in fifteen years . . . "They will pass . . . they can't last forever," he whispered. "*Au revoir.*"

"And as he tottered away," recalls Max, "I called after him, idiotically, '*Bonne chance.*'"

The ashy taste of those two outrageous words.

Marie-Berthe Aurenche became Max's second wife. She was scarcely eighteen and dazzled everyone, even surrealists, with her blue-and-gold porcelain beauty. And Max dazzled her. They ran away together. So that the bitter objections of her infuriated parents were too late to repair the damage. Seething, they had, like it or not, to take him in, more as a fresh closet skeleton than as a son-in-law. But more of them in a moment. Meanwhile it can be stated that the girl, though in love, seemed elsewhere.

Not Max. Encouraged by the way all the gaily colored threads were weaving the spiral of his artist-life, he painted and pasted and wrought fast-drying plaster, drawing the shape of his thought into a monument that marked his victory over dreary adversity. The studio in the rue des Plantes, time to paint, the friendly collectors who left with pictures under their arms, the plash of glinting surrealist voices at the favorite café, the beauteous wife.

Only, it was sometimes disconcerting the way a new painting would disappear. On these days Marie would come in toward evening with her hair elaborately curled, her nails pointed and painted. The little pictures paid the coiffeur, as it turned out. Was it not lucky that he liked them?

Perhaps it was, if that had been all. But there began a hazy series of retreats into the sickly past, a pattern but dimly comprehended by the bewildered husband, who fought a losing battle with uncomfortable evidence. For behind the pretty face was a victim, all warp and no woof, fashioned to conform to the insane caprice of a pair of lunatics who happened to be her parents. Indeed, outlandish as it may seem, all her young life the girl had been groomed for sovereignty. Incredulous Max heard her tell of the legend—oh, but it was true!—that she was destined to be the future queen of France. Yes, a letter was lying in a secret place. It was written by Madame de M.; it had waited a hundred and forty years already; it traced the lineage in no uncertain terms, there was no doubt, no doubt at all that Madame A. herself was in direct line and that her daughter would ascend the three velvet steps to the throne when the moment came. The letter was to be opened (a day was mentioned) and she would be crowned queen. The monarchy finally restored, she would be Her Majesty Marie-Berthe.

At first he laughed, hugely. "And me, then what would I be—the prince consort?" He was all amused indulgence.

"I suppose so," she answered absently, dreaming perhaps of what sort of vehicle she would choose for her ride from the rue des Plantes to the Louvre.

They had sent her as a child to a "very exclusive" con-
vent school on the Isle of Jersey—only girls of "noble"
birth were accepted. In this school, presided over by nuns
who were, of course, equally noble, Marie-Berthe, the little commoner was scorned and snubbed unmercifully by
her playmates until one day the entire school body was
summoned to hear an announcement. The mother superior swept to the podium:

"Young ladies, there is, among you, a girl who may
seem undistinguished in your eyes and worthy of only the
merest consideration. By these words, my esteemed girls, I
now tell you that the person in question is of the noblest
lineage possible and that she is destined to rule over you
all as the future queen. You will now return to your rooms
to ponder carefully these words, and to make the adjust-
ment in your minds that such an announcement
demands."

In the rue des Plantes, 1927, the famous letter was
somehow forgotten. But its effects hung around the studio like noxious fumes from a nepenthean admixture
designed to keep the world at bay. In some incomprehen-
sible way the spiral was upending, turning into a tunnel.
There were, to be sure, fine moments with surrealist
friends who, at the peak of their powers and their conquest of large chunks of the knowable present, counted
the beautiful couple as a living proof of the positive ethos.
Too, there were invitations to the opulent tables of what is
still called *le tout Paris*, where the dishes were often so-so,
but richly composed.

But although life in the rue des Plantes was not particularly stringent, Marie-Berthe proved otherwise, and her religious fervor spilled and soaked into every corner of their shared space, spreading an odor of sanctity that pervaded even the conjugal bed and so rendered lovemaking a sorry exercise, not only joyless but somehow unseemly. For the abiding shape of her every action and the color of her every thought were formed and tinged by a medieval fanaticism ever more melancholy and soul-deforming. The lifelong prop of her royal destiny having evaporated like holy water left in the sun, she threw herself into a blaze of self-castigation. She was "filthy." She was abject, a sinner. Like a tormented witch she flung their hard won pennies into the cathedral cauldron and raised her voice in public confession.

Only minimally daunted, Max painted daily. While Marie-Berthe's afternoons were a steaming broth of orgasmic devotion flavored with coiffeur philosophy, his own passed in the blissful pursuit of his personal chimera. But there wasn't enough money, sometimes not quite enough food.

It happened once or twice that Amal, their Senegalese friend, blew in at such a dire moment. He too was without a sou. But he grinned, "Wait an hour. I'll do the boulevards." And an hour later he was back with bags of groceries and wine, his wonderful white teeth triumphantly bared in a beatific smile. Saving the day but not the morrow.

Scolded about the purloined pictures and not being able to contemplate a future without a regular coiffure,

Marie cast about and found a job. It was during one of those *mondain* luncheons that Schiaparelli, the great dress designer of the place Vendôme, sizing up the girl's face and figure, said she could use a receptionist. So began a specious interval, specious because, though the work was amusing, more or less, it did not last long. In fact after only a few days it was all over. Her mate did not know what had happened, why she didn't go back. Probably he did not want to know. It wasn't mentioned. Until a friend brought it out to him: Madame S. was not pleased about the way Marie-Berthe had sat in the window (she had to mind the salon during the long lunch hour) painting her toes. One morning Max asked her if it was true, and she said yes, it had been very peaceful.

From then on there was no talk of employment, a demeaning word in any event. And soon it was clear that even an errand could not be undertaken. Once in the street the wretched girl would give the money she carried to the first beggar encountered, if he would pray with her.

It happened that a portrait, commissioned and paid for in advance after a discreet glance by model and hus-band (Jean and Dominique de Menil) around the bare studio, was to be delivered by Marie-Berthe. After a few weeks, Max, hearing no praise, assumed it wasn't too suc-cessful. The lady sitter, not seeing it appear, assumed the artist had his reasons. Until one day, twenty years later, and passing a Parisian framer's dusty window, she saw her own eyes looking out from a heap of frames in the corner. The eyes were waiting to be claimed, if one paid for the frame that had been ordered by the person who brought it in, said the old framer. Politely, no one had ever mentioned the absent portrait to the other, though artist and model met rather often after those hectic times.

Drift and dust blew everywhere by now. The studio was an island or a cell, it didn't matter as long as brushes and colors were there, furnished gratis by a generous merchant—all he took was a picture now and then.

A word about the Lefebvre-Foinet family, purveyors of artist's materials, French and traditional to the bone, monumentally dedicated to the users of their (hand-ground) colors, their (hand-sized) canvases, even hand-made papers, Russian sable brushes, little tin pots to clip onto the edge of palettes—oh, let us just say the things that artists do not use anymore.

In their resin-colored, oak-lined shop, behind a window full of immense jars of paintbrushes and one of those energetic jointed wooden robotlike dolls that are fondly supposed to help beginners learn figure drawing, out of the shadowy back room where packages were made of unpackageable bulks, or from his pocket-sized adjoining office hung with tiny pictures, would appear Monsieur Maurice Lefebvre-Foinet himself, full of jollity for the gents and gallantry for the ladies. Monsieur Maurice never failed to make this distinction no matter what kind of a painter you were, and his smile was shed upon you in direct or oblique rays according to your gender. One imagines that in earlier days female customers were rare indeed, unless one counted the probably silent, tousled model-companion who would appear, huddled shyly against her blustering artist as he chose his tube of raw sienna and muttered something about putting it on the tab before lumbering out in the cold, his pink-nosed girl close in his wake like the muffler wound twice round his neck and fluttering in the raw wind. To all of them the shop dispensed warmth and encouragement along with brushes and tubes of paint. The all-too-often indigent artist knew that there he would find credit, in exchange for an occasional work from his hand. To this day, hundreds and hundreds of pictures (some of them ours) stacked against the top-floor walls of their ship's-prow-shaped house (no longer theirs today) bear dates from the grandfather's time.

At one point an invitation came for Max from London, a good gallery, friends of friends, would he like to show? It was full of promise. He prepared, pictures were sent, tickets bought for the boat train. When the time came to leave, Marie-Berthe would not go. She was ill. She was unworthy, unclean. She was adamant. He was obliged to go alone.

Arriving in London he found a telegram from her: "Please." So a ticket was sent (it would have been folly to send money) and careful instructions added as you would for a child with her name pinned to her coat. They waited, he and friend Roland Penrose, at Victoria Station. The train came in and stopped, sputtered and released a cloud of steam while Max and Roland scanned the pas-

sengers looming out of the cottony stuff like hurried
phantoms. But no Marie-Berthe.

As they stood there, Roland saying that she just might
have missed the boat train, the last shreds of steam blew
away to reveal a solitary porter struggling with a trunk
that had lost its handles. Beyond him, from far down the
platform, a miniature female figure drew closer and they
wondered aloud, could it be . . . ?

It was. Advancing slowly up the platform, not smiling,
not running, and with a slight limp: Marie-Berthe.

In filthy rags and lace, ancient rubber shoes, her white
face drawn, eyes like craters, she carried a wilted bunch of
violets in one hand, a string bag in the other. That there
was nothing at all in the string bag probably seemed to
these two baffled males an appropriate detail of her
apparition.

Roland balanced on his heels and smiled uncertainly.
Max stood embarrassed. Their banter tarried, their grin-
ning faces sobered like those of scolded schoolboys.
Roland hailed a cab.

"You are so kind, so kind. I don't deserve it," she murmured as, flanking her tenderly, they swooped down to
push her in.

"Shhhh."

"Ah, but it's true . . ." By this time there was no trace
of intimacy in her voice, only the litany of her sinfulness,
her uncleanliness, as she kissed his hands or knelt down.
For two days they reasoned with her:

"Please forget all that, darling. You're a good girl, you must be nice for Max. Come now, we must get you some clothes for the opening."

And Roland brought her to a dressmaker, where she gazed at the models swinging and twirling, gazed sadly, hunched in the borrowed coat, and murmured her broken-record obsession:

"Unclean, unclean . . . why bring me here . . . I am filthy, a whited sepulcher . . . the holy Virgin knows, she understands . . ." And then dully, "Take me back, take me back. . . ."

They questioned, they reasoned. It was impossible for them to find the slightest cause for her self-abhorrence. Sin was as real in thought as in deed for such as her—and I must confess a fascination with what were surely the ravening inventions of her mind.

Back in Paris her closest friends were converts to the faith—perfervid zealots whose piety, as is often the case with this very strange category of human wreckage, far outstripped that of the tepid, born regulars of the confessional. Except for Marie-Berthe. For her and her suite the confessional was a tingling bath of fire and flogging, as frequent, as intoxicating, as irresistible as is the local bistro, with its "shot of red," to the alcoholic. They approached the baring of their souls with eager step on the cold flagstones of churches and cathedrals alike, where booths of wild sorrow waited behind sin-stained wood.

There in London confession was problematic. Catholic churches were few. And in what words could one cry out? The hour of the opening arrived. She would not go.

"Leave me here in my room." She would meditate, she would pray. But when they returned from the gallery she had vanished.

The night passed without a sign, and, fevered by exhaustion, Max slept. At dawn the doorbell brought Roland down the stairs. Marie-Berthe was there on the curb with the taxi driver, who demanded his fistful of guineas. They brought her inside. She had found her way to a priest far out of London, a French Catholic priest who had consented to hear her urgent confession. Mercifully she then slept for two days.

In the London week that followed, while he kept appointments, was interviewed and invited, Marie-Berthe was losing all contact with the real world. And still there was no one willing to lead her away. She was so pretty.

The breaking point loomed and advanced, with its seductive promise of oblivion. Foundering, the artist breathed heavily and without joy until, one rainy day, Marie-Berthe, drained and absent, asked to be taken to the boat train for Paris.

So once again Max was at Victoria Station. He saw her into a compartment. Farewell. For they both knew that her departure from London was the departure from his life.

Firmly identifying with his pictures, with *Loplop, Bird Superior* (the name he gave to his alter ego, using it regu-

larly in writing as well as pictures), and knowing that all
nightmares come to an end when night backs away, he
stayed on, attentive to his exhibition and to the picture
that was London, 1937.

Looking up from a dinner plate one evening, he saw
his dazzling reward—English this time, a Leonora (Car-
rington), undaunted by imminent breaking points, seductive though they might be. Menaces are made to be
foiled. And so they carried each other off. And landed in
a high windy house in the south of France. The town?
Saint-Martin-d'Ardèche, where olives grow and the mis-
tral blows your past away.

I could not pretend to know anything of that time except
for the mute testimony of myriad creatures in cement and
paint and iron that he left there forever and for all to see.
And a few more stories. They have to do with vineyards,
dogs that ate grapes, and the denizens of the local bar.
There was a rotund, elderly priest, a kind of abbot, I think
Max said, in a neighboring village, one of those places
that lie upon the earth just as they did in their prehistory,
the hills and stones undisturbed by frenzied stabs at mod-
ernization, their inhabitants as rooted as old trees. This
ecclesiastic was their protector in the eyes, they said, of
God, and they tolerated him as such. His only fun was an
occasional visit by donkey-back to Saint-Martin, the big
town for him, where, in the café, he could forget his savage flock and exchange words with several sophisticated

philosophers: the barman, the wine grower, the olive pressers, the village bum.

Sometimes Max was there and a kind of friendship sprang up between artist and divine that resulted in an invitation to dinner by the genial priest, who assured his friend that cooking was his hobby.

The day came, the artist came, the five-course dinner came to the table in all its glory.

"*Bon appétit,*" smacked the host as he dipped a spoon in the sepia soup. It was indeed a spread, copiously *arrosé* with superb wines and a special cognac as tailpiece.

What intrigued the guest was the satin-smooth way the same plates were replaced by his host, padding from kitchen to table with that buoyant, almost levitational ease fat priests have in their cassocks like old sailing vessels complete with slanting tack and full furl. Especially admirable, he thought, must be the discretion of the woman in the kitchen, who never once showed her face. And for reason. Because, strolling in at the end of the repast, as if to take a bow, and licking his chops, was the host's faithful helper: his dog. He it was, together with the roly-poly man of God, who cleaned the plates between courses. How else, said the man simply, could he do it all alone?

Un Peu de Calme, a little calm, *A Moment of Calm.* It isn't hard to imagine that calm, tanned and fanned by the hot Provençal wind, careless as the cicada. Indeed, the calm flowed down the hill from the stony house with its crazy beckoning sculptures and friezes, a whole population of chimeras and prodigies in cement, not salt, and from the light in a makeshift studio where he stood immersed in his phantasmal world, master of canvases redolent of bog and swamp and rotting forest, lush triumphs of his brush.

It was 1939, spring-calm, a precarious calm and so much more precious. It was a drop of dew, a perfect world sliding slowly down a leaf and hanging there for dear life, a golden life with a beautiful companion, only a little mad if you were careful. So in that lull he painted the big canvas and glued it onto the far arched wall of the garden room, open-ended to the winds.

Here was a sad, spiny forest hiding the specter of war, for he would not summon the brutality to bring doom out into the open, though he knew the smell of blackened leaves from long years before. So he knew there was no life in the spiked, tangly trees. Where were the green veins; where the swarming life of *La Joie de Vivre* of 1936? Where were the caterpillars, walking sticks, the mimetic jokes, the wood lice, moths? Where were the birds? Instead, the iron branches. Motion was laid, and the drop of water hung. The picture was an omen, not a warning. With eyes wide open but not blazing, he mutely saw and mutely recorded. There in the high house, with its olive groves and its grapes, a place that to this day wears the raiment of its reliefs, its sculptured phoenixes, its frescoes, he stained the wide canvas in blackened green and blue and rust, uneasy colors of fading hope. Thus ravished, the rectangle gasped and held its breath. *A Moment of Calm.*

Bon Soir, *oil on canvas, shaped painting, 1951.*

TOP: *My parents, Andrew and Amanda Tanning, 1903.*
ABOVE: *I am mugging for "elocution" lessons, 1918.*
BELOW: The Truth About Comets and Little Girls, *oil on canvas, 1951.*

TOP, LEFT: *Andy Tanning and hometown friend, Carl Sandburg, 1939.*
TOP, RIGHT: Voltage, *oil on canvas, 1943.*
BELOW: *Galesburg Public Library.*

ABOVE: On Time Off Time, *oil on canvas, 1948.*
BELOW, LEFT: *Catalogue cover for my first exhibition at the Julien Levy Gallery, 1944.*
BELOW, RIGHT: *My cover for the Ballet Russe de Monte Carlo programme, 1946.*

LEFT: *Julien Levy.*
BELOW: *(Left)* A Parisian
Afternoon *and (right)*
Birthday, *the paintings he
saw on his first studio visit.*

ABOVE: *House-building in Sedona, Arizona, with Max Ernst, 1946.*
BELOW, LEFT: *Eskimo totem pole, part of Max Ernst's collection of tribal art.*
BELOW, RIGHT: *We stand in a would-be window of the house during some of its growing pains. It never quite grew up. As if under a spell, something willed its windows crooked, willed its steps to lead nowhere, willed it ever romantically unfinished.*

ABOVE: *I paint the local landscape and Max named it* Self Portrait, *1947*.
BELOW: *Max Ernst and Dorothea Tanning, photograph, 1949.*

ABOVE: *A contest at the Julien Levy Gallery, 1944, pitted seven intrepid chess players, (left to right) Julien Levy, who has left his board momentarily to snap these photos, Frederick Kiesler, Alfred Barr, Xanti Schawinsky, Vittorio Rieti, me, and Max Ernst, against blindfolded chessmaster Koltanowski; all boards monitored by Marcel Duchamp.* BELOW: The Philosophers, *oil on canvas, 1952.*

ABOVE: Palaestra, *1947.*

BELOW, LEFT: *Colorado River canyon, 1957.* "Shooting the rapids" *is what we were doing (not at all the same thing later after the dam was built).*

BELOW, RIGHT: *Our incomparable guide, Elmer.*

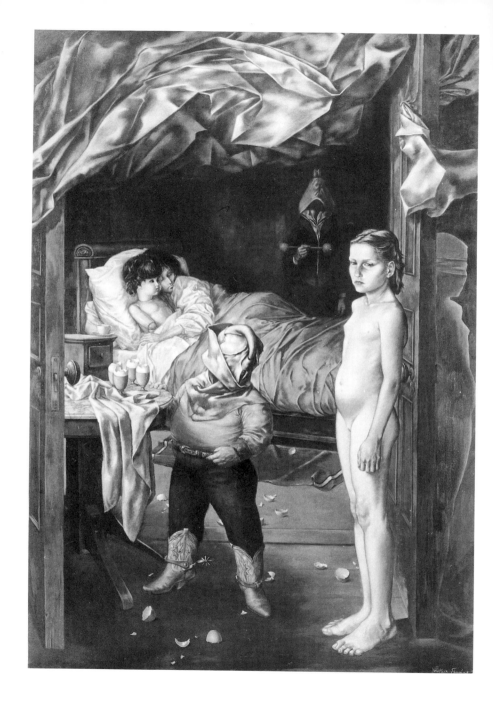

The Guest Room, *oil on canvas, 1950–52.*

ABOVE: *One of a series of chilly, secretive paintings,* Interior with Sudden Joy, *oil on canvas, 1951.*

BELOW: *With the dog, Kachina, about 1958, Max and I stroll beside our house in Touraine, France, an area generally known as "the chateau country" or by an even handsomer sobriquet, "the garden of France."*

ABOVE: *In Monte Carlo with Teeny and Marcel Duchamp for the chess tournement. Equal time was spent watching the greats and playing our own boards.*
BELOW: *Back in Paris, I impersonate my dog.*

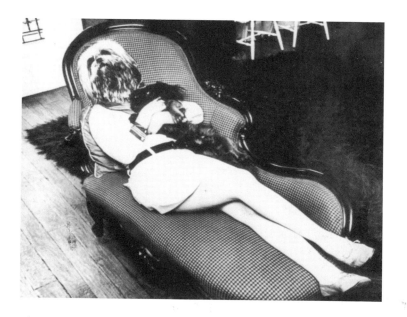

Insomnias, *oil on canvas, 1957*.

LEFT: *Max Ernst, 1915, soldier, wounded and wandering.*
BELOW: *I paint him,* Max in a Blue Boat, *oil on canvas, 1947.*

ABOVE: Fatala, *oil on canvas, 1947.*
BELOW: Eine Kleine Nachtmusik, *oil on canvas, 1946.*

LEFT: *(Left to right), Andre Breton, Elisa Breton, Max Ernst, and me, 1958, in St. Cirque la Popie, Lot, France.*

BELOW, LEFT: *Cover of* Les Sept Perils Spectraux, *my first album of lithographs, Paris, 1950.*

BELOW, RIGHT: Sisters, *oil on canvas, 1953.*

Death and the Maiden, *oil on canvas, 1954.*

LEFT: Family Portrait, *oil on canvas, 1952.*
BELOW: *Max is pulling me out from under the bed in Hans Richter's surrealist movie,* Dreams That Money Can Buy, *1947.*

Family Portrait, *oil on canvas, 1977.*

ABOVE: Rainy Day Canape, *sculpture in tweed, 1972–73.*
BELOW: Maternity Five, *oil on canvas, 1980.*

ABOVE: Hotel du Pavot (Poppy Hotel), *installation of tweed sculptures for Dorothea Tanning retrospective at CNAC (later, Pompidou Centre), Paris, 1974.*
BELOW: Table Tragique (Tragic Table), *sculpture in wood and stuffed tweed, 1974.*

ABOVE, LEFT: *Paris studio 1979, working on* Fetish *(large version).*
ABOVE, RIGHT: *Detail of* Xmas, *with Eskimo potlatch bowl in background. Seillans, 1972.*
BELOW: Notes for an Apocalypse, *oil on canvas, 1977.*

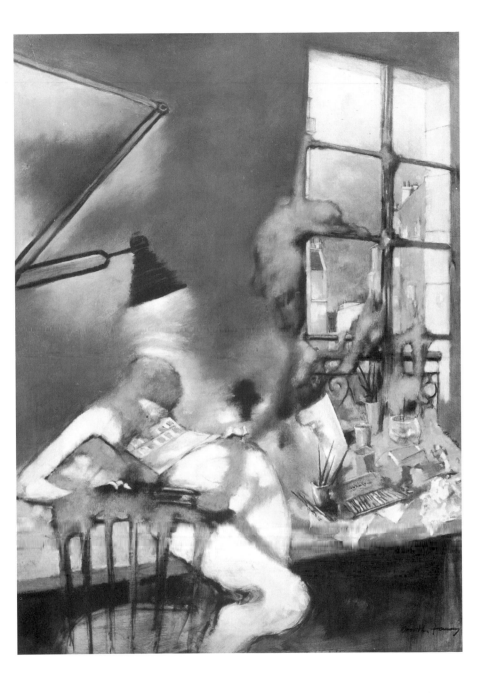

Still in the Studio, *oil on canvas, 1977*.

ABOVE: *The ladies of Seillans (any nice day).*
BELOW: Emma, *cloth sculpture, 1970.*

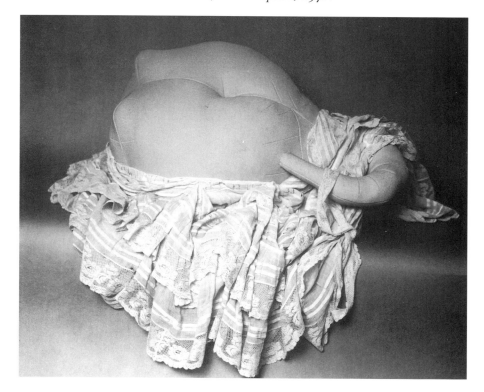

Some souvenirs: (Left) In Nonza, Corsica, with Leonor Fini. (Center, left) Clowning with Marie Laure de Noailles. (Center, right) With René Magritte at my retrospective in Belgium, 1967. (Bottom) With Matta and Octavio Paz, Paris.

ABOVE: Even the Young Girls, *oil on canvas, 1965.*
BELOW: Poses Dans un Ecole d'Art Qui N'existe Pas, *ink on paper, 1965.*

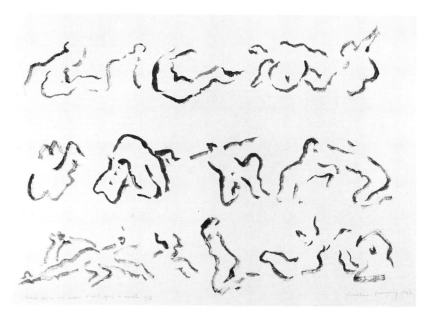

ABOVE: *With Merce Cunningham in Paris, 1971.*
RIGHT: *George Balanchine shows off his ballerina cat.*
BELOW: *My scenery for* Bayou, *music Virgil Thompson; choreography Balanchine. New York, 1952.*

ABOVE: *Our village of Seillans, France.*
LEFT: *Eleanor Clark and Robert Penn Warren visit. Seillans, 1967.*
BELOW: *The house I designed. Here we had five glorious years, 1970 to 1975.*

Tango Lives, *oil on canvas, 1977.*

Mean Frequency of Auroras, *oil on canvas, 1981.*

ABOVE: *John Cage and Robert Ashley, New York, 1983.*
RIGHT: *James Merrill, Key West, 1992.*
BELOW: *I bask in exoticism, Podor, Senegal, 1978.*

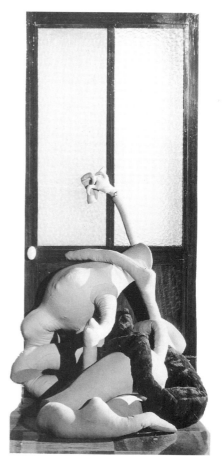

Open Sesame, *1970, cloth sculpture with wooden and glass door, both sides.*

Indeed, the storm that had been eyeing him from the north came one day in the form of handcuffs, two local gendarmes, apologetic: "We're sorry, Monsieur Max . . ." and he was led away, he, the enemy alien still carrying the dread German passport. He was, in fact, interned by French authorities, as were thousands of other German nationals, considered enemy aliens, living in France— a parallel with the hapless Japanese-American citizens interned in wartime California.

With firebrand fervor surrealism had drafted manifestos against Franco, Mussolini, Hitler, Stalin, colonialism. These Max Ernst signed and signed again. So when in 1941, after the seizure of Paris, the invader descended to blot the sun from the southern hills of France, one knew the imperative: escape. Rumors soaked and spread. Max was wanted back there, some said, back in the fatherland, even though Der Führer had been photographed beside a Max Ernst painting, *La Belle Jardinière* ("The Beautiful Gardener"), in an exhibition of "degenerate art," and the painting then ceremoniously burnt, an auto-da-fé complete with flashbulbs and banners. Ah, yes. Bring him back to the Reich, chastened, obedient, some body said. No wonder, then, that his face was turned westward.

Meanwhile he is in the wrong place, and the result, incarceration—in the form of camps, four of them, from each of which he must flee, thereby becoming not only an alien but a fugitive, describing a thousand narrow escapes outlining his trajectory as he plunges toward the sea.

Such is the way the dewdrop life slides and falls, crashing like a fragmentation bomb around bereft Leonora. She sinks gently into a cognac oblivion fed by the local innkeeper, he who will afterwards take the house in payment for the booze.

He is an enterprising man. He will turn the place into a bordello for the customers from Avignon, the big town, a hideaway from wives and spies. Meanwhile he lets her stay, alone in the house, until along comes one of Leonora's compatriots from England who, taking charge, will lead her friend away, away from this grubby farm, away from nasty France. Listen to her as she paints a screaming picture of rape, rape, rape that is sure to arrive with the Nazi advance. Packing in haste, just time for a note:

"Dear Max, I have gone with C. and will wait for you in Estramadura."

Off they flee, across France and Spain. But the sorely tried girl shatters like a mirror along the way and is taken to stay in a Santander clinic.

For the third time he escapes from the camp (Largentière? Loriol?) to find his way home once more. She is gone. The house is not his.

There are heavy men sitting around the table in his kitchen. Each one of them has a fifth finger missing (a precaution against conscription). They are genial in the main; why indeed not, since they don't have to go to war? They are even sorry for the poor *boche*, who has not been very clever. He is allowed to stay, an overnight guest, as it were, at the house of friend and collector Jean Ducellier.

Because next day the local police are there, embarrassed about the handcuffs. "*Allons, Monsieur Max, sois gentil. Tu sais que c'est emmerdant. . . .*" ("Come on, Monsieur Max, be nice. You know this is a shitty job for us. . . .")

And the horror goes on, hilarious. Another camp, Les Milles this time, a former brick factory. The ovens make splendid cells, full to bursting. A motley population: legionnaires wearing chestfuls of medals; traffickers in everything from cigarettes to opium (indifferent grade), wine to foie gras. Hans Bellmer—his cell is in the same oven—draws Max in profile, his fellow artist and all made of bricks, a brick profile from the brickmaking oven. And behold the splendid commander who, approaching the artist politely but firmly, would have him make the portrait of the camp, of which he is proud. (In fact, twenty-four years afterward a letter arrives from the old bastard. He is still alive out there. He has heard of the artist, his former internee who so ably painted the portrait of the camp. Would he mind signing the picture?)

There is a nightclub run by the plucky pansies; their loves and lovers provide blessed distraction from the bricks. While they sing and play and swish their ruffles, the digging goes on dogged and hopeless, in the brick cell walls, slyly watched by the guards until their triumphant ripe moment of discovery; so that the diggers, thin, blinded rodents by this time, can begin again the only thing that by now they knew how to do.

It is dark in the brick oven. Drawing is harder than digging, but then, you see, you are *required* to draw. They want their portraits, the vain posturing officers of Les Milles, for after all, who is not intrigued to see himself on paper instead of in the spiteful mirror?

As a reward for the portraits, Max is assigned a flattering task: to wheel out the garbage beyond the gates. A promotion, really. A distinction nicely concomitant with his talent, you might say if you were an officer in charge of the mangy prisoners. You might also say, if you were the trusty in charge of garbage, that such a distinction implies, even demands, one thing: escape. So he takes to the road again, this time with a poet cellmate who, as it turns out, cannot swim and so becomes a drag, an abject, jittery lump to be carried across streams, to be hidden from beady-eyed farmers who, upon seeing them, would— or would not?—turn them in.

Back to the high, empty house, a silent evening errand this time, a lightning visit, to remove his pictures, oh, some of them, from their stretchers; only the smaller ones, to be sure, to roll them in newspapers, anything. Goodbye, goodbye to the warm wind, the olives, the wine. Goodbye to the calm that was. For now he will not come back.

See him running across the hills, hiding in barns, avoiding the roads, the towns. Bridges are the worst. A bridge is guarded at both ends. The sleepy drover lets him hold the reins; the sleepy horse pulls him across. Just twenty more kilometers to B. de L., *sous-préfet.* My old friend will help, will give me an exit visa. But Monsieur de

L. was not there, they said. No. But there is Georges, *préfet* of a neighbor province, perhaps sitting in his castle, for it would be hard to imagine him leaving it for anything so ephemeral as Nazis. On to friend Georges. What is fifty kilometers?

Georges is there and goes to his library to write out an exit visa, an impressive piece of paper that he hugely enjoys decorating with his illegible signature and every last rubber stamp on his desk. There follow a hundred and one more escapes, a thousand ironies. At last the frontier, the station, and a train for Madrid.

The border guard is full of zeal. He studies the pretty stamps while Max breathes, an eternity of careful breathing. The guard looks up.

"This is a very strange exit visa. I have never seen an exit visa like it." He is called to another desk and comes back frowning. "I'm sorry. I will have to send you back to the prefecture in Pau."

At the same time another uniform, a customs inspector, barks: "What do you have wrapped up in that paper there?"

The package is unwrapped, the pictures unrolled, held up for all to see. So takes place the exhibition of his life, with the unrolling of those wild and sumptuous canvases that, in what seems like a few minutes, get tacked to peeling walls of the dreary little station. Travelers look and marvel.

There before them are the forests and their glistening basilisks, the green eyes of rampant nature that stare down the officious customs inspector; the totem excrescences that speak urgently to a little flock of fluttering nuns who all clasp their hands and murmur in awe, "*Bonito, bonito.*" Imagine those pictures there on the station walls with their bursts of iridescent life that mock and woo the border guard and the customs inspector as he gazes, walks away and back again. In the general commotion he has made a decision. He plants himself before Max, his voice perhaps trembling slightly:

"*Monsieur, j'adore le talent. Vous avez un grand talent. Mais je dois vous envoyer à Pau. Voilà la direction pour Pau. Voilà à gauche le train pour Madrid. Voici votre passeport. Ne vous trompez pas de train.*" ("Monsieur, I adore talent. You have a great talent. But I must send you back to Pau. There is the train for Pau. Here on the left is the train for Madrid. Here is your passport. Don't take the wrong train.")

"*Adieu, Monsieur.*" Wouldn't he like a souvenir, a little picture? He did not hesitate in his gruff murmur.

"*Non, merci.*"

From the train window glazed eyes look out on glittering Spanish hills. At towns thin, wiry boys crawl over the cars. Great moist eyes and thrust-out hands seem to be everywhere. Swarms of boys that fall away when the train picks up speed.

Then one day there is Lisbon, and Estoril, where the hapless refugees wait for papers with rubber stamps. For weeks, months. There too is Peggy Guggenheim, the gentle collector of painting who will effect a rescue, will bring him to America. Here during a few bewildering days on Ellis Island (July 1941), he enjoys "a splendid view of the Statue of Liberty." Then, with Peggy Guggenheim and his son, Jimmy (born of that first marriage to Louise, and already a New Yorker), as guarantors, he is freed.

CHAPTER FIVE

*Cactus
and Stars*

IF DURING those Arizona nights we picked our way through the teeming forest of our memories, during the day we picked at the stubborn desert. In the cool mornings Max tended his garden, digging little trenches and dams to make a firm intention for water. Only, the rain never fell. Until the big well was dug, canals and trenches gaped like toy-sized arroyos remembering water they had never known.

But, first, there was an event to attend to. Man Ray thought it was funny. With the intention to marry, we had come to Hollywood, where he lived. Getting married in Hollywood! We all laughed about it, but the interesting thing he said, "Maybe we'll go too. If Max can do it so can I." And added, ruefully, "Though I've never done anything so rectangular."

On October 24, 1946, therefore, a double wedding in Beverly Hills united, *in the eyes of the law,* Max and Dorothea, and Man and Julie. There. It's said and done. Painless, forgettable, but fun. The Stravinskys gave us a wedding champagne toast; the Arensbergs, whose art collection contained works by both Max and Man, did the same; and that evening saw us with Albert Lewin, film director best known for his *The Picture of Dorian Gray* (the film that featured the first painting ever on-screen in color, and still the most horrifying: Dorian in the last stages of decay, painted by the Chicago artist Ivan Albright, who, it almost seemed to me, had existed for that purpose).

After our movielike events, and back in Sedona, I found my "studio" (it was one of the house's three rooms, a kitchen and screened porch, for sleeping, being the other two; Max had built a separate little structure for a studio), with its canvases, stretchers, mediums, brushes, and paint tubes waiting for me to wake them up. Here, in this two-hundred-square-foot (about) rectangular space, where the temperature hovered around ninety degrees and sometimes made me cry, I nevertheless painted: *Palaestra, Max in a Blue Boat, Maternity, Guardian Angels.* And later on: *Interior with Sudden Joy, The Guest Room* (a largish work, lying, since its sale, in 1954, in some bank vault). And then *The Philosophers, A Very Happy Picture, Avatar.* . . . Sedona, where nothing happened, was happening.

Guarding the flimsy house, our friends of the wilderness: masks, totems, and potlatch bear, the ones we had brought from New York, mingled with new ones from the reservation, which is a whole story in itself. "Where did it come from, Max?" I would ask as he hammered a nail for some new find. Answer: "They made it for you." And I, insisting: "But who did, what does it mean?" Then he, losing interest, "Oh, it's Tlingit" (or maybe he said Kwakiutl). He was already elsewhere. And when photographer Henri Cartier-Bresson came from Paris to Sedona, accompanied by John Malcolm Brinnen, he considered the wolf mask, its hairy ears and wide copper eyes. "Elie would never sleep in the same room with that," he remarked of his Balinese wife. As he spoke, the mask seemed to flash its terrible abalone grin. From that time on, if I didn't actually fear it I was respectful. So was Tchelitchew, who came out with Charles Henri Ford to spend the summer:

On a visit to New York, I had seen them, just as they were wondering where to go really away. I told them about our very first Sedona friends, Bob and Mary Kittredge, who rented out cottages (built, incredibly, of giant boulders by Bob, an Atlas of a man) in their earthly paradise of Oak Creek Canyon, adjacent to the village of Sedona. Though beautiful, it was a rather savage setting: a rushing stream, high pines, and red cliffs. "Come on out, Pavlik. Persuade him, Charlie." They came.

When, one day, we had to leave for a short trip—just two days—I asked Pavlik to keep our dog, Kachina. But dogs were not a part of his world, oh, no, not at all. Tchelitchew's world was one of spells and powers and menaces where animals, if any, were mythological and rarely benign. Still, she was a *little* dog, I pointed out, and a quiet one. So, with a troubled sigh, he agreed.

Two days later, coming to fetch Kachina, I found an excited Tchelitchew. And while Charlie looked on, amused by it all, I listened to Pavlik, marveling at the wonderful

creature who had saved his life. The dog had, in the middle of the night, begun to whine and scratch at the bed.
Annoyed, its occupant sat up and turned on the light—to
see a rattlesnake lying on the floorboards; clearly, said
Pavlik, all curled up and waiting to give him the fatal bite.
From then on, his regard, even reverence, for Kachina was
assured. She was, indeed, a spirit from the gods, a holy
Tibetan emissary, sent to save him, Pavel Tchelitchew, for
the world.

Back in New York, he told Russian friend Vladimir
Nabokov about Oak Creek Canyon, and soon after he,
too, spent some time at the Kittredge hideaway; alas, I was
by then in France and so missed the great man—one of
those I had longed to meet.

Between Sedona, Arizona, and New York City lies most
of the U.S.A. Two thousand five hundred miles were spun
out and counted by our Fords, eight times in twelve years.
Each time our two-wheeled mail-order trailer carried a
load of pictures under its tarp, and all too often the beautiful, hapless pictures went both ways, going and coming.
Gaily loaded under the desert sun. Stoically loaded to
come back, minus one or two. An abiding image of that
time, stamped upon the red-dusted pellicle of my memory, is of Max, hammer in hand, crating pictures. It is a
fragile thing, the painted canvas. How securely it has to be
fitted and fastened, nothing touching its skin, a helpless
infant born of mind and gesture.

Lumber, hatchets, nails, wrenches. The plumb line. They were as essential out there as colors and canvas. In league with saws they built our wooden (no running water, ergo no cement) house just as they built the pictures' crates. So that we, fragile creatures like those pictures, could be enclosed, roofed, locked inside, nothing touching, unbruised and intact. Except that, unlike the pictures, we could go out at will. A fast dive into the pounding heat to chase away a cow, fill the birdbath, pick the two brave zinnias that had bloomed overnight.

Nature was not always open-armed. Yet, the innocence of country living had us in thrall. We cooked outdoors on stones, flaying scrubby desert twigs to get a blaze. Playing house, the artist's way, in the crystal air, the charming weeds, the true mud.

Mud, weeds, indeed—merely a dip into another kind of quagmire, Mother Nature's kind. Far from the city: our adventure. And adventures need quagmires. They bubble and simmer, enzymes making things happen. Implacably garrulous as to voice, unashamed, in league with the maternal deity just mentioned, they are even friendly when possible. Was I, then, knowing them firsthand? Oh, I had seen them in movies—but those were *movies*. They were fantasies peopled by celebrated actors who drew water from wells, forded streams barefoot, chopped wood for fire, lay exhausted but valiant on straw pallets— although with lovely hairdos—and planned the next day's triumphs over adversity. I wondered about that word "adversity." There was something familiar about it. And about "quagmire." If there wasn't a city kind, then what had I been sunk in for so long without quite knowing it? Or was there simply some deep and ancient longing that spoke to us, to Max and to foggy me, that led us out of town and into green light, red stone—the land. But only after we had waited for each other. You don't do it alone like Thoreau. You don't ask for that much solitude.

At night candles and chimney lamps were carried from room to room, pushing back the immensities that hung around the dark. An electrical storm could hang a ball of white fire in the doorway. But it was only for a moment and did no harm. There might be a week of red wind that tore at our wooden house. Kept us inside. Multiple veils of ruddy dust rose high, so high in the air that we could stare without blinking at the perfectly one-dimensional white plate that passed for the sun.

In that camera-sharp place where the only electricity was in such thunderous lightning, there were no sounds in the afternoon save the hum of the heat. It was so intense, so lurking, so aged, that we the intruders felt also quiet, intense, and strangely on tiptoe, as if in peril. The heat bounced like coiled springs off the burning red rocks and melted the tar on our paper roof. It came inside to sit on my eyes. Breathing was important, an event.

Day after day, surrounded as by an enemy who dares not deal the final blow, we doggedly painted our pictures, each of us in our own shimmering four walls, as if we were warriors wielding arms, to survive and to triumph. Big gestures such as covering a canvas with quick paint were reserved for evenings. These began early. Four-thirty or five o'clock saw the sun dip behind our hill and in half an hour the temperature dropped twenty degrees, a theatrical quick-change. Crystalline air drawn into burned lungs produced somersaults of energy. One pounded, wrestled, scraped, dragged, swabbed—making art is not a silent affair—until night dropped too, like a clapped lid, and it was time to watch the stars.

Reader! Imagine the pure excitement of living in such a place of ambivalent elements. Overhead a blue so triumphant it penetrated the darkest spaces of your brain. Underneath a ground ancient and cruel with stones, only stones, and cactus spines playing possum. The evilest creatures of nature crawled, crept, scurried, slithered, and observed you with hatred, but saved their venom while you kept your distance, when warned. It was then that you gave yourself up to that incredibly seductive wafture that, try as you might, you could never name. Its components? The red dust, the junipers, infinitesimal desert blooms, the stones. Even the stars shed perfume with their light when we watched them slide slowly across the sky.

There was always something attractive in the offing. A visit from Marcel Duchamp meant chess, a lot of chess. Lee Miller, who so suffered from the heat that even (beautifully) bare-breasted she did not find the heart to take the photographs she had come to do. But on the last day of her stay, galvanized into activity by a sudden temperature drop, she took four hundred pictures, all of them splendid, some of them in this book. She also gave me some invaluable advice: noticing my disappointment on reading some review of my work, she said, "Don't read it, Dorothea. Just measure it." Advice I didn't need after a while in Sedona, Arizona, where you could very well wonder what an art critic was: species, appearance, habits, means of communication, etc.

In Hawaii, during a summer interlude several years later (1952), we were invited by the art-critic-less University of Hawaii, there to lecture on art (Max) and to teach a class in painting and drawing (me). Teach! Me, teach! To say that I was not cut out for teaching would be a nice way of saying that my six-week tenure at the University of Hawaii was a total disaster. My students were mainly fun-loving dropouts from the mainland who had heard about how they could chalk up an easy credit or two while taking care of their suntans and other needs on the beaches of Honolulu. Besides, not having studied painting in a *school* (those three weeks back in Chicago with the charcoal?), how could I know what they say there? I couldn't tell them about my hand, its secret pact with my brain and how it had found ways to paint the visions it found in there. I simply could not convey this procedure to a roomful of students waiting to be instructed in techniques. I wanted to say: "Go to a good museum of art and look carefully and with emotion at the pictures. Then go home and do the same thing as you have just seen. You now have craft. The rest is up to you." But something told me this kind of talk might not go down. So, after lurching through most of the sessions with these gifted but mostly absent students and just as the last day drew near (they all miraculously showed up), I had an idea for our end-of-term exhibit: I would try a new take on the *cadavre exquis*.

Here I will ask the reader to picture a roomful of students seated in a circle around a nude model on a central stand. Starting at the top of her head, everyone draws her first four inches, then folds the paper and passes it to his or her neighbor, who draws the next four. By the time the drawing is complete, it has made the full circle; thus, sixteen drawings have made the tour of the sixteen students. (Try this. Just divide the height of the object by the number of persons who must be in a circle around it.) Needless to say, the results were outrageous. Even Picasso at his most defiant could seem mild by comparison. But the *cadavre exquis* was not a form of expression much appreciated by the officers of the University of Hawaii when they paid us their stately end-of-term visit. In fact, they walked by our exhibit with averted eyes. And I had thought the experiment so successful! But never mind. I basked in the gentle island lifestyle and even peered into erupting Kilauea before heading back to Sedona and our home-made house, its thirsty plants, its welcoming pool bar.

The Tanguy visit, Kay Sage and Yves, long awaited and planned, was ruined by a cruel period of rain, sleet, wind, and perpetually lowering skies. Kay with a raging toothache was obliged to submit, after the forty-five-minute drive to Flagstaff, to a no-nonsense extraction, something that, had she known in advance, she would have viewed with horror. And Yves spent most of the time in bed with flu. Oh, I was personally responsible, having cautioned, "Don't come until March when the uncertain weather is over." Instead, February had been balmy and sun-drenched. Even Man Ray, his car stalled in the mud for three days, had wondered, "Maybe the Arizona climate is overrated?" Balanchine and wife Tanny Leclercq were luckier: a sunny day at our place, on their way to Stravinsky's in Hollywood. Dylan Thomas, on a reading trip to California, stayed a week (waiting wonderfully for money that was slow to arrive) and regaled us with violent declamation and bibulous monologues.

Dylan Thomas. How could anyone resist his bardic exuberance, his dithyrambs? I can still see him, vibrant boomer, swaying down the main street of Cottonwood, our nearest town, repudiating by his very existence any hint of mortality, any rent in the fabric of flesh and fantasy. We look into a lively bar, called the Bridgeport Tavern. This delightful haven for the likes of Dylan Thomas was next door to a revivalist meeting house, with a neat lawn on which was a large signboard bearing the words WHERE WILL YOU SPEND ETERNITY? One evening after a few beers next door, Dylan and Max carefully placed beside it a reply they had cooked up that afternoon, a big sign that read IN THE BRIDGEPORT TAVERN. They then rollicked back home, well content with the day's work, Dylan singing his bawdy hometown songs while Caitlin, his wife, remained superbly aloof and uninvolved.

She, by the way, was not happy in Sedona. Was it too rugged? Too boring? Exasperated, she seemed to do everything to disrupt plans, moments, events. When some excursion or visit was in order, and everyone ready, she would disappear among the junipers or hide behind big rocks, while Dylan, like a fat Pan, wandered hopelessly, calling, "*Cait*lin, oh *Cait*lin . . ." The trouble, I believe, was our dogs. She couldn't bear them. "Ugh," she said, "In England they make bloody little gods out of them." I supposed that such was not the case in her native Wales. And that Welsh mothers of children *tolerate* dogs, just barely. Little dogs she found especially obnoxious. Something fundamental, I think, about who or what gets into the lifeboat in the crunch. How many moms like Cat Thomas ground their teeth when Noah brought in that mangy menagerie and left their kids behind to swim?

Another of those who found their way to our remote escape hatch was a girl named Sonia Sekula, who brought a white rabbit, with the admonition "Give him a little love." Easy to say. For the first night he slipped out of the cozy dwelling we had devised for him and ate, down to the ground before morning, twenty-four Parma violets that we had set out that very day in defiance of cactus and cutworm, but on hand was Caresse Crosby, ebullience rampant on a field of extravagance, who said: "Catch him and I'll make you a *civet de lièvre* [jugged hare] to remember." No friends of white rabbits by now, we finally caught him, although it took days of luring and baiting. Because he was no innocent Easter bunny; he was a wise old rabbit who knew a thing or two about the wiles of humans—after all, hadn't he graduated from a pet shop? More days were spent marinating him once the butcher had achieved him, and another day was spent on his cooking. That rabbit! How to end the tale? He was not only mean but aged. And who is tougher than an old rabbit? His revenge: besides being inedible, he caused us a bitter sort of anguish that had nothing to do with appetite.

Caresse soon returned to Italy and to a vast, moldering castle called Roccasimibaldi. Here she could indulge her latest fervor: some impassioned thing about world citizenship, surrounding herself with vigorous young idealists like Garry Davis, who made news by traveling with his "world passport" (or trying to). In Roccasimibaldi's giant rooms these adepts, males mostly, happily slaved to repair or create plumbing, to plug holes, to carry wood and water, cook spaghetti—endless chores, all quite gay and optimistic despite the constant need for sweaters and firewood. Caresse even acquired this monstrous pile of stone as big as a town, then she died. Roccasimibaldi showed up in the *Times* yesterday, some forty years later, for sale!

But in Sedona, there in the red world of jagged souvenirs signed by the great glacier, castleless pioneers named their scenic views to bring them down to size. Cathedral Rock was a ruddy mass imitating for those childlike settlers a cathedral. Courthouse Rock, noble giant reduced in name to a reminder of fiefs and files. Just west of Sedona was Cleopatra's Nipple. It isn't known, of course, who named it so, nor why anyone as remote as Cleopatra should occupy the imagination of an American cowboy—for it must have been a cowboy—but it was often thus pointed out to us, just as naturally as the other poverty-stricken titles.

But, coming back years later, and encountering an entirely different population: retirees hoping to live ten minutes longer than they would elsewhere. Old doctors with cloudy pasts (That would be Dr. Woodcock, Princeton alumnus. Wispy but trim in his buffalo plaid shirt, he lived alone with his horse on the other side of the creek. Riding the horse at a walk—never a trot, much less a gallop—to the general store, daily, he picked up his mail and other sundries. One day I asked him to dine with us. The dinner must have been good, for he said afterward, "Max, you married a cook," something Max loved to quote. Two years later he ordered a shotgun from Sears & Roebuck, shot his horse, then crept into a pine box he had had built, put the gun in his mouth, and pulled the trigger. The price tag was still hanging on the gun when they found him.), the usual undaunted, unpublished writers, painters with camera eyes and a penchant for scenery, fevered adepts at new religions, or, in general, people who didn't get along with their relatives back home. Coming back then, we found that Cleopatra's Nipple no longer existed. Its name had been cleaned up by less giddy imaginations; it was now known as Chimney Rock and had never, in anyone's memory, been called anything else.

It is well to remember that this rugged land was peopled mainly by what we have called pioneers; some of those of their descendants whom we knew were surely as colorful as their ancestors. When Charlie Brewer, patri-

arch of a sprawling tribe that occupied the land down by
Oak Creek, and from whom we had bought our three and
a half acres, came around with his dog to pay a call, it was
always a memorable event. He told us about the things
and people that piqued his curiosity, such as the man who
had told him about a vision he had had.

Charlie quoted him: " 'Yessir,' he says, 'I seen God.' He
says, 'I was standin' there with that old red dog of ours and
the dog lookin' up at the sky and barkin'.' And he looked
up to where the dog was barkin' and he seen God. Stood
there and lookin', he says, and down come God. 'Well,' he
says, 'I'll venture to say He had shoulders that was thirty foot
across and He was holdin' out to me a gold key. He gave me
this gold key,' he says. And I says, 'What'd you do with it?'
And he says, 'Why, don't you see? That key He gave me, that
was power. And I can put a curse on anybody I want to
because he gave me that power, and that curse will really
curse everybody.' And I says, 'Well, that's pretty good.' "

That God's gift of power was a malevolent one is a
thought too gloomy to be pursued here. Anyway, it was easy
to see that surrounded by such grandeur, a mere man
could long for power. Then, as now, the decibels of nature
could crush a human brain. That is what happens. So I
lock the door and paint interiors. Great events. A white-
and-dark picture would muffle the red world outside. Big
bare rooms with white frozen figures, like Sodom and
Gomorrah. There is opalescent light and velvet dark. Isn't
that the artist's best joy, to control light? To rival the sun
and moon, to turn their logic upside down with brushes

and paint and monstrous ego? I am here. Arthur Rimbaud, mad poet, is here too, on the blackboard in my canvas. What you see there are notes from his secret notebook. Private, impudent signs. The door is not a door on the wild red garden, just on a little something personal, like the door of a house looking in. Schoolgirls invite a frosty beggar and his dog; they all peer inside and make me think for some reason of the way certain birds tuck living ants among their feathers. Only, we are on the inside and the birds are outside swinging in the scrub firs and equated with stones and scorpions. In here, out there. It is all something see-able but removed, and brings to mind, you might say, a rare iridescent bug, which is also a victory of a kind. *Interior with Sudden Joy* is the title, mentioned earlier.

"This is Capricorn Hill," I said one day. Max looked for a while at the stony, cactus-armed rise, the cleared track where wheels could turn. "Yes."

It was a great day when water was brought from under the hill After a year of hauling we had only to turn a spigot. So that next day Max could begin a monument to our Capricorn Hill, a king and queen in cement and scrap iron regal guardians for our house, our two heroic trees, our paints and brushes, our precarious peace. What else could he call it but *Capricorn?*

More than just an extra feature of a house is its name, I thought, regretting that in my country most houses had only numbers. Solidly planted in the books I had dreamed over since school days were those houses with names that not only proved their existence but chastised the geography surrounding them, so that river, village, hills, lakes and even mountains were hardly more than shifting background in the mental picture of the house with its magical name.

In Arizona there was nothing about our made-it-myself two-room house that visibly merited a name. Capricorn Hill. Alone it stood, if not crooked at any rate somewhat rakish, stuck on a landscape of such stunning red-and-gold grandeur that its life could be only a matter of brevity, a beetle of brown boards and tarpaper roof waiting for metamorphosis. Up on its hill, bifurcating the winds and rather friendly with the stars that swayed over our outdoor table like chandeliers.

On those evenings when there were visitors we might have been Magnasco pirates reveling on a sea-sprayed deck, sails furled, candle lamps steady, while the world spun backward and our voices hung upside down in the desert night air. Tales were tall, arguments were musical, philosophy gave pause. Remembering the voices I record a bit of their vehemence, their irony, their music:

Max Tells of Mozart and Others

To him the last real European
Amalgam of all sweet sound
Green gazes came and made of amalgam a potpourri.
Green glances came heralding
The tender giant chauvinist thundering fatherland

Panic for chords, celestial choir
Based on a bag of hope.
And then that hope broke down in him
While students came to throw their tearful caps
Into the air.
They came in brandenburgs out of the brick wall
Tossing caps.

Thus came the weather change.
"Thus came Wagner after
To creep to the cross with Parsifal."
All this churns an inner maelstrom
Brought to the simmer by sound finespun.
There is some element in it
Some consequent hallucination
Still green, a kind of intimate solstice.

You would think that here ends the story, that those velvet nights, preludes to each passionate day in a landscape so charged that "if Wagner had seen this his music would be louder than it is already" (somebody was saying) were more than enough. Did not this paradise dimly hold us in thrall, sustain us hilariously in our ongoing combat with need, the creature kind, and provide the sweep of background—a long luminous brushstroke upon which to pin, plaster, paste, and paint our questions and our answers for the rest of our lives?

Cowboy Elmer Purtyman helps put on the tar-paper roof while watching the artist's progress. "Better git on the ball, Dorothea, and fenesh that petcher." Cowboy Elmer, who had once, years before, served in the navy, and who walked with a rolling gait like an old sailor with the sea bottled up inside him, and who, exuberantly in league with the primordial, guides us through the Colorado River rapids (replaced now by concrete dams) in rubber boats. He pitches tents, makes cowboy biscuits, and shows us Indian hieroglyphs in fastnesses where the invader (we) had never walked.

Studded with discoveries in nearby Indian caves, canyons, pueblos, aged and wise, and precious as silicate arrowheads, of which we found several, is the memory of that nine-day river passage, eighteen miles on the torrent that cut skyscraper-deep between sheer stone. The shiny autumn silence that listened to water, black shadow that swallowed light and hid our bobbing boat in a seeming underworld ready to be drawn by Gustave Doré, a paradise lost, no artist's tricks needed, not even imagination; it was all right there before our eyes along with the phantom presence of Indians, eyeing us from up there on their rim or waiting in cave and cranny. Uneasily. Because it was theirs, and even at this late date we were intruding.

These were the canyon walls that are now so cleaned up, rerouted even, arranged, photographed, advertised, that their lofty reticence has become no more than a movie backdrop for organized tours. Deplorable? Certainly, but that being the case, one must deplore the entire human presence with its long history of conquest—of nature, of other humans: Indians, Israelites, Vikings, Muslims, Aztecs

. . . And if we, gliding downriver in an unreal chasm, were silent and discomposed by its pristine beauty it was a thing that even in the memory is a treasure beyond words.

Guide Elmer moved respectfully through the gloom. For hours on end no one spoke. Arriving at Lee's Ferry two days late—we had played at moviemaking in a hidden canyon—we were hailed with relief by the locals, even newsmen, and our movie footage was nicely integrated, back in New York, in Hans Richter's avant-garde film *8 by 8.*

It all showed, alas, that paradise was indeed a some-where not quite believable, or—can it be?—desirable. Were Adam and Eve really chased from the garden? Or did they leave?

In our time and circumstances, however, staying or leaving was not so simple. So when, in 1949, a competi-tion was launched by that very same movie director (of *Dorian Gray*) for a painting of the temptation of Saint Anthony for his next film, we accepted, being two of the twelve painters invited to participate. Result: the money for—leaving. Hung about with valid reasons, if such were required, we locked our flimsy door and left for France.

CHAPTER SIX

Paris with a Patina

AUGUST 1949. Antwerp, where we dock, is in full carnival delirium. An Ensor carnival—how conditioned we are by pictures!— a Turner sunset, a Vermeer light, pale Friedrich mountains, a line of Daubigny trees, a Schwitters billboard, a green apple for Magritte, a Percheron by Rosa Bonheur, the list is endless, nature is seriously compromised—the perfect recreation of his grotesqueries, the brass noise, the brassier colors, the hideous grinning masks that are loathsome caricatures of their wearers, dead or alive.

Death is dancing in the streets, death is a bear, death is a dwarf running on tiny feet, a paper hat trampled by fat sunburnt legs, all swarming in the great town square. Around the corner suddenly. Quiet, airless-seeming, a narrow street of ground-floor bay windows offers an impassive consortium of death. In each one, framed in ocher varnish, lace, and potted plants, a leering orange-haired, yellow-haired, black-haired woman placidly knits or crochets. Or fans herself. She is of course one of the masks like her neighbor. They are not young; indeed, they appear eerily respectable, a strict sorority in their placid, interchangeable calm, one after the other, all the same, the same, and provoke in me, the awed passerby, that maddening uncertainty of place felt when wandering in a hall of mirrors.

Then a train ride: hot, sticky, and smelling of sweat and an orange that my neighbor peels. And finally France. It was to become, for me, a space of twenty-eight years and could never be confused with counted time, filled as it was with astonishing myths in the making that came to stay. People were unique and poetic. In this giant space—for Paris was only part of what seemed like a vast, enchanted park where there was always room for more eucalyptus-lined roads—headlong living shared hours with monuments living and dead. Shall I ever forget the rose that Picasso broke from his dooryard bush for me? Of course he knew I would not. But, to begin—again.

The Paris winter of that first year froze everything but human hearts. These remained warm and courageous in spite of plummeting temperatures that were only slightly higher in rooms than in the streets—central heating being largely unknown. Poets and painters alike, hunched in stiff, hard overcoats, haunt the café, hoping to hear of a room, half a room, somewhere, anywhere except the hotel—also hunched and stiff with cold, as I found out.

Optimist, I looked around for a place to work. Thus, while Max worked in a borrowed studio, I found a forgot-

ten hotel room in a forgotten hotel and brought my canvases and paints. But the radiator turned out to be a ploy,
for no heat ever came from it. I sat there for several days,
bundled up before my easel, and cried.

One such day was cheered by an afternoon date with
Truman Capote, who was in Paris for I don't remember
what. Along with Jane Bowles, Themistocles Hoetis, and
some others, he was holed up in the Hôtel d'Angleterre
(they must have kept each other warm), on the rue de
l'Université. Truman and I met in an English-style, and
warm, tearoom on the boulevard Saint-Germain, a space
much later occupied by the Alexander Iolas Gallery.

We drank a lot of hot tea while Truman complained
to me about *Vogue* magazine, which had never printed his
article on Hollywood, although it had paid for his trip
and expenses.

"Can't you get it back?" I asked. "Surely you could
place it elsewhere. . . ." No, alas, they had paid him. It
belonged to them.

"But what did you say in it?

"Oh it was just *straight reportage.* On some stars. Joan
Crawford, for instance."

"Joan Crawford! Wasn't it even fun?"

"Fun! First of all, a *little girl*"—a moue here—"answers
the door. She shows me into this *museum* and says,
'Mommy says I'm to entertain you till she comes down.'

" 'Well,' I said, 'So entertain me, then.' She started
pointing out the things in the vitrines, built in along the
walls.

" 'This is a Louey Sez tea set. It cost Mommy seven thousand dollars. This, over here, is a Ming Dynasty vaz. It cost mommy eighteen thousand dollars. This one—' She went on and on with these pricemarks until I changed the subject:

" '*My*,' I said, 'you have a lot of beautiful flowers here.'

" 'Oh yes, Mommy has a standing order with the most expensive florist in Hollywood. . . .' Just then, thank heaven, Joan Crawford *swept* down the stairs, you know: in a drabby sort of housecoat, no hairdo, no makeup—just lots of black around the eyes—she held out her two hands like this"—gesture here—"and said, 'Oh, Truman, darling, I'm so sorry to keep you waiting. I was just upstairs making the beds.' "

Me: "You wrote that for *Vogue?*"

"Of course. It's just *straight reportage.*"

"Who else did you see?"

"Lana Turner, for one. A dinner date at Chasen's. I couldn't get her to *say* anything—just 'mmm . . .'—but I kept trying: 'I hear you've just been to New York?' I thought this might wake her.

" 'Mmm . . .'

" 'Was it, well, what you wanted? You must have a lot of friends there. Who did you see . . . ?'

" 'Mmm . . . saw some shows.'

" 'Oh, that must have been exciting. What did you see?'

" 'Mmm . . . saw *Medea.*'

" 'Of course. Judith Anderson. Isn't she great?'

" 'Mmm . . . I would have done it differently.' "

Truman sipped his tea. I asked: "Truman, is this what you wrote for *Vogue*?" He was still disgusted, just thinking of it all: sitting in that outlandish room with a *little girl,* waiting for the great star of motion pictures.

"You know, they don't recognize good copy when they see it," said Truman Capote sadly. He was right, I thought. It must have been a lovely *straight reportage.*

A month later, Max and I are lent an apartment with studio on the quai Saint-Michel. It has damask draperies and handsome rugs. From its lofty balcony we look down at the superb sweep of the Seine, flowing between us and the Cathedral of Notre Dame. This stylish pad that we were privileged to inhabit for two months, January and February, is dependent for heat on two delicate porcelain stoves, pretty little things called *mirus,* which have a distressing way of simply going out instead of burning the coal *boulettes* we heap into them. Outdoors, on the side of our number thirteen, a tall column of yellow ice (from the top-floor toilet) clings like an amber waterfall. As pipes burst, so does our bubble. Braving the icy studio, Max says his hand did not thaw enough to grasp a brush.

In the salon we sit tight on the satin chairs, bundled in sweaters, coats, boots, a cold marble chessboard between us. Mirrors sparkle like ice cubes while in the kitchen drops of grease congeal white on the pans. We make tea, gallons of hot tea, and Max scratches a hole in the frost on the windowpane. Yes, the Seine is frozen over.

"*Allons! Les misérables.*" There she is, Madame Guyot, our concierge, our lifeline, who, a week later, wangles us our own space: two tiny rooms under the mansard, our first Paris home. Attained, they would say, by means of five flights of stairs. Not minded at all, especially going down, for it means that we will sit in the warm café, glassed-in for winter, with stove, stovepipe, chessboards (you bring your own pieces), and gray, milky coffee.

Soon, more chess players arrive. Handshakes all around. Playing, I am cowed by a fellow named Dédé who defeats me with ease and much gloating. Damp overcoats huddle in the corner like sheep out of the rain. The lovely, steamy silence is broken only by the hard-thinking sighs of my opponent and his drumming—unfair, I think—of his fingers on the Formica table while the short winter afternoon gives up trying. Lights go on in the boulevard and out in the boutiques across the street, where tradesmen bring down their iron curtains with a grinching crash, lock them at the bottom, and walk away. Time for dinner, more handshakes, *bonsoir,* and the Restaurant Charpentier around the corner, a place of high understanding and low prices. Our own Man Ray is there. So American in his beret, our wedding twin, with his Julie, diminutive New Yorker whose French, after six years in Paris, consists of the word *petite.* It is fascinating to see her in conversation; that is, listening to French tablemates who are obliged to trot out their own eight words of English.

"They smashed the window," Man is telling us. A little gallery had been showing his objects. The by-now-famous metronome, the housewife's iron sprouting tacks, the *pain peint*—a loaf of French bread painted blue. And in

the Paris night, hooligans have destroyed them. DEGENER-
ATE, they have scrawled. "My things utterly ruined," says
Man. He always said "my things": objects, photographs,
paintings.

Scion of this restaurant dynasty and whirlwind waiter
was Ern*est*, who knew everything, it would seem, about the
U.S.A.—mountains, cities, populations, rivers, presidents,
the sort of information found in almanacs and reburied
in them at once. "Hey! Can you name your state capitals?"
And he would duck his head to my ear as he set down the
steaming ragout, to reel off the names of the capitals of
our states, thus embarrassing us all who knew not. He
would go there one day, he said. Perhaps he is here now.

Moving through those bone-chilling evenings in Saint-
Germain-des-Prés, we rarely failed to find our surprise.
There, lit by the glow of café terraces and cruising cars,
would loom the face of some friend: Wifredo Lam, Roland
Penrose, in town for a day, Sam Francis or Katharine Kuh,
who represented the Art Institute of Chicago and was
pleading with it by telegram and telephone to buy, for
twenty-five thousand dollars, one of the big, lately discovered Monet waterlily canvases on show at the Katha
Granoff Gallery. Thus would begin for us all an unexpected evening over couscous or pot-au-feu, with or without tablecloths, but always supplied with wine and the
funny story.

Little by little the French language became not only
possible but easy. It can be said with truth that I learned it
in the first years from Madame Guyot, our concierge.

With her dovelike voice, her immense gentleness, her superb *blanquette,* and her expert way of finding the flea in the bed, she quite literally kept us alive.

In fact, she is, for me, only one of a vast sisterhood of heroic human beings: the French concierges. I have never understood why these patient, defeated women, glued to their miserable loges day and night, at the beck and call of a great houseful of tenants or proprietors, fallen upon and vilified at every inconvenience, torn from sleep by late arrivals (they have to buzz them in), are doomed by fate to remain in their *merde* forever, maligned and ridiculed by worldly travelers and silly japes who never seem to speak of them as anything but "quaint" and disheveled witches to be borne with, figures in a Punch and Judy, *bizarre.*

Much later, in 1959, I went daily to paint in a studio I had acquired on the rue Saint-André-des-Arts, really a tiny apartment that had one wall ten feet wide. So I worked on a ten-foot canvas. Arriving at eight in the morning, I was buzzed in by Madame Turpin, the concierge. I can close my eyes and see her now. Yes, you, Madame Turpin, with your great phlebitic legs, your glistening white arms that end in little hands like butterflies, are you still there in the jaws of your recliner, behind the window that looks out on nothing save damp cobblestones and courtyard windows? Does your husband still come home from the weekly cross-country grind of his truck-driving haul to make your bed and swear that you are still his beauty and his light? Reader, let us thank heaven for the TV.

Madame Deleuze has a very off-white dog. Madame Bertin has three cats. Our Madame Guyot has one too, Kiki, a real monster that loves her. That is, there is no other way to explain his behavior when Monsieur Guyot comes home (he too is a truck driver) and Kiki jumps up on the table and urinates in his soup. *"Il fallait le faire couper"* ("We had to neuter him"), sighs gentle Madame Guyot. Every morning she padded into our attic to light the fire and grind the coffee while we struggled out of heavy sleep, reluctant to affront the shivering day. It was our second winter. Max now had a borrowed studio in a not-too-distant quarter. I painted my pictures in a room adjacent to ours, and worked at etching in, of course, an etcher's atelier, described later in this account.

At last April, a rudimentary spring and with winter forgotten. Our evenings were surely what "spring in Paris" is all about. Balmy and electric, with people looking for trouble or just company. Saint-Germain-des-Prés, where one evening we ran into Marcel Zerbib with Lam, and, on the way to our place, Lucien Freud with his wife, Caroline. They had been wondering where to dine. "Come up to our pad," I said. "Marcel here will cook up something Tunisian." (He made great ragouts with peanut butter.) They came along, they huddled wide-eyed in a corner of our eyrie. What, I wondered, had they expected, poor things? They must have felt trapped—the quai Saint-Michel *sounded* like Paris's best. But to get to our two maid's rooms, you went in by a little door next to the camera shop; you climbed those five steep flights of hollowed-out stairs to find us under slanting ceilings at the very top of the old house. There was a glassed-in partition of sorts to separate the "kitchen," a two-burner gas plate and a tiny sink with real faucet and real water, from the dining area. I wish I could remember some of the succulent ethnic meals that were made and served in that primitive pad. There was our lumpy bed and flickering fireplace to go to sleep by. And another miniature sink to keep us clean (you really can do it). All of it dim doings for London visitors on the fast track.

Others were sometimes intrigued and even seduced by our reckless strategies. We were often at the Hersants', later changed to Hersaint—the real Hersant actually managing (this is France) to legally forbid our Jewish friend to use the name. Their château was called Villebon, a grand house built by Victor Hugo that, over the century, had fallen into disrepair; the sort of dank, lumbering property that owners can't seem to get rid of. But it was in this place, sumptuously renovated and refurbished by the Hersaints—Madame being gifted in the matter of interiors—that occurred some of the most sparkling receptions of 1950s Paris. I am sure that some of my American contemporaries would remember evenings at Villebon. Hélène Hersaint was a modern Madame Verdurin who, I believe, would have preferred to be thought of as a modern Madame de Staël. She aimed to receive everybody who was anybody in the arts as well as in the "aristocracy"; it was her abiding passion, as for many gentle beings who are neither very creative or very titled, but who recognize

and revere those who are and who hope that, with contact, some of the magic will rub off on themselves. There
were interesting lunches with friends who, like her, surrounded themselves with books, garnished their furniture
in books, and came to think of themselves as having deep
wisdom. Did you not, in buying a book, receive knowledge? Of Muslim origin, she later became a Catholic con-
vert. I found this not in the least surprising, given her
penchant for extravagance and general gorgeousness.
There are people in whose lives no Charlie Brewers or
Ronnies or Doc Woodcocks ever appear, only princesses
and geniuses. Dear Hélène was one of those people, per-
sisting in her very personal definition of human worth.
She would refer to the Virgin Mary as to a particularly
darling and close friend, adorned in her mind, I am sure,
as in a sumptuous van Eyck painting, with plenty of
damasks, ermines, and precious jewels.

For Hélène's evenings you could justifiably use the
word "ball," for *bals* they were. The five crystal chandeliers
in the ballroom blazed with *candlelight*. How could I forget
them when remembering the drops of hot wax falling on
my head as we danced? Another time, at one of Hélène's
luncheons, I saw Claude Hersaint smiling in his plaid
waistcoat as he received us. A fellow guest, celebrated for
his fantasy-based pretensions (for example, he claimed
Lord Byron as a relative), observed him scornfully, actually saying: "How dare you wear my plaid!" Clearly, life was
colorful at the Château de Villebon.

Like everyone, we went to the movies. And there found

the famous Paris fleas. "They live mostly in the Champs-Elysées cinemas," said friend Claude. Madame Guyot was inclined to agree. Sure enough, it was usually after an evening at the movies that I would thrash the night away in an uneven battle with one or more of the wretched beasts. Not Max, who remained superbly asleep and unbitten.

Fleas. That summer we knew slightly a writer of novels, the Parisian kind: Menilmontant at night, plenty of Paris's brawny, untranslatable local *argot,* and girls who wait. He was the sort of macho fellow seen in French films of yore—tight suit, bedroom eyes, white teeth in view—and had written a heroic and hilarious chapter on these insects. At an art opening I shook hands with him. "Why did he scratch the inside of my hand?" I ask Max. And he, laughing, "Maybe because he is so used to scratching his fleas." So saying, he takes me to the other side of the room.

When you are in Paris you are out. When you live in an attic you are out. That is what it means, "coming out." For it is an outgoing process, innocent, the need to know the others. In our case, the need to escape the two slanting little rooms with their *boulette*-burning stoves to warm us, the gas plate where savory dishes got put together by friends, the walls empty of pictures in these first two Paris years.

Even most of the Parisians we knew—artists, poets, shoestring publishers—seemed not much better off behind their crackled dormers and crumbling walls. And then I would think of Leonardo's famous lines about how, upon looking fixedly at a ruined wall, imagination could deliver to the eye horses, battles, processions, landscapes. Except that we of the glorious present might distinguish other visions drifting up through the flaky surface like photographs wavering in a watery developer: monsters of outer space, rockets, bombs, devastated cities. Behind these frail façades, then, are the poor poets, always the first victims of upheaval, collapse. Living out their uncertain lives in houses that lean, on leaky top floors in attics, with water faucets on dim brown hall landings, in rooms formerly occupied by servants and reached by flight after flight of tilting spiral stairs, complete with clammy handrail, broken-hearted hollows in the steps, and bare bulbs over the doors.

Another winter, another lunch, this time with Tristan Tzara, who has invited us to his place. Poor poet, poor Tzara. He refutes his poverty with that monocle. Like all of them behind their abject walls, he dreams big, and all externals fall away before his thundering poem. He fathered dada in Zurich. Now Paris hides him, a card-carrying embarrassment three flights up a murky staircase. —Or so I thought.

We pressed the bell, heard the tinkle. The door opened and a maid in frilly black and white made way for us to pass into the salon. A blaze of eighteenth-century rooms of inordinate height (of course: those stairs) where winter sunshine played with the chandeliers and caused lavender-yellow-rose beams to tremble on the worn seraglio carpet. Long windows giving on a sepia garden conversed with the bare tops of ancient trees.

In a library of leaves: pamphlets, tracts piled high, magazines, catalogues, manuscripts, gray-labeled boxes, albums, papers, books, and standing among his treasures as if in a paper nest, there was Tzara, amazing Tzara, just as I had wanted him to be. His knitted vest bore a hero's darns and spots. From his thatch of pepper-and-salt hair to the baggy tweed pants there was nothing, I felt, that could ever be changed. He wore not a monocle but shell-rimmed glasses.

African carvings hung high on the walls, along with Papuan spears, Polynesian masks; a collection living in harmony with pale Louis Seize chairs and an ormolu desk.

"Lunch is served."

We sat, just us three, at a round table graced with fanciful Bohemian glassware and placed, curiously, in the big entry hall. We ate sardines and drank wine served by the pretty soubrette, and after our diminutive lunch we looked at mementos, drawings, letters, poems on ruled paper, and a number of those sketchy sketches on paper table covers. This, by the way, was a well-known formula for the assiduous scavenger-collector: after the jolly bistro dinner, toward the end of the talk, the wine, the laughing, the antics, at some point there appeared from nowhere a pen, a pencil, or even colored crayons. *"Allons, Pablo, comment était ce drôle de flic, comment il t'a montré du doigt"* ("Come on Pablo, draw that dumb cop, the way he pointed at you"). Everyone drew and wrote and signed. *"C'est ton tour, Alberto, hah, regarde, Portrait d'un Cloche"* ("Your turn, Alberto, hah, Look! Portrait of a Bum").

When the bill was paid (a great bluster here) and chairs pushed back and leaves taken, someone during the merry bustle would turn quickly and tear the "tablecloth," the drawings, signatures, and doodles landing safely in his pocket—why not, instead of in the restaurant garbage or restaurant pockets? Tzara's beloved collection, what will become of it?

Full of ferocious wit, he could also be cruel. To a fellow poet passing the café where he sat: "Ah, my friend, I found a rare book of yours, *rarissisme* [super-rare]—all the pages were cut." In those days publishers always left it to the reader to cut the book's pages.

Now his dada charm had turned to communist clout, and in *Fuite* ("Flight"), one of his plays, I heard the actor say: "Better my chosen chains than a found liberty." Max was NOT *d'accord*.

It doesn't take very long then to realize that left-bank Paris, where everything, for us, seemed to happen, wears her rags and tags on the outside. A perpetual carnival where disguise and discretion are one and the same. As the caliph of Baghdad donned pauper's tatters to ride among his people, so the Paris street wears her uniform of humble grays that add up to pearl and amethyst, precious as a patina.

So that was it. They all lived behind scarred walls and leaning stairs. Imitation-wood-grain varnish everywhere, sticky-smelling, better than none at all. Terrifying little elevators into which you squeezed your fatalism and your elbows graced the more affluent apartments and *les hôtels particuliers* (private houses). We are all brave passengers. *"Pardon, madame." "Ooh là-là."* "Five!" "Are we not too many?" Someone leans to squint at the notice. "Three hundred kilos capacity," he reads on the brass plate. General laughter among the ladies, who are, of course, so svelte. Once through this gauntlet, we are let into rooms which, as they appeared to my American eye, so often resembled Versailles—mirrors, gilt chairs, gleaming parquet, and all.

There were two worlds in the Paris I knew: the one just noted and the other one, as I was to see. Alberto Giacometti, for instance, resolutely embedded himself in his tumbledown alley, a place that, for its air of seedy resignation, defied comparison with even our quai Saint-Michel perch.

Alberto Giacometti, genius. But should I not mention rather earlier than later the young wife, flower-faced Annette, who kept him company when he wasn't too sure . . . who posed and posed and smiled and smiled, undisturbed by what seemed a mysterious penury, by hovel living, by the cold wind in the cracks blowing on her flower flesh in the tiny room? We went to visit them sometimes. You went in by an alley, narrow, gray, but, one felt, a little Paris space cherished comfortably by those who lived there. After finding Alberto in his closet-sized studio, we were led down the weedy path to another door, which he opened. There sat, convincingly, in a little space that resembled a sturdy and continuous nightmare, Annette, her beauty fixed like a collage image on my vision.

Annette, a wife, surrounded by little more than a bed and a gas plate. Much later, I ran into Alberto one morning at Lefebvre-Foinet's art supply shop and I felt a colder wind. There was not the usual badinage. His face was gray. *"Je ne suis pas content"* ("I am not pleased"), he said, knowing he was ill. Soon he was gone.

But where in this book shall I speak of Matta, Roberto Matta, painter, who is all over it, from New York to Paris to New York and back again, who has colored this story from my earliest surrealist days? Before that, his arrival in Paris from Chile was like a sighted comet for the surrealists in that café on the place Blanche. One imagines him: irrepressible exotic and seminal artist whose cosmos-inspired paintings challenged even André Breton. Not one of those who became too famous, like Picasso—whose stairway on the rue des Grands Augustins was so clogged, votaries on every step, that one had to give him up, we said sadly, not to have to squeeze past the bodies. But Matta, whether in Paris or New York, where his ebullience and his vision dazzled our own young artists, merging in his big canvases the architecture of outer space with the conceits of earthly technologues, is indelibly here. And there; pursuing art and the elusive feminine with equal fervor. Matta, worth a hundred pages of fantasies to match his own imagination. And though he doesn't know it, I cling to him as to a spar of that surrealist ship some of us sailed, long since unmanned, now a phantom vessel leaking badly, with Matta and me all that's left of one antique New York evening and the game of murder.

*   *   *

But this was 1950s Paris, and although the surrealist meetings continued, the place Blanche was becoming as remote from me as a dry lake. Simmering under my cap at these meetings and in other surrealist encounters was an ever-growing, questioning impatience, adding up to an imperative: break out. Around 1955, my canvases literally splintered. Their colors came out of the closet, you might say, to open the rectangles to a different light. They were prismatic surfaces where I veiled, suggested, and floated my persistent icons and preoccupations, in another of the thousand ways of saying the same things.

Meanwhile, frivolity was not out of the picture. At François Hugo's one evening I met two ancient queens of the Paris *beau monde*: Maria de Gramont and Elsa Schiaparelli. Both had lived energetic lives, with plenty of iced champagne and stardust, both were somewhat bitter about the nasty way that nature had turned them into has-beens, both were tensely polite. When Schiaparelli, who was the first to leave, was safely out of the room, Maria snorted with derision. "How gross of her to wear a plunging neckline like that, at her age!" And Monique Hugo, our hostess, deprecatingly: "But Maria, she is after all a great couturière." And Maria, snapping back: "Maybe. But that doesn't make one want to see more of her flesh." Both of them were, I am sorry to say, examples of that peculiarly Parisian tendency among a few of her inhabitants: nostalgia for the perfect princely past. That it has been far from perfect does not deter these dreamers from their airless play-acting. But no matter. They are harmless in the main, no more dangerous than children building sand castles on the beach, bless their little hearts.

One is perplexed, however, to see a few artists join in the game. What are they up to? Or rather, what are they? Their faery world of power and aristocracy melts European history into a sticky mass of titles and brocade dressing gowns. They are in deadly earnest about the gilded centuries in which they place a few of their ancestors, and about their own preeminence in the here and now, their bodies cared for in the unavoidable present, their minds awash in the perfumes of the prestigious past. When remembering Flaubert's remark "Honors dishonor, titles degrade," his unpopularity among these rare and precious birds is, indeed, understandable. I have seen not a few of such people at art openings, book signings, cafés, or receptions. They see nothing. Or if they do, it is with disdain.

Our fief was, of course, Saint-Germain-des-Prés, with sallies to Montparnasse where another nostalgia was the prevailing malady. It is utterly impossible to walk along the boulevard Montparnasse on a brightly brave autumn day without seeing on its café terraces the petulant ghosts of former denizens haloed by that determined glamour that only intervening time can confer. *Montparnos* of old, French, flavored with British and American, hang around the wicker chairs, sociable spooks full of droll stories but spooks all the same. Even in spring the place looks autumnal with its pale new leaves and paler sun, and some fragile survivor eager to talk about Hemingway or Henry Miller, or Man Ray's Kiki.

One sat at a table for hours, a forgotten glass of something paying the way. In winter, tattered poets drank café-crèmes to keep warm. Seedy youngish men with exploded hair wrote in smudged notebooks. When they looked up, which they did rather often, they did not see you. When they looked down again, their pencils scribbled self-consciously. Sometimes they were joined by girls in heavy makeup and thin jackets.

According to street names we were in a city of saints joined by an occasional profane. The rue Guillaume Apollinaire was a subject of much jesting among literary buffs and artists, who would point out to you its doll-like length occupied by two massive gray buildings without numbers, without entrances, these being located around the corners on its two busy right-angle streets. You could *walk* on the rue Guillaume Apollinaire but you could not *live* there. Surely Apollinaire would have laughed and loved his phantom street. In any case, he soon had to lie back in his tomb. The subject was so unmercifully taken up and ridden, in disrespectful sheets like *Le Canard Enchaîné*, that a few years later the city *conseil réuni* got busy when no one was looking and had a couple of doors punched in the side of their building—it belonged to the town—and numbers conspicuously added to dress them up.

The daily down-to-earth life in Paris involved treks to

the local market for fresh produce besides the usual pâtés, butter, and eggs; and woe to you if you forgot your string bag, for you would have to get your victuals home wrapped in newspaper. Here, too, is the acid test of the sophisticated shopper: anyone not speaking French must take what is handed over without a murmur—or even a mutter. My pride knew no bounds the day I snapped back *in French* at the hag selling carrots, and got an awed *"D'accord."*

Most colorful of these markets was the Marché de Buci, where if you were lucky you might see artist Leonor Fini, already a legend for amateurs of sensational Paris, sweep into the bustling crowd of comparatively drab shoppers. Picture her striding across the rue de Seine, an imperious flash of taffetas and perfume and feathers, seeming to illumine even the cobbles under her very high heels. A firebird among the crones and frost-bitten vendors of sausages and cheese and sorrel, all of whom would turn briefly to stare after her as at some sudden, mythical apparition. In her studio it was a different matter. She painted tirelessly, canvases inhabited by elongated, unearthly females and an occasional girlish male. But, like a canoe in a tidal wave, she fought hard against incarceration in the ghetto of Women Painters. Her mythology was the Italian eighteenth century with all of its sinister extravagance and sensuality. From it she took only what she wanted: the *outrance* and the willfulness that reflected her refusal to grow up. *"Jusqu'a se raser les poils pubiques,"* said Max. (Hmmm . . .) Her triumph was to remain the dazzling little girl who painted, with the technical brio of a master, her world of sylphs and monsters. Her self-absorption was authentic, unwavering. It included an obsession with cleanliness that meant inside as well as outside and was defined by purges, a necessary ritual for absolute perfection. Moreover, the purges were not only for herself but also for her numerous angora cats. That was harder to take. You had to love Leonor a lot (I did) to put up with the cat miasma that accompanied whatever perfume drifted through her beautiful rooms on any given evening.

Her acquaintance was large, including as it did a few glamorous people: Jean Genet (in Leonor's well-heated apartment he wore an immense turtleneck sweater that covered his hands and gave an impression of robotlike dexterity to the eating of his dinner), and on another occasion Anna Magnani, whose burning gaze caressed me but briefly, for it was turned off like a switch at my insisting that I could not adopt her dog.

If ever there was a resolute "dream world," Leonor Fini lived there and managed, amazingly, never to leave it. In a conversation about a current movie, *Mondo Cane* ("Carnivorous World"), she said, primly, "Kot"—one of her two male companions—"says I shouldn't see it. *Ce n'est pas adapté à moi*" ("It isn't adapted to me"). And later, with her in Nonza, Cap Corse, we all played at the water's edge while the sea slammed against black Corsican rocks, and water slid between stones to make doll-sized lakes, the pebbles shining up in all their colors before they were caught like iridescent fish. At sundown, back on the promontory before the black ruin, a former monastery without roof that Leonor called home in summer, we displayed our wares like jewel merchants in some rug-shaded souk, proud of our finds.

"Ah, yours is the best. . . ."

"No, that one, the green and blood red, the find of the day. . . ."

Then with the dark they are forgotten, as the dry wind bears away their colors.

When, in 1977, I was alone, a few friends for dinner could sometimes fill the emptiness. Leonor came with her two companions, painter Stanislao Lepri and aforementioned editor Kot Jelenski. James Baldwin, our American firebrand author, was in Paris and would also come, making for an exceptional evening, I told myself. We all waited for Jimmy, who did not show up before we had given him up and had already begun our dinner. But when he did arrive the evening began to be "exceptional," for he positively danced in, all wound up like a golliwog, in checkered pants and big yellow bow tie and wide green hat. He never stopped talking—in English. It was the only time I ever saw Leonor Fini upstaged. She visibly faded before this glorious American jack-in-the-box who, though he had been living in France for some time, did not speak French—exactly the reverse of André Breton in America, perhaps for the same reason—and, were he alive today, would probably remember his Paris evening at my place as a bit of a drag.

Throughout these Paris years I was often at Georges Visat's etching atelier and at Mourlot the lithographer's. There I would meet other friends: Joan Miró, for example, in Paris from his island of Mallorca. He brought drawings and projects to be turned into prints that became rectangles of pure delight. I seem to hear his voice again—*"Comment ça va?"*—and to see his round eyes in a face that was always lighted with an inner smile. That smile was the color of him, it was in everything he did; every painting, drawing, sculpture, that grew from under his hand wore a smile somewhere, mocking or happy, ironic or indulgent, and often enigmatic. He didn't talk much. Why should he? There seemed always to be plenty of talkers around to fill the air with sounds of importance. His own were quick and soft-spoken. Cordial. *"Comment ça va?"*

One late afternoon, we were gathered in our Paris apartment, rue de Lille: Miró, wife Pilar, Max Ernst, and me. It was the day after the opening of his new exhibition at Galerie Maeght, where an eight-page magazine, *Derrière le Miroir*, was published for each show. At a break in the conversation I showed Miró my copy from the opening. A black-and-white illustration made from a Miró drawing was on its cover.

"Dear Miró, would you sign this for me?"

His face beamed. *"Mais oui."* He jumped up. "Do you have some colored crayons?"

And would you believe it? I found only two scraggly wax pencils, red and blue. But Miró closeted himself in the next room, and remained there during the rest of the visit. When he came out with the page, he had not only signed it, he had transformed his black-and-white drawing into a glowing picture in three colors.

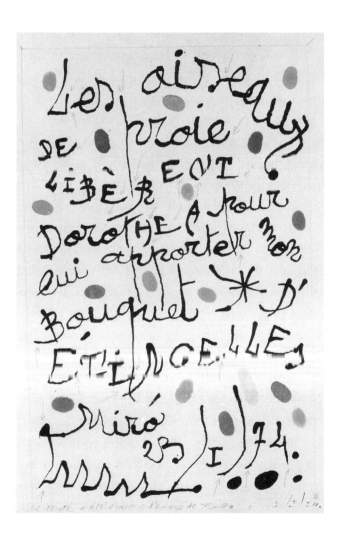

*   *   *

Surely someone else remembers our Patrick Waldberg of
the comely prose (somewhat rare due to the author's
indolence) and portly stance; the way he danced at the village fête, seeming to levitate despite his comfy bulk, his
feet scarcely touching the ground. Born in California, on
exactly the same day as I, he was almost immediately
brought to France, where he lived and died a Frenchman,
despite the American passport that he kept in his pocket
like a warm, furry friend. A Jewish father and an Irish
mother. That lady, a devout Catholic, had given the then
pope ten thousand dollars for his little cap, a searing fact
in Patrick's inheritance. His own precious memories:
young, he had danced with Rosita Dolly of the Dolly
Sisters (who today would remember them?), and older,
came with us to Sedona, and older yet, would hunker in
the night bistros with Sam Beckett or Yves Bonnefoy. A
raconteur, he knew the recent past and its denizens,
whether in poetry, art or theater.

He would have told you what he thought of Jean
Paulhan, *éminence grise* of French lit-crit, a frisky, gray
mouse, in a way, munching on the paper of books, especially books about books, so that his own prose was often
lavished on names that few people would remember today
if he had not written about them. Unlike Sainte-Beuve, his
inspired predecessor, he watched and weighed most often
without mercy. "Taste, beauty, and other confused ideas,"
he could say with quiet scorn. It must have been amusing

for him to demolish some puny penman in just four words. Elegant, tiptoe words to match his woodwind voice and the way he bounced—or was it pounced?—from his side of the dining room to ours, while rather offhandedly outlining a book project with, he hoped, artists' illustrations. He was one of those people for whom language was more precious than life. Wanting to know more about him, I ask:

"Max, tell me, what do you think of Paulhan? What is so great about him that everyone is in awe of?" Pause. "Is he really the gray eminence that people seem to imply? Or is it only the NRF editing?" (He had become the guiding spirit of the literary review *La Nouvelle Revue Française*).

Answer: "*Un hibou défroqué*" ("An unfrocked owl").

Of course, that reply was not serious, for he and Paulhan were friends; but it was attractively outlandish enough to change the subject. So that it was only much later that I could try to satisfy my curiosity (and never quite did) about the great mandarin of French language, Jean Paulhan, and his unrealizable exigencies for its users. Was it not he who said, "Only new words don't yet sound like insults"?

It was Patrick who loved to discuss everybody, their achievements, their foibles, their dramas. Patrick, who knew much of the present because he swam in it. He cared not at all for the future, considering it already mediocre. But he loved the past. Rich in anecdote, he could tell you what everyone had done and painted and written (with generous quotes) and said and acted (with accurate miming). His own writing: allusive, fragrant, the kind they call *belles lettres*. He did not compose poems, as so many do without knowing what they are doing. And if Sam Beckett was a writer, Patrick was his ideal reader, listener, arguer.

Sometimes they were joined by Oscar Dominguez, a hulk, as unforgettable as he was immense. The head oversized, everything—great globes of eyeball, great nose, great wavy lips. Even the penis, a heavy, idle appendage that, at some dinner party or other, he was said to have displayed. Rising and opening his fly, he had taken out its shy but immense occupant and laid it on his dinner plate. The ladies did not faint; this was the 1930s and everyone was a surrealist, impervious to shock. Besides, giant Oscar, unhappy Oscarito, was to be indulged. He it was who had investigated a fascinating new take on the process known as decalcomania by using it as a painting technique. His variation consisted of covering a surface—canvas, paper, glass, or any smooth support—with an oily or wet paint, laying another surface on top, pressing down firmly, then pulling it slowly away. This method was later explored by others, notably Max Ernst, who used it as the basis for many of his paintings.

Young *coqueluche* (darling) in a prosperous Tenerife family, he had arrived in Paris, his pockets full of money that was soon exhausted by *la vie Parisienne*. People remembered his appearance in full evening dress, weary of champagne, at three or four a.m. in Les Halles, the

great market, now gone, that supplied Paris with its produce. Here, with pals, he would sober up with a bowl of
onion soup. This was a short period. For soon the evening
clothes disappeared, and Oscar Dominguez was a dedicated surrealist painter, whose pranks, along with those of
Picabia, an earlier golden boy, from Cuba, were never
dainty. He painted furiously, between bouts of depression
and failed suicide attempts, surrealist pictures whose fearsome contents recalled the writings of Lautréamont or
Gilles de Rey or Sade, and contained, mainly, an inordinate amount of torture practiced upon female nudes.
This was a general feature of many of the surrealist pictures at the time, painted by mostly quiet souls who loved
their often rather eccentric surrealist wives so faithfully
that they did not even have lovers like the rest of the male
population.

Devoted to Oscar was Marie Laure de Noailles, *grande
dame* and patroness of the avant-garde, a painter herself—
it seemed everyone was. We met often, with and without
Dominguez. How to describe Marie Laure without failing
to convey her rather puzzling uniqueness? To the *beau
monde*, which she typically and socially owed her allegiance, she preferred us, the rootless, the reckless, the
hilarious wreckers of her native establishment. An illustri-
ous ancestor, the marquis de Sade, gave her, in our eyes,
an added aura, and in hers, his phantom blessing. There
was Charles, her elegant, estranged husband and ongoing
friend, who in 1932 had been dropped from the Jockey
Club for having underwritten Luis Buñuel's scandalous

film *L'Age d'Or*. They said he took it hard. In any case, he left Paris to live thenceforth in Grasse.

The patronage of these two visionaries, who were viscount and viscountess *incidentally,* saved many other seminal works of the day. Their baronial Paris mansion welcomed all those in the arts who defined the mood of their time, whether in three-piece suits or patched tweed. Can we forget those great marble stairs, their walls lined with Goyas and Burne-Joneses, big rooms muffled by the thick scatter of damask draperies, pictures, *objets de virtu,* glowing carpets, and, in a doorway, Charles himself on a visit, smiling coolly above his velvet collar, greeting you, her friend? *Mondain* indeed were the lunches where everyone talked fast before moving to the library for coffee and rushing out strictly before three-fifteen like white rabbits. What they could possibly do with the small remnants of those winter afternoons was, for me, an idle contemplation that always ended with the cozy thought of *cinq à sept*, a favorite name for the hours reserved for extramarital fun.

Some other Paris receptions were just as baffling. At one of these, in a salon studded with great art—Memlings, Sassettas, and Giottos—that the frustrated visitor was not encouraged to dawdle before, I was fascinated to see the princess's tiny beaded bag lying beside her plate during the entire dinner. She lived there, didn't she? It was her home; and yet the bag stayed in full view. What was in it? Pills? Jewels? A tiny revolver? I would have given worlds to know.

And at Louise de Vilmorin's place just outside Paris,

oddities abounded—albeit pleasant ones. Invited there for dinner, along with a scintillating bouquet of sophisi-cates (mostly men), we ate *pot-au-feu*—Louise liked to play at country-style living. Later, in the salon after dinner, I asked for *le petit coin*—the toilet—and Louise herself got up to show me the way. It involved passing across the big entrance hall, and while we were there the doorbell rang. She turned to me and said, "Get out." Like that. I hurried on as fast as I could but not before seeing her open the door to—Orson Welles! Of course I understood: my presence there obviously would have spoiled what she saw as a very romantic moment.

And I did not in the least resent her order. It was direct and expedient and quite in keeping with her dis-arming little-girl persona. Incidentally, during the evening that followed I did not exchange one word with the great Orson, who, as I remember, stood leaning in the classic mantelpiece pose and scowling while his hostess was moving among her other guests. He was probably not too at home in this roomful of blue-and-white Delft bibelots (her passion) and French conversationalists— maybe falling a bit upstaged by André Malraux (Louise's boyfriend), who, surrounded by an awed little circle of admirers, was holding forth on the glories of some obscure Greek sculpture. How did Orson Welles come to be in this party, anyway? (He seemed to be asking himself the same question.) I remembered that, young, Louise de Vilmorin had actually spent some years married to an American and living in the American far west. And that her book, *Madame de*, had recently been made into a hit movie. It was also known that Orson Welles was on his uppers and scouring about for money to realize a project. Alas, I thought, he will not find it here.

Surrealist lore told of the late 1930s at Marie-Laure's rambling château in Hyères, a seaside town on the Côte d'Azur, its house parties, seemingly frivolous but always with purpose: a Man Ray movie, *L'Etoile de Mer*, being filmed on the local ramparts; or a symposium, a happening—happenings are age-old—desperate high jinks imperfectly hiding the melancholy anticipation of war. The Marie Laure that I knew later still kept her grand memories locked away in mother-of-pearl so she could go on living as she pleased: in the present, gathering the motley and the near-famous around her, involving herself more deeply than ever in the artistic ferment of 1950s and 1960s Paris with Oscarito Dominguez at her side. Until one day the blood oozed out from under his door on the third-floor landing in the rue Campagne Première. He had finally pulled it off, the only thing he really wanted to do.

Now, with the slow tread of this summer night, memory serves me ill. Try, try to remember at least some of the thirty-four times three hundred and sixty-five nights. They are the ones to be cherished. Try, try to remember them and the same number of days to match, all shine and opalescence, before they turn to black. For it is not always possible to notice when you are in orbit. Moments snowball to years. I watch them whirl around us with their processions and silences, their peripheral nebulae, famous and infamous, mortal and wistfully immortal.

One of the latter, still there for me, is Paris's Henri Langlois, Turkish it seemed, and cinema hero; for he saved, during the long war years and after, countless film masterpieces from oblivion. I see him like a photograph: Henri with Mary Meerson at his side, both of them of enormous girth, both in sneakers at Jean and Krishna Riboud's, each of them in Krishna's most capacious chairs. Mary: straw hair, long dress in a time of minis. Henri, possessor of the most fervent eyes I have ever seen, great dark amber lamps framed in an immensity of flesh; eyes straight out of some Turkish zenana. When they looked at you they doubtless saw the movie screen with, perhaps, you in it—though not necessarily. He was perhaps fifty-some, yet aged, as an oracle is aged. As words were for Jean Paulhan, movies were his life. Since then, everyone involved in them knows how he scrounged and salvaged and stored—stacked in their cans to the ceiling in his rooms, everywhere, even under the bed, in the unused bathtub the films that today we take for granted, never dreaming that they might have been lost forever without Henri Langlois and his passion: for they later became the core of Paris's Cinémathèque, Henri Langlois at its helm. Not, however, before interlopers, seizing the credit along with the cans of film, tried to ease him out. Scandal. Indignation. The protest was led, discreetly, by Jean Riboud, art collector and unofficial force in cultural matters; and, vociferously, by most of France's best film directors, who marched up—or was it down?—the Champs-Elysées to defend their hero, Henri Langlois—and to win his reinstatement.

Heroes, too, in their way, were the Americans who arrived to astonish languid Paris with their very American brand of verve and invention. Watching Robert Wilson's *Deafman Glance,* I watched, at the same time, *le tout Paris* audience watching in amazed silence as that remarkable spectacle unfolded without a sound. Soon after, the American Center in Paris, along with a young impresario enterprise called Artservices, brought more of the real avant-garde back to Paris, where, after all, it had started so long ago: Merce Cunningham, John Cage—dance, music, and more theater. And even though I was embedded in my own universe, striving after my own goals, they marked my Paris life with something resembling solidarity. Meanwhile (and sometimes still) I am a tourist, a condition endemic to us all and known to be incurable.

From our secondhand car's windows I am shown measureless intervals filled with the stretch of passing lands, rivers, towns, mountains, craters, ruins, and walls, thousands of them, piles of stones, millions of stones that define every definable space; cut, uncut, crumbling, bombed, restored, blackened; and fainting in the carbon monoxide stealth that mocks dead centuries and their fallen monuments. I am the perfect blotter. My eyes never get enough of looking. Greedy tourist eyes, they tell me seeing is believing. The past is everywhere I turn; it will seduce the present if I am not careful. Frescoes tell incomparable stories, tapestries sign history in blue and blood and purple. A fortress sheds its anachronistic frown on the motel and gas pump below. Without clanking armor, tired limping horse, lice, suppurating wounds, I might all the same be seeking some absurd grail, so imbued am I, so annihilated by the evidence, so flattened against the martyred wall.

Moreover, tapestries are fragile and tend to fade. Captive weavers must have known about that, weaving against time to break evil spells or to save their necks, in drafty stone chambers like this one at Angers. Here, trembling in a perpetual twilight gloom, dreaming and indifferent to the ever-changing pairs of eyes that glide over them while the tour guide's voice drones through his dim spiel, apocalyptic episodes in pallid blues and reds have lost their fire. Yet I know of one pair of eyes, mine, that is misty with looking at them. So old. So fragile. Their glorious days so long gone. It is perfectly thrilling to think of this lapse of time. Centuries come close because you are drawn in by standing there; you are part of the circle, the mystic signs are traced for you alone; the fanfare, dim but just audible, prods like the elbow of your neighbor, craning to see.

Up and down the zigzag of French roads, weaving its own tapestry, shuttled the little *deux chevaux*, "two-horse-power," our steed. Open on my lap as Max drove, and providing food for thought, was the guidebook, indispensable bright red companion of timid travelers, carrying descriptions of every hotel *worth stopping in*, with petite line drawings of bathtub, toilet, telephone, bidet, a flowery little star if the food was deemed especially nice. Monuments, churches, curiosities boasting centuries of history to be visited—between meals. Because clearly it was the restaurants that fascinated the guide-liners, pitiless compilers who graded food mills as schoolmasters grade student exams so that, given the guide's authority and the French penchant for rich and sophisticated eating, even the remotest three-star establishment received each day its quota of devout diners.

Such "temples of gastronomy" were not to be taken lightly. In fact, entering one of these dining rooms at mealtime—you must observe the rigid time slot in which you may be fed—was very much like entering one of the ancient churches on your itinerary: the same respectful silence, no one laughing or talking above a murmur, the same beatific ministrations of acolyte-waiters who seemed to stifle an impulse to genuflect when uncovering your mystic nourishment, the Specialty of the House, or pouring out the ritual splash of wine for monsieur to taste (why always him?). In putting together his humble materials the starry cook introduces a little bit of this, a little more of that, a handful of those things over there, a whisper of the other, until something decidedly odd yet palatable has been cooked and served. He has thus produced a secret which he guards as preciously as the old Prague alchemist kept his gold-making formula from leaking to the ears of his rivals.

It is the eating experience that looms large on the road. Cars are driven from restaurant to restaurant, ports leading all the way to the Mediterranean Sea.

On we went, always south save for small deviations— Tournus, Albi, Hauterives, where a postman, "Le Facteur Cheval," had left his dream palace (worth the detour, says the smart guidebook). Coastal barrens and folded flat lands crushed by immense cloud dramas that were some-how always unsmiling, if not actually tragic, filled the eye's frame, with only a rim of earth to anchor it to our concept of gravity.

The Losère, France's wasteland, raised its steep hills to bear an occasional ruin: stony wind-lashed manor or gap-ing chapel, abandoned by God and man, epitome of loneli-ness? No, I thought; earth is earth, the sky is kind and this manor can live again. Surely we could replace windows and doors. They would be painted blue, of course, to match a clear day. There would be smoke from the chimneys. There would be trees. We would find water, yes, if you are deter-mined. . . . Three or four trees on the leeward side. Oh let me stay, let me live in this place! I could make it breathe again. But no. Look back. It is still there, with its howling holes for windows, small now, and then a speck only.

White mountains like party hats reared at our left, grad-ing to blue and then green; from cruel to kindly they came down to us, to envelop the precarious wing of road that offered a bottomless plunge on one side and lo! a cottage on the other. Enough to set the mind on mountainside dreaming, each cottage beckoned: "You there, come in.

Here is a cake to eat and a magic mirror." And then, each time, we were around the bend, we dipped to lose sight of it with a stab of regret, something like abandoning a faithful dog. Yesterday, beside a stream, the black granite stones of a waterside mill asked me to stay. "Take me."

Lest pure pleasure overtake us there were Max's calls on people nobody would remember today, little links in the many *réseaux* of the 1941–43 Resistance to the Nazi occupation. How many times my heart broke hearing their shattering accounts of deportation and murder— the bursting into a kitchen, the husband hiding in the closet while she irons and irons until the ironing board is knocked over on the floor and her husband dragged away. . . . Oh, this was far, far from our tourism. . . .

It is also with some emotion that I remember the day of our visit to Joë Bousquet in Carcassonne. Imagine a hot summer afternoon in one of the most fabled of cities and an American girl being taken to meet a First World War–wounded man, paralyzed from the waist down. The two men, Max and Joë Bousquet, were hapless conscripts on opposite sides in the war, one of them emerging whole in body, the other bedridden for life. He had triumphed over pain and despair with an indomitable weapon: his pen. And pen it literally was, covering thousands of sheets of paper, year after year, with dense, lacy handwriting that I can still see on those letters that came to Max from Carcassonne. In his way, Joë Bousquet was known. Literary reviews eagerly published him—essays, philosophy, criticism, poems. But in his writing, perhaps the most attention was lavished on letters to his friends and contemporaries in Paris's intellectual and arts community. It must have been a truly voluminous correspondence. Such was the man I was about to meet.

It was a big dark house with that peculiar hush of the city *immeuble,* cool after the blazing heat outside. We were shown into a high room, curtains drawn, a sense of still air like held breath. And there, at the far end, was the bed, an oasis in a brown room. The only glow: a small shaded lamp, so that in the great spaces of the place I saw just one golden pool of light, and on white pillows the pale dome of his head; on the bedside table, the opium pipe that eased his pain and that, with his devoted nurse, Jeanne, kept torment at bay. He greeted his old friend, Max, and me. "Tea? A glass of something?" and then, "That will be all, Jeanne. We'll be all right. "

The two men talked in low tones. I didn't try to listen, infused as I was with a melancholy that seemed to ooze from the heavy drawn curtains, the walls, even the little shaded lamp. My throat felt tight facing the sorrow of this room and the man in its bed. To think that these two poets had been caught in a murderous web of war, maybe even obliged to shoot at each other! (Though in fact they had established, to their relief, that they had been in different sectors during the conflict.)

Wanting to include me in their talk, they pointed out the paintings that Joë had bought (some of them by Max) while their paint was still fresh, now prized as masterpieces and that I felt rather than saw in the shadowy quiet of that big room where our voices had no echo but stayed by us like secrets.

Coming out into noise and brash light I felt I had dreamed it all.

Tooling south, we pull up one day toward noon in Saint-Martin-d'Ardèche, the home from which Max was removed in 1940 by the Vichy police for having the wrong identification card. Here is the usual village square, the same patchy high houses, with a cat in one wide-open window and a few crusty boule players in baggy corduroys lopped off at the ankle, the beret that literally clings, an integral part of the head, playing in a torpid slow-motion game. Always the dog in a hurry with clearly someplace to go, crossing the line of roll so that the player must wait, only a weary *merde* escaping his preoccupation. The same scene, like a movie cliché, at every town. And always the deafening cicada din muffles the click of steel boules. Plane trees show their knotty roots and knottier branches in perfect harmony with the knotty, arthritic, hobbling citizenry: grandmothers and grandfathers and great-uncles and maiden aunts of restless beauties and ambitious boys gone to the city. What youth hovers there does so as absently, as lightly as the migrating bird. The hotel lunch under green leaves: "No! It's M'sieur Max!" marvels an old waiter who is still here. "And it's you, M'sieur Gazette," teases Max, and with reason. For the garrulous old fellow fills us in. The crooked hotel keeper who confiscated Max and Leonora's house in the confusion of its foreign owner's wartime plight is now behind bars, so the waiter tells us. For obscure crimes, something to do with pimping on a grand scale.

"It's still yours, M'sieur Max, you have only to take it to court." He does not know, as so many were to know to their satisfaction, that M'sieur Max does not go to court. For anything whatever. We climb up the stony lane that serves as a road to the house.

At first I do not like it. A stern silhouette. Ah, so that's it. There is something grim and harsh about its grayish walls, aslant and holed with narrow eyelike windows, rather too serviceable-looking for all its haphazard angles and additions, and denoting in the frown it presented to my eyes some long commitment to expediency. A mill? An oil press? No one lives there.

Surely he will feel some special acuteness in this place, will show me, along with the house, and however obscurely, at least by a silence, a queer change of tone, or just a sad gaze, some glimpse of inner disarray huddled inside him like a crumpled ghost. So that climbing the hill to his house (for was it not still and always his house?) will be heavy going, a fraught, dogged pursuit of demons that he is determined to meet head-on. Oh, even if it is for me, the whole detour: showing me the house: a place, as I soon saw, of indescribable wonderment.

I have expected a certain postcard picturesqueness combined, of course, with the natural bounty of olive grove and vineyard, a few sheep on the hillside; I am prepared for that. But not for the magisterial presence of its

totems. Max's totems in cement, iron, plaster. From every
parapet, every stair ramp, doorway, and wall, they lean
over me like a tribal council, sizing me up, I feel, to my
disadvantage.

We move nearer the house, silent save for an exchange
of *bonjours* with two urchins who are playing on the porch
and who run down the hill as we walk into an open garden room, almost under the house, a lower level. Its stone
interior is vaulted, and there is the usual moldy smell that
quite suddenly becomes part of a strange dreamlike
moment in which we see at the far end of the room a
dense, high forest, black in this shadowed cavelike space
where all is now very quiet, the children's voices gone,
even the cicadas having momentarily stopped their eternal rubbing as they will sometimes do.

"This," says Max with a kind of gesture. He turns away
and I go nearer.

It is then that the picture shows me its tattered edge
peeling from the wall. I pull, only a little. The canvas
clings to my hand. Obeying some sort of righteous
impulse that needs no question, gripped by a swarming
rage at seeing the paint flakes on the floor, intent, determined, I pull and roll, while he looks on, saying nothing,
nothing at all, as the picture is finally, no, not finally but
immediately, rolled in my grasp and I am running down
the lane, where, overtaking me, Max says it is too late to
save the paint film, in any case. But his voice is in pieces,
lost in some neighbor's machine-saw roar while a yelping
dog that I know is on a chain somewhere half-menaces,

half-cries, and a quick succession of hot gusts tear at my
crazy burden, tipping me and blowing hair in my face.

The rest of its history may be told in a few words: for
two years it waited in friend George's château in windy
Ucel. Then in 1956, when studio space was ready in our
own house in Huismes, it was rebacked and brought
home, where, for a season, Max restored and painted
more of his forest, visited it with birds of dazzling
plumage, and rode a watery moon over the trees. Was it
the black forest of his German boyhood? Or the stunning
memory of America's northwest? Whatever the reason, *A
Moment of Calm* was truer than ever. "There!" he said,
standing back. "You saved it. It's yours." A strange and
perfect moment.

The picture is now in the National Gallery, in
Washington, D.C., where I believe it belongs. The reason: at
the most perilous time of Max's life (1941), after surviving
one concentration camp after another—Largentière, Les
Milles, Loriol, Saint-Nicolas—and escaping to Spain, he was
rescued, literally, by Americans, and it was here that he
found asylum at last, from Nazis and from their puppets. To
live safely, to paint, to meet one. To give him that "moment
of calm." The picture is a token of gratitude, as I see it, to
the country that saved him from total moral defeat.

For the next few years, domicile was a matter of exigencies that sent us both ways: Sedona, Huismes (pronounced "Weem"), and, of course, Paris and New York.
For in 1955, no longer frozen in poses of doubt on the
quai Saint-Michel, we go to live in Touraine—the garden

of France, they call it—where we will dive into verdant fog to dig our second septic tank.

1953–54. France for a year or two is punctured with desperate returns to Arizona. It was on one of those lavish meanders (we mapped a different itinerary each time through the well-known rainbow that stretches across our states) that we came one day to a windy crossroads in the New Mexico desert. A sign pointed: ACOMA, Indian Pueblo, forty-seven miles. Should we? We did. Those miles were slow and grinding with bumps and holes, the washboard surface, if you could call it a surface, that marked all roads in Indian reservations and that were rarely negotiated without groans and coughs by any but the toughest vehicles.

Heedless travelers in low-swung city cars drive their delicate steeds onto beds of stone and stratum. So that by the time you have arrived at Acoma, high, high up on an unearthly mesa, the radiator is boiling, the sun is slanting across from another constellation, and you have somewhat lost contact with your planet.

"The first thing we saw," said Max afterwards, "was a church." True. It dominated the place, rising on the empty flat clearing like a clearly un-Indian monument in the full face of the afternoon sun. There was no sign of life on the central plaza, no one at all. Cameraless, we were nonetheless wistful. Max stood gazing in disbelief.

"Imagine! A Catholic church in a pueblo!" While we were taking it in—the raw adobe of houses and pink belfry, the empty square—a priest in black cassock hurried from the church accompanied by a small boy. They stopped to speak for a moment and then separated, the boy moving in our direction. "Hi," said Max. "I didn't know you were Christians here."

"Oh, no," the lad replied, "we aren't. We are Catholics. Over there"—he pointed westward to a neighboring mesa—"they are Christians, they dance without masks. Here we dance with masks. We are Catholics."

He smiled suddenly. "Want to see a dance?"

Oh, yes! "That will be a dollar." He had a no-nonsense businesslike air. Would there really be a dance? Now?

"Yes, yes, they're getting ready in the kiva." True to his words, the place soon filled with masked dancers and their fellow tribesmen. Onto the dusty agora adobe houses spilled dogs, silent mothers, children, the old and lame. And in the last flames of a superb sunset we watched a dance that, though full of grandeur, was neither Christian nor Catholic.

The ocean liners that carried us across the Atlantic—four, six, seven times—are blurred into one. Always back again to the little house, anticipating grace in the form of preserving Max's proud citizenship as an American.

Each time we climbed the gangplank, forward-leaning into the slanting ramp, in the highest possible state of excitement (what other mode of travel can compare with the boarding of a ship?), shedding, as we did so, all imminent threats to our peace, we knew that outward bound was in the delicious here and now. For six days we rocked beyond commotion's reach. Time then was a big lazy eternity, round as a ball with spume and spray always in front and behind us, a benign amphibian not terrifying after all. It did not care how long you took for your next chess move. Until, unperceived and most wonderful of all, eternity drifted off into the mist, and it was landing day, bringing another kind of commotion, other eternities. For instance, a beloved city is always good to come back to even if, as in the case of Paris, there are frequent failed summers: autumn approaches while you are waiting for the heat wave that passes you by. American summers of curling temperatures in league with a pounding sun cannot be expected in this rather northern austerity that doesn't sweat under its arms or leave its sweater at home. A good season, however, will bring such days of blissful blue and gold that the only place to be is out.

It was on such a day that the bus took me on at the place Saint-Michel. I carried a small flat package under my arm, a painting, a *Forêt* by Max that I had long wanted to have framed; now was the time. The bus lumbered, lurched, leapt, and dropped me at the place Saint-Germain-des-Prés. One of those days with summer balancing just above the rooftops, not quite coming down to warm us, and I hurrying up the street until a heart arrest, a complete turnover that shook my chest and brought me to a standstill. The little package was still in the bus, alone on the seat. For how long?

I watched the crazy monster tooling away up the rue de Rennes utterly unmindful of my package and of me standing upright in the street among crowds of people, none of whom I knew. Go after it, take the next bus, which would probably veer off in some idiotic direction as buses are wont to do? Report it? To whom? Where? How to find the number? And what was the use? My picture would be picked up, had already been picked up, a package is always fun, didn't we know it, a mystery, a stroke of luck, who knows? All these futile workings of the mind just as the decapitated fowl or landed fish pursues its useless jerkings before giving up. Moreover the disappearing bus had now a positively guilty look, running away like that with my package, its very outline the silhouette of a clumsy thief. There was something sickening about it like bad news from the doctor. One thing was hideously sure: my little forest wasn't mine anymore.

We had both been so pleased the day he gave it to me, a sunny moment of the kind possible only during the flutter of a gift. Oh, don't panic. Oh God.

Probably I walked on, probably the day went by, not so very blue, not so very golden after all, its fabric tarnished and a growing hole in it through which I saw a little phantom forest that would have to be mentioned that evening, a nasty confession. Disagreeable, surely, an evening destined to scorn and disgust, why not? How could I expect anything else? How not to agree with him? In the shop windows I saw myself as two-dimensional, flat, without substance in a waver of bungling loss. Another wrong turn. Irredeemable. Could it be otherwise? Yes, it was otherwise. That evening, laying aside *Le Monde,* Max listened in silence. Then, after a pause, not at all exasperated at being told something unpleasant, he said, mildly and very offhand, "Never mind. I'll make you another one."

It is 1954, a banner year of events. In May I have my first Paris exhibition. A little gallery in the beautiful place Furstenberg, presided over by Simone Collinet, first wife of André Breton and staunch lover of dada and surrealism. I was euphoric. The place, the absolutely dreamlike May afternoon (Why "April in Paris" when the month of May is the real seducer?), and my paintings on these walls—crowded rather close together, since I was showing not only new work but things I had already shown in New York, very satisfyingly finding enthusiasm and buyers. For me, an artist living in the shadow of a great man, it was somehow crucial: the shadow lifted and a gentle but steady light shone on me. I was now an artist that Paris newspapers wrote about, Paris collectors bought, Paris friends recognized. The catalogue I had designed was a tiny book with pictures, an etching and friends' poems such as:

> *Quand sa famille a pris le thé*
> *(When her family takes their tea)*
> *La douce rit et se met nue*
> *(She laughs and drops her clothes)*
> *Pour la rose et pour les velus*
> *(For the furred and for the rose)*
> *Dans le miroir de Dorothée.*
> *(In the mirror of Dorothée.)*
> *(André Pieyre de Mandiargues)*

*   *   *

Soon there is Venice. The incomparable. The mere name is enough, like a mask over a smile. It is a lacy word that, if you're going there, promises you certain reward; indeed, it is the one city on earth that is absolutely predictable. Here behind heart-catching façades, their filmy reflections fluttering in the dirty canal like fragile altar cloths hung out to dry, lie all the secrets you could wish for. Here filthy water is beautiful. Here all rooms are lofty and the worms in the walls have no more work ethic than the gondoliers. They wait while we wander.

Of course you don't really believe in the people who are put there, or the dogs and cats, like those tiny dolls on architectural models just to show the scale, because the real Venetianos you see when gazing at the Carpaccios in the museums will surely come back soon (tonight?) from their long absence.

This was the Venice Biennale of 1954, in those days still an event. We were assigned a princely hotel room, golden chairs, royal expanse of bed, a funny telephone, damask walls. Our two dogs were not overly impressed, being concerned with the menu. On the second day the waiter at the door made suggestions. But I said no, he would please bring carrots, rice, and ground beef, as usual. It was really what they always had. Dogs do not need change in these matters. But the waiter's eyebrows lifted and he said, "But, madam, they had carrots yesterday!" I took this in for a moment, but prevailed for carrots.

Unashamed sightseeing: museums and palaces, streets, canals. Back at the hotel a telegram: "Max Ernst: You have won first prize in painting. (Arp for sculpture, Miró for graphics.) Please come to the Giardini at eleven tomorrow."

Next morning, arriving at the gate, guarded by two splendid guards in white and gold, we are stopped. Oh, Max! He has forgotten his telegram. He rummages in his pockets, a key chain in the shape of an owl falling in the sandy path. As he recovers it, he is trying vainly to communicate with the magnificent guards, Italian being a language neither of us can deal with. Gestures. "But we are invited," pointing to the distant crowd. "We forgot. I forgot it at the hotel. Danieli. Hotel Danieli."

Here a few rapid Italian words from the guard, with negative shake of the head and a finger pointing to the town.

"But it is too late to go back. Don't you hear, the ceremony has already begun." We hear the distant applause, the loudspeaker. Adamantine, the beautiful guards. A last effort: *"Ma sono primo premio"* ("But I am the first-prize winner"), pleads Max, touching his chest. The handsome soldier stares. There is a short staring moment while he considers the cheeky pronouncement. Then he steps aside to his colleague where we cannot hear. But we see his all-too-plain gesture: right hand raised to point with index to his temple, the finger describing a circular motion. *"Primo premio,"* shapes his disdainful mustachioed mouth, as his pal rolls his eyes to heaven. Frowning, he returns to invite us to the exit.

So we did not, after all, bask in glory, Max's *primo premio*; he did not, except in laughing, even refer to it, while we dipped instead into Venice's older glories, and in the darksome nave of a cool church peered squinting at the great shadowy Tintorettos, loving them without quite making them out—they could be fakes for all we knew but it wouldn't have mattered. Not on this day. For the reference and the moment combined to provide enchantment of a very superior kind, we said, to what was droning on under the sultry wet sun in the Giardini. Some who had been there said afterward that no names of laureates had been pronounced to dim the grandeur of speeches that exalted not modern art but the municipality of Venice, as well as an honored guest from Rome, Clare Booth Luce, our ambassador to Italy at the time.

"Mrs. Luce," I said the next day at the American consulate party, "Please meet our first-prize winner."

She looked uncertain.

"The first prize in painting," I said, a little louder but still smiling. "The Biennale. For art. Painting and sculpture. . . ." (After all, this was an art event.)

"But what is it? she asked helplessly.

"The first prize. It's for lifetime achievement in painting."

"But what . . . ?"

How to get through to her? I tried another tack: "Oh! It's twelve million lire." I had understood at last. And, indeed, she was all happy congratulations.

The first American to win the big prize! Its concrete

results were twofold: banishment (exclusion) by Breton and his new friends from the surrealist enclave, for so stooping; and the money to buy a farmhouse in Touraine. Just in time, as it happened. Because Max was not to be an American for long. Once more we are back in Arizona. Once more involved with lawyers, and writing darling letters to congressmen who just might see the grotesque error of the McCarran Act. It was McCarthy time, and Max was a naturalized American; as such, somewhat second-class and certainly not permitted, like the rest of us, to stay in a foreign country. A familiar refrain, it must have seemed to him, sung in three languages so far, and always off-key. Knowing that indignation would be sterile, ah, but patience rewarded surely, our hope ran high. Did we not have a fancy lawyer who had literally promised? Had not exception already been made for von Stroheim, the moviemaker? Could not an artist, a *primo premio,* expect the same?

He could not. After sixteen humiliating months of dreadful effort, trips to Phoenix, money running out, a decision had to be faced. The pictures did not find buyers enough to keep us. So we gave away our crooked little house, built with Max's hands, and returned to Huismes and to the process of making art which did not demand any precise lieu except the studio. There might be some point here in mentioning something that was happening to my work during these years.

To go back: The first exhibition of my paintings had occurred at the Julien Levy Gallery in the fall of 1944. I

remember nothing at all about it. It must have been suc-
cessful (three pictures sold), for he gave me another one
in January of 1948—his last, as I recall, before closing the
gallery.

After the initial delight of realizing what I could do
with paint and brushes; after the heady whirl of acquiring
surrealist friends; after seeing that I could transfer my
inmost desires and enigmas to pictures that could be read
like books; after contemplating hundreds of surrealist
works, I began to wonder at certain similarities of concep-
tion in those paintings and drawings. I began to chafe just
a little at the reliance on precisely painted elements of the
natural world in order to present an incongruity. The
peerless Dalí, for instance, wasn't he a later Maxfield
Parrish but with a different imagination? It struck me that
with some of these artists—why name them all?—everything was *collage*. Upon a vista of endless sand or in a bare
room you could put anything. You could turn night into
day and vice versa just by using light and dark colors. You
could paint a sad giant dog (I did). Gradually, in looking
at how many ways paint can flow onto canvas, I began to
long for letting it have more freedom.

Beginning, roughly, in 1955, after a period of painting
direct, simple images as statement (*Tableau Vivant; The
Blue Waltz; Death and the Maiden* . . .), my painted composi-
tions began to shift and merge in an ever intensifying complexity of planes. Color was now a first prerogative: a white
canvas tacked to the wall in Sedona would be blue and violet and a certain dried-rust red. It would have to be verti-

cal. It would also be not quite there, immediately. I wanted to lead the eye into spaces that hid, revealed, transformed all at once and where there would be some never-before-seen image, as if it had appeared with no help from me. I was very excited and called it *Insomnias*. Finished just in time to be carted off with the rest—pictures, totem poles, dogs, memories—to France, where Max was to become a welcome citizen.

Before long, once more in Paris, life was rainy with money: a brand-new commodity after the Venice event of three years before. It had begun to roll in, I believe is the fat, opulent expression, and Max was soon accustomed to walking around with cozily bulging pockets (French bills being big as flags, tastefully tinted and bulky). Many days saw him presiding at the bountiful tables of three-star restaurants, treating with the chummy new money his less fortunate cronies, *bons vivants* all, to those monstrous gourmet meals that last for hours while the talk flies and the wines flow.

At last it is time to pay the bill. He reaches into a back pocket for crumpled paper notes, some of which fall on the floor like dried leaves. He peels off a few and stuffs back the rest, very slowly, absently, into his hip pocket, perhaps finishing the anecdote while pals struggle to their feet, all laughing and talking at once. It is then that the waiter runs after him, flushed, and proud of his shining honesty, waving a bank note.

"*M'sieur Max!* You dropped this. It was under the table."

Max turns, quiet, embarrassed, vexed. Accepts the

object with a careless air of disdain and indifference that
says, Why did the fool have to spoil my fun? Making me
awkward, ridiculous. I hate this. No one likes to be caught
doing something wrong. I believe he would have preferred less zealous, yes, less honest waiters, for it happened more than once to quash the gaiety if only for a
moment. There is something terribly sobering about a
bank note on the floor.

At another restaurant repast years later it was Jean
Cocteau who beguiled me. Cocteau, whose "dreams will
soon go down into the street," a precious gem, perhaps an
amethyst or sapphire, still splendid, with his Orphic sublime, age maybe sixty-seven, still unassailably fine. I
remember that it was the occasion of their meeting, Max
and Jean, after a forty years' *brouille* (rupture)—that is, if
two people could be said to have a rupture when they
have never met; and now the dénouement. Amid gentle
laughter their story rolled out. It had to do with a long-
ago correspondence, and must have appealed to Jean in
his play-writing heart. A real guignol, complete with mis-
chievous friend and purloined letter and faked reply. The
sequence. To the letter of admiration from Jean Cocteau
to Max Ernst—this must have been the late 1920s—it was
friend Paul, intercepting it, who replied, Paul Eluard,
writing in his careful schoolboy hand, a wicked letter of
taunts and insults and signed with Max's name. Showing
it to someone, Cocteau had scoffed, "*Que je suis déçu! Il a
une écriture de bonne!*" ("What a disappointment! Such
handwriting—like a housemaid's!") Thus the forty years.

Now in the restaurant, all is explained at last, and two aging artists are wreathing garlands of celebration around our table, both perfectly satisfied with themselves and each other and the wine and the evening—in that order. I see the paper tablecloth, receiving its customary doodles. We are all earnestly occupied. I draw a two-headed snake, "Not an eagle," I say to Jean's delight, thus proving I know his play *L'Aigle à Deux Têtes*, and giving myself a semblance of participation.

Seeing this man of the theater, my mind leapt back to twelve years before and my first Paris theater evening. The play: *La Seconde Surprise de l'Amour,* by Marivaux, performed at the Théâtre de Marigny. It was my first sight of France's first lady of the stage, Madeleine Renaud, who, with her husband, Jean Louis Barrault, reigned energetically over French theater. The curtain rises: there she is, enfolded in a black cloudlet of a gown, with pale shoulders and a halo smile, a permeating smile that is the emblem of Marivaux and of herself. Hearing the players speak their lines—not lines but lilt, for quite aside from the chesslike combinations of the drama, surely it was music that Marivaux, his very name a bar of lovely sound, had in mind—I wished, more than I had ever wished anything, to understand the words. Picture me, poor mute visitor, backstage in their dressing room, silently vowing to learn. So that years later, when she was Samuel Beckett's Winnie in *Happy Days,* I could follow and marvel contentedly. More years passed before I was at last *in* French, and, together with Jean Louis Barrault, this time involved in directing (he) and designing costumes (I) for *Judith*, a play by Jean Giraudoux, to be presented at the Théâtre de l'Odéon, France's national theater. Backdrop by Max Ernst. For this, Barrault comes to us in Huismes, where he talks, croons, paces the floor, mesmerizes me, *sotto voce*, presses an arm for accent. Our house catches the fire of his voice and his involvement. After all, is that not what he has come for, all the way to Huismes, Indre-et-Loire?

Then, in 1968, Paris student revolt caught the heart of Barrault and turned him into an unlikely firebrand. The Odéon was a mutinous ship with Jean Louis at the helm. "'Sixty-eight" in the Odéon, '68 in the boulevard Saint-Germain, where the buses are stopped in their tracks, sideways, helpless pachyderms in the tear gas and the churning May smoggy air. And Jean Louis at the Odéon, surrounded by sit-ins; Jean Louis and Madeleine, truly the avant-garde, if ever the word had a meaning.

And now a little postscript to this chapter of various strivings. At one point in the game of addresses (this was back in 1958) we had bought an apartment, a Paris pad that was really the second (top) floor of a small house in the Fifteenth Arrondissement, a severely unfashionable quarter. Max peeked into the attic, a kind of crawl space. Could he buy it too? "You can have it," was the owner's amazing answer. Work then began; it would be a studio. A young architect friend, plumbers, carpenters, the usual bills, the struggle for a telephone, yes, if you knew someone well placed in Communications. Oh, but it was all worth the effort: the roof raised on the north side to make way for light; smooth pale floor; banks of drawers under the eaves. A proper studio, reached by our very own stairs, where we were soon at work as if nothing could happen to interrupt the steady flow of exhilaration.

Exhilaration's underside, however, did not take long to tinge our bower with first unease, then anguish. We heard it one night when awake at four-thirty in the morning—the sound of horses' hooves on the pavement outside in the rue Dutot. It always happened at the same hour: I would be torn from sleep by the bright, rhythmic clop-clop, I would hear with excruciating clarity the jaunty steps of unseen horses, obedient and all-unknowing, trotting nicely through the hushed streets, breathing in sharp morning air and exhaling snorts of rumination, perhaps liking the smart sound of their hooves on the cobbles as they walked to the slaughterhouse a short mile away. Again and again I told myself that they were oblivious of their doom. But how to accept it?

An occasional evening could provide distraction for a few hours. One special time, at our apartment with Jacques Lacan, psychoanalytic spirit (bristling with hang-ups), and his Sylvia, formerly Bataille, the unforgettable heroine of *Parti de Campagne* ("Picnic Party"), by filmmaker Jean Renoir. As for me, what was I except an observer, fated to write this down in other space and other time? Marcel Duchamp, also present, with wife, Teeny; Marcel, sly and enigmatic with Lacan, both of them like heads of state avoiding collision under the watchful eye of Robert Lebel, chronicler of great thoughts.

It was all so satisfying, or would have been had I been able to forget the horses; for they would come before me in the night, toss their heads, and exhale great plumes of steamy breath, just as they were doing in reality, out there in the frozen and all too near street, while I held the pillow over my ears. Until one day release came in the form of a knock at the door and two *messieurs* who floored me with the news that we had six months to remove ourselves. Ah, yes, the house was slated for razing.

"But this cannot be! Indeed, it is ours," I told them.

"Madam, you must have known. All property owners were notified. Repeatedly. Why, here is the decree. The sector has been on the demolition program for eight years."

A stunning revelation for us, feckless Americans. It was one year after we had remodeled it. Shaken but unvanquished, we looked around for another Paris apartment (would we want to give up Paris entirely?), but this time, far from homeless, we had our Venice-prize-bought farmhouse, just a three-hour drive away, to return to.

CHAPTER SEVEN

In "the Garden
of France"

Huismes, Indre-et-Loire, is in Touraine, long called "the garden of France." Creamy stone punctuates the all-over green fief of ancient kings and modern Americans, two of whom led us to this house not far from friend Sandy (Alexander) Calder. We readied it, saw it fitted up with plumbing; we scraped and plastered and windowed, stairwayed, heated, gardened, and walled. Into this house that we called Le Pin Perdu (it had been Le Pin, but no pine tree was to be seen) came everything we owned. Six thousand miles of land and ocean were traversed by our fantasies and foibles, further swollen by more of the same, found locally

The nests we have made! That, like birds, we have feathered, floored, furnished. The flea markets we have drawn from, the antique fairs, the sublime junk, not old enough, just too old. Each time believing it was the last and each time moving on, our gear a growing mountain in spite of doleful losses. These pare our history to just this side of amputation.

Letters, photographs, books, objects, even documents, big and little things treasured like breath—impossible to live without them—move with me and the beds and the casseroles from house to house, yet some of them and always the wrong ones inevitably vanish, a diminishment at each upheaval (that photo there, why has it only one eye imitating a windy tunnel?) hinting at loss. A little lost each time, not much, absorbed into the mysterious space to which you willingly confide pieces of your reckless life, your memory deeply troubled and faulty without them. Because even memory can lose its key like that of the last house, and upon what recall then can you depend to enter the next one? After a while I could not remember what I didn't have anymore.

But why worry about the inanimate? Only life was not trivial, only love could be truly missed, and I had both.

Morning walks in the steamy green of our Touraine garden brought us surprises: the first lilac—so soon!—a peony that would be white, and then one day the toad, life-less, with his hands chewed off—a feline amusement surely. What a way to die. We had greeted each other every morning. Our toad. Our friend, on hand in the same place, maybe glad to see us. Until that day on our usual round. "Don't look!" Max said and tried to turn me away. But how can you forget a maimed toad? And why his *hands*?

Down at the far end of the garden where the sky held a sweep of dominion over a small unshaded territory, we built a greenhouse for the provision of potted flowers to bring in during the long winter spans and for starting (we would beat Monsieur Blondeau, our neighbor, by at least three weeks) early lettuces and tomatoes and basil. In this greenhouse puttered and pottered our dapper old gardener, Monsieur D., beret aslant, clipped mustache, bright pink cheeks proudly framing a magenta nose (the wines of Chinon and Bourgeuil being famously irresistible), who regularly wore clogs and a knitted vest from the busy needles of his invisible Madame D. We never in all the years he was on the place laid eyes on Madame D., and with reason. For coming back unexpectedly, one soft May afternoon from a stay in town and after ringing at the gate a rather long time, we were admitted by a beet-red Yvette, our housekeeper, and glimpsed at the same moment Monsieur D., issuing from our ground-floor bedroom down at the far end of the house, arranging his baggy corduroys. So the knitting needles belonged to Yvette, just as did the gentle May afternoons. And to think we had always called him old Monsieur D.!

For eighteen years this Yvette held our daily life together. Widowed early on, she had raised four daughters from scratch. Scratch because it was hand to mouth, a factory job. Until on a dim day her boss disappeared, with three months' back salaries. Thus we inherited Yvette. What she did for the following years is a litany that could interest no one anymore. But the armloads of flowers from the garden and her thin voice, so at odds with the solid body, as she answered our compliments, *"Oui, on dirait des fausses fleurs"* ("Yes, one could mistake them for artificial flowers"). Or telling of her brother who had drawn a dog so lifelike that *"on dirait qu'il allait parler"* ("you'd think he was about to talk").

Joining in our occasional foolishness—dinner sometimes saw us all gravely costumed and unrecognizable—she would dive with the rest of us into a wicker trunk of rags and jetsam to come up with the colors of our evening. Decked out in fireman's *casque* and black lace knickers, this hardworking Yvette served the ragout, attentive and unperturbed. To see her bouncing down the lane on her *mobylette*—the wide expanse of her girdled behind forming just one firm imposing cheek miraculously and, you could perfectly see, comfortably resting on the little triangular seat, a long loaf of bread strapped just under it—was a sight to either distress or amuse, depending on who was watching.

It was a stunning event when Yvette won a Solex motorbike in a farm journal contest. The contest: Guess the Correct Age of This Dog (fuzzy photo). I could imagine them leaning together on her oilcloth table cover. Evening. Monsieur D. argues for his guess, then when all agree and it is settled he gives it to her, to his lady, his first guess. Because he sent one too, in his own name. They wait. The farmers of the whole French nation are waiting; every farmer has guessed the age of the dog. Then a telegram for Yvette. Stupefaction! She has won first prize, the Solex. And he, Monsieur D., amazingly, wins the second, a shotgun. After the excitement he asks, would she, Yvette, trade? Would she give up the Solex for the gun? After all, she already has a motorbike. Ah, no!

He was a sort of intellectual or thinking man, this Monsieur D.; he read the *Canard Enchaîné* but kept his ideas and his opinions to himself. In fact, he was not an ear-bender, or talker, at all. He trundled his wheelbarrow of manure down the nave of our garden path as if it were an offering of lilies to be consecrated at the chancel. On rainy days he stayed in the greenhouse, that hotbed of optimism as redolent of green buzzing life as the shores of a pond. In March it was a moving thing to watch the seedlings push up in their slats, first showing their bent pale necks like tiny wickets and the next day pulling the rest of themselves out of the mysterious dirt. Max wanted nasturtiums, happy flowers, happy to bloom, happy to be eaten in the salad. But all too soon their glassy prison, like so many prisons, went wild and wrong. April, May. By June it would be almost impossible for Monsieur D. to get through the door, so choked it was with rampant verdure grimly waiting to be set outdoors. The chlorophyll was overwhelming. Unwatered pots began to line up around the outside walls like garbage cans, hoping only for invisibility. Compost, he told us, it would all make fine compost. As for the transplanting, it had rained too much. Or it had not rained enough, the ground was hard. You could always count on one or the other. Monsieur D., like the sorcerer's apprentice, had each year started something he couldn't finish.

We respected his thinking life; how can you help it, confronted with such dignity, such mystery? It was Yvette who brought it all together, she whose brother had been carted off in 1942, to God knows what concentration camp, along with the rest of the vigorous males of Huismes, resistants all, never to be seen again. Denounced they were, by a slimy local *collabo,* someone with a "de" to his name, the town's *grand bourgeois.* She told it with fatal simplicity. The *collabo* had stayed up there in his moldy manoir, doing for himself, she emphasized, because certainly no one would work for him. After the Allied victory he was dragged like a rat from his walled garden to the village square to be judged and shot.

Yvette sighs. "But when the time came, *eh bien,* no one in that crowd would hold the gun. We were all together, maybe a hundred widows and old people. None of us wanted to be the one. So he is still up there in his house. *Et il y a même ceux qui lui disent bonjour"* ("And there are even those who still speak to him").

One of the survivors, because he had been only a boy at the time of deportation, was Giles Chauvelin, who, as he grew up, became a master stonecutter and official restorer of national monuments, notably the châteaux of the surrounding countryside: Amboise, Chambord, Chenonceaux, Villandry, Azay-le-Rideau. More and more elements of ancient carvings—a helpless gargoyle, an acanthus leaf— were crashing down in response to the bangs of supersonic planes training for some future war. (Humbler victims included the pile of old stone across the lane from us, a hovel occupied by Madame Pihouée, aged eighty-one, who could sew and read without glasses and whose abode, with herself inside it, simply crumbled one day, fell about her like a dropped petticoat. Miraculously, she was untouched—"like Cologne's cathedral in the World War II bombing," said Max—but never seen by us again. We were told she was now "in a home.") Chauvelin was thus never in want of projects and commissions. As far as we knew, he could count on full employment, keeping up with the damage wrought by the prideful aircraft cruising our luscious countryside of Touraine. Sound-barrier blasts never failed to loosen a stony saint or two from its niche high on some façade. So that, visiting Chauvelin's cavernous atelier, you saw the heart and soul of medieval architecture still in the making: trefoil and capital; even whole entablatures in creamy *pierre de Vilhoneux*. And still today, when the supersonic blast rips away another stone dream from the "garden of kings," I wince a little as if it were my own skin. Now stone returns to stone, transformed as warehouse or garage. Even the guidebook often has nothing to give but absence.

There are certain luxuries which, taken all together, make a modest life big: killing a day on a useless social gu by before answering a letter, saying one isn't at home; telling the best ideas to the dog; crying for fun. There in Huismes, after Venice and the *primo premio*, we had become once more dedicated country mice, planting American corn, dealing with molehills, and, on the shiny side, having our old friends the Alexander Calders living near, in

Sache. We shared our fun and games. Seeing the tall brown-paper-bag mask moving among the dancers at our party one knew that Sandy Calder was under it.

And in Rome one day we met at his rooms. I had been to the coiffeur. Sandy took it in, especially the two corkscrew curls, a sort of retro hairstyle much seen at the time. "Huh-uh-uh!" Impossible to convey his private laugh, followed by "Too late. The bottles are already opened." Apparently dozing during most of the restaurant dinner, he would suddenly comment on or correct some remark by the hardy convives—we and Louisa Calder, Alberto Moravia and Elsa Morandi—who all thought he was in dreamland. One glass of wine was enough to put him to sleep or lift him onto an antic plateau of delight hardly known since the innocence of Bacchanalian days. He was, at these times, the very emblem of his sculptures, weight-less—and unpredictable.

It may also be said that from this time on, between letters and visits, life in the country was a far cry indeed from the dreamy dawn of Sedona, Arizona. Our Pin Perdu opened its pale blue gate to admit a fairly steady procession of every sort of visitor, from the bosom friend to the merely curious, from the personage in his long car to the postgraduate with backpack, from the collaborator (book, theater piece, exhibition, print) to the bearer of messages from home. Dominique de Menil, our American collector, broke bread with our Swiss carpenter. An orphan housemaid from Paris posed with Man Ray, our American photographer; Georges Bataille, Arp, Roger Caillois, Matta (with wife and baby), to name a few names. Chess was played for two days nonstop with two Duchamps.

One day, to match a moment's levity, I showed Marcel Duchamp our *Mona Lisa,* a handpainted copy, actual size, that had been a mock "prize" for Max at a party in Marie Laure's Hyères retreat. The *Mona Lisa.* Here she was, a sinewy, all-wrong creature, powerfully painted on a wooden panel, her crooked leer a categorical repudiation not only of Leonardo da Vinci but of all artists. "All she needs is a mustache," I said, to prolong the fun. Duchamp: "Well, give me two small brushes and a little white and raw umber." That afternoon our *Mona Lisa* became a treasure after all, for he painted every hair of mustache and goatee, just as he had on his famous original. Another golden moment.

The next day we drove down to Lascaux to see the cave paintings, a project dear to Teeny Duchamp's heart and pleasantly shared, though with something like fortitude, by Marcel. Arriving at the little hotel in Montigny, near the caves, the next evening, we sat at dinner (we were the only diners!) and watched Marcel calculate in his notebook the time needed next morning for the caves:

"Let's see, if we get up at eight, take twenty-five minutes to dress, about twenty-two minutes for breakfast . . . it's twenty-five minutes from here to the caves, ten minutes probably to stand in line if we get there early, and

seven minutes should be enough to spend inside. That's
one hour and twenty-nine minutes altogether." It worked
out pretty much as he said.

I believe he was serious, although one never quite
knew. Marcel Duchamp's sense of humor was his sixth
sense and far from the least important. In fact, everything
he did was tinged by this treasure; it is no exaggeration to
say he allowed it to determine the course of his entire life-
work. As William Anastasi has pointed out, he felt close to
the French writer Alfred Jarry, a late-nineteenth-century
gleeful absurdist, dear to the surrealists—and to me.
Proposer of outrageous acts and martyr to his own brand
of iconoclasm, Jarry was Marcel's secret garden, Jarry's
writings his secret bible, Jarry's humor a model for his
own. (All this is still being argued.) In Breton's surrealism
there was not the smallest hint of humor; it was deadly
serious, moving in on dada like a rival team at the
Olympics. Marcel, on the other hand, collaborated with
them both. Indulgent, helpful, and with a bemused kind
of affection, he enjoyed, with that sixth sense of his, playing their games.

As for Max Ernst, never was a man so solicited to return
"home." *Bitte!* Visitors, authors, interviewers, filmmakers.
Sometimes, to substitute for conversation, I would get out
my camera. "Do you take real pictures? Is there film in the
camera?" "Nearly always," I reply, unwisely. Because one
day, on the terrace it was, with a brace of rollicking

callers, two directors of something artistic or other who, with guffaws and chortles, had donned flowered straw hats for the photo, a bad moment occurred when I discovered there was no film in the box. My sitters did not hide their disgust when I (oh so stupidly) announced the funny discovery; peevish and sarcastic, they hardly spoke to me when making their farewells.

Droll souvenirs, recited poems (seductive, indeed, those lines from Bürger, Hölderlin, Novalis . . .), rousing school songs. Old cities showered him with new honors accompanied by medals and colored ribbons. They installed a Max Ernst fountain in his hometown of Brühl; they named a school after him. Commemorative coins for his birthdays. A bronze plaque on his birthplace. And, needless to say, retrospective exhibitions.

During my thirty-four-year tenure we traveled to openings of a number of these exhibitions in Germany and beyond. I saw the capitals of the occidental world. I saw their sunny or shiny-wet streets and vacant lots, their cathedrals, castles, canals, their parks (ah those spooky parks! "We have put you in the Park Hotel, very quiet." And I, who longed for local Life, looked out, instead, on dark trees), monuments, and, naturally, their museums. I wanted to go home. (It must be remembered that these were postwar years and many towns were sad, gray, unrestored. I wandered through some of them, their unlit squares, their blind foreign alleys, thinking, "Here, crime is self-inflicted; for everyone, from the age of five, must be planning their escape.")

But exhilaration was always the order of the days in the museums, lit, as they were, by adulation, so natural and gratifying to the artist. And to the artist's wife, naturally. Assiduities I had come wonderingly to accept. Oh, the good people I have tried to communicate with! Their boundless love and admiration for him—and his wife. They coddle her, coo over her. She, caught among the ladies, sits frozen, idiotically demure, as they marvel, "Did you hear? She paints too!" And what comes bobbing to the surface is the fact of the devoted mate, the last—and lasting—in a long line of tryouts for the job. She cares for the warrior who is quiet at last, and needful. Unsung heroine in her mythic devotion, she holds in check an only occasional moment of frustration. She knows that her man is the true immortal and that she is envied by numberless members of her sex who are waiting to replace her should anything go wrong.

February 8, 1959. In the kitchen of Le Pin Perdu, our world, Max opens champagne, a fire is crackling in the big chimney, and nobody cares that outdoors is dark and wet at five o'clock. Monsieur D. has stepped inside in his stocking feet, clogs left by the door. Yvette turns down the gas under her *poireaux* and comes to take her glass. They both hold the stems delicately, little fingers aloft. We are just four, and we drink to Max, French citizen from this day forward. Stateless for a year, he had gravely accepted when the prime minister said: "France would be honored. . . ." So now at last he has a home.

As for me, I wanted to be glad. But he had been an American. And my country had repudiated him, meaninglessly. So, yes, I was glad, sadly glad. Moreover, I find irresistible an impulse to include here a final document, received five years later:

American Embassy
Paris, France
July 20, 1964
Mr. Max Ernst
19, *rue de Lille*
Paris, 7e

Dear Max:

As you undoubtedly know, the Supreme Court on May 19 *ruled unconstitutional Section* 352 *of the Immigration and Nationality Act (and similar Sections under previous legislation). Thus, naturalized citizens now have the same rights and privileges as native-born Americans and may reside abroad indefinitely, whether in their country of origin or elsewhere, without endangering their American citizenship.*

Furthermore, decisions on loss of citizenship based on that Section are thereby voided. It gives me great pleasure, therefore, to tell you that if you wish to verify your continued United States citizenship, to receive a passport, or to register as an American citizen, I shall be delighted to see you. Please telephone me whenever it is convenient for you, and I shall see to it that you are given prompt attention at any time that

you would care to come. I don't think I need to tell you how
happy I am personally to be writing you this letter and I hope
to have the pleasure of seeing you and Mrs. Ernst again.

> *With kindest personal regards,*
> *Sincerely,*
> *Perry Culley*
> *American Consul General*

Oh, too late, too late.

To have consciously turned away from his country at
an early age after having worn, willy-nilly, its military uniform in the most lethal war the world had yet known and
to have recognized its ugly destiny during the slow
approach of further madness must have been for him an
abiding horror. And then to become again a victim of that
same horror along with millions of surprised and helpless
human beings—all this must have demanded of him an
unshakable faith in art as salvation. His own art, certainly,
along with that of the others who did not survive the
horde. (That, too, he had painted: *La Horde,* over and
over in those menacing years.)

On the flagstones under the wisteria, sunspots are small
and round to match the ones on the table. The soup
steams in the shade. A glassy sort of hour, fragmentary
talk in German, this rolling language I do not understand. Some small argument, desultory, as blurry as a

warm snowy day, the words quick to melt. Oh Max, with your absent *ach, so,* and your hair blowing over one ear. Now the sun has gone and gusty wind takes over. I bleat a verb from time to time, unexotic. What am I doing here? You look to me for rescue; I say let's go inside for the coffee and this we all do. The tiny argument has melted, a puddle on the table, left behind along with crumpled napkins. Coffee is sipped in silence because you are all at once a statue, eyes turned to the ceiling; you are a million miles away and you will not come back. For the thousandth time I leap, filling the breach with trusty amenities—smiles, gestures, sign language dredged up out of old habit as you knew they would be. It is nothing to what I would do for you, in truth. Just ask me.

At last they are gone, have waved goodbye. The next hour—spent cleaning up, piling dishes, emptying ashtrays, feeling my way back to myself—passes in that cottony, timeless state known to those emerging from anesthesia.

"Das Leben ist kein Traum". ("Life is no dream").

One of them, laughing, had quoted the line from Tikhonov's poem. Ah but it was, it was. They had only to remember the next line, "But it can and will become one." My love was so anchored, so final, that a wisp of regret sometimes swept over it, an odd little cloud: I would never know love's despair, its changes, its vanities, its hopes, its anguish; love's pain would not be granted me. It was like the time I had wanted to be mad, not knowing my good fortune.

Max painted my portrait then, in his way. "Hell, I could die now," I thought, seeing it. But what can I say? I'm glad this did not happen.

Because of language confusion our shape as a pair was not sophisticated. We did not have what is known as repartee. What we shared was, to the casual observer, predominantly emotional, even primitive. But it was richer than that. Three languages, two of them more or less shared; three ways to say the same things, simple, fundamental things. Like tools in the hands they became kindly helpers as the years passed. We had wished so earnestly to make them so. If poor in syntax they made up for it in color—and fun. We found we were able to adopt and adapt current or referent expressions to furnish conversation with everything we needed. We could give adequate well-shaped reasons for acceptance, rejection, admiration, or indifference. Determined to speak and understand French when in France, I chided Max, who always addressed me in English:

"*Allons, Max, il faut qu'on parle en Français dorénavant.*"
And he: "*D'accord.*"

But a few minutes later, to my question "*A quel heure sont-ils attendus?*" he replies, "Eight o'clock."

A friend explains this to me later: "The language you have used in your first days, first lovemaking, can never be replaced by another."

We could fight respectably. Of course there were

fights. Accusations, reasonable or unreasonable, it never matters. Without the anger, the crumpled hour, the clouds of adrenaline, the floods, the quiet gloom while it is going on—he couldn't eat, I couldn't think—our lake would have filled with swamp grass. What oral communication we had was quite good enough for our purposes, and we had so much else. What's more, accents were a source of delight. My French had enough inadvertent clumsiness to amuse all present. (As an American I would never be able to say *truite* when ordering trout. With that one word, an enemy would easily unmask me. Treet? Tweet? We must choose.) His English was a treasure of funny words. Bushes and cushions rhymed with Russians. "Ah yes, Dorotaya."

There hovered, however, a persistent, medium-sized cloud in this great wash of blue, and it hung around to blur our edges and provide a little frustration. In the area of books, only the French ones were shared, and those not always. There was no use pretending I could hear their nuances or savor their styles even though I could read *Bouvard et Pécuchet* with delight. For what was I to do with the wildly convoluted prose of André Breton? Or Malcolm de Chazal's so very French maxims? I loved the gentle heart of Marcel Schwob, and the perverse extravagance of Villier's *Axel* is still a real peril to my precarious equilibrium. But the others, all the others . . . How little time there is! How could I find enough of it to learn to read the German ones too?

Max lived in an ever-widening pond of books. There was not a day that failed to deliver its book, that did not see a new one float into view: on eddies of mail (American), brought by hand (German), or from the bookstore (French).

My own library was a smaller corner. In it those smoldering former companions, pushed aside like cast-off schoolmates, slouched in the background and assumed the easy poses that only words can claim. They all knew their turn would come. The defiant American paperback with its peppery pinup cover that has nothing to do with the inside. (All you have to do is tear it off.) And the faded hardcovers, how had they managed to stay by, to turn into seasoned travelers, discreet and huddled where you could lay a hand on them?

My shelf, my books: mostly fiction—American and British classics that, very quietly, began to appear, in their translations, among Max's French books. *Jude the Obscure, Ulysses,* and *Moby-Dick. Typee,* too, and *Mardi.* Hawthorne, Thoreau . . . How, I wondered, would they translate Henry James? Ambrose Bierce, okay; Fitzgerald, okay; Henry Miller, I could see that all right. But *Finnegans Wake?* Good God. Yet they all slipped, gleeful masqueraders, into that other company and took their places graciously, like expatriates rather proud to be able to give the time of day in a foreign language.

The effect on me was stunning. My book friends were all at once new and naked. He wanted, then, to know what I knew, read what I read. It was a startling thought. I felt oddly nervous and responsible. Random phrases from this or that book surfaced in my mind. How would they sound to him in French? How would he *see* them? The first real sharing of that part of our lives was taking place at last.

Besides the bookshelf books there were the home-made ones. In the kind of life we led, bookmaking was as necessary a part of it as buttons on a coat. I cannot remember any painter acquaintance who did not at some time engage in collaboration on a book.

Editions were never more than one hundred and twenty copies—they depreciated in value as the numbers rose. Ardent publisher of some of the best of these was short, round, Swiss Monsieur Louis Broder, whose demanding profession left him only time to eat, and it must not be assumed that he did so out of mere hunger. His obsession with *le beau livre* was juicily matched by his devotion to *la grande cuisine*. I am sure that in putting together his elegant books he considered himself a kind of superchef.

One day he asked rather casually, "What kind of books do you have in America?"

"Oh, very good books," said Max.

"But how are they made?" he wanted to know. "Who buys them?"

I explained about how the book is generally hardcover, printed in many thousands, "and after they're read you put them on the shelf. . . ."

"Oh!" Monsieur Broder did not disguise his scorn. "Oh, you mean they buy *reading* books!"

Texts often came from poet friends. Or there might be some long-forgotten manuscript to be brought gloriously to light, with Japan paper, elegant handset type, abundant flyleaves, and, most important, lovingly pulled etchings in limpid colors that melted into the petallike paper the way mauve and carmine soak into the sky at sunset.

A well-known master etcher in Paris was Georges Visat. With his virtuoso bag of tricks under control—his scumbles, acids, chemical wonders, coaxed accidents, his waxes, varnishes, sugars, resists, spit, and resins, followed by hours of scrapings, polishings, inking, proofing—all the arduous passionate sweaty process of etching on copper—he brought out glorious deep-diving images in floated spectral colors for which other people got the credit. I suppose that's the way it should be: artist, artisan. But both words seem obsolete in this context. As the first of the two I experimented with it all; until, that is, it became clear to me that the process was so overwhelming, so fraught, it would be better to drop it instead of going crazy with the possibilities.

Constantly on the prowl for new techniques, Visat one day borrowed a little painting of mine and, by some latest method, made from it an etching. It was perfect. But was it wrong? Was it a fraud? Would a collector find it a cheat? Would Georges Visat, with his special hands, his good-natured genius, his light under a bushel of artists, reap opprobrium for keeping the flame of etching alive? As the years passed it became even harder to consign Visat to the caste of mere craftsmen, for he waded into editing, producing not only etchings but the whole book as well.

An interesting number of these books were fiercely

and explicitly erotic, with rich descriptive passages and a wealth of invention. They were written by mild, over-refined men and women whose swollen imaginations doubtless consoled them for grim reality. Even such books were *built,* like cathedrals, with an inordinate amount of creative fervor and dedication. Erotic or not, emblems so strong in their collaborative ardor were bound to become objects of pure magic.

Such were the books made by Iliadz, another shoe-string editor, with his artist and poet friends: bouquets of words, printed with love, to hold in your hands. Artists writing, poets painting. A "free" sort of adventure, serious fun without the dedicated preparation, without the drudgery and without too much concern for what other people might find to say about it. If Artaud or Apolli-naire—or Henry Miller or e.e. cummings—decided to draw or even paint, was it only in response to the creative urge? Or might they have wanted a simple change of pace and gesture, as erratic and *irresponsible* as the capers of birds in air? It was this airy freedom that prevailed in those ateliers where even I made etchings, and wrote poems—in French!—over a period of twenty years.

In May 1958 I traveled—alone—to Turin for an exhi-bition of my paintings in the Galeria Galatea. De Chirico's city of arcades looked satisfyingly Chiricoesque to my eyes: severe, melancholy, and sleepy, so contrasted to the roar of Rome or Milan. At my opening everyone seemed to be at least a count or a duke if not a serene somebody. I didn't mind, for they bought a few little pictures (my pictures at this time were mostly little), and after their initial disappointment at not seeing my husband, they really went to some pains to show me around.

These years—1958 to 1962—are so jumbled in my backward-gazing eyes, so full of eventful sojourns in the rue Mathurin-Regnier and in Huismes, our village home, that their patterns flow together as unpredictably as the swaths of paint on canvas. Upon our losing the Paris pad, as recounted earlier, rooms were found somehow for our work, both of us working daily at the easel or, lacking that, on canvas tacked to the wall. Exhibitions followed, mostly Max's, already noted earlier here. And two more of my own.

Although country living was what we loved best, and did most, a Paris headquarters could not be forgone. For indeed, what artist could bear to be constantly away from this place of seminal activity, friends, projects, bookmaking ateliers, even the ubiquitous cafes? In late 1962, therefore, our search was brilliantly rewarded by a new Paris address: five rooms in a splendid building at 19, rue de Lille. A friend who knew all about Paris's past told us its early history, worth repeating here. It was built in 1720 for the comte de Lauraguais, duc de Brancas, enlightened patron of the sciences, law, medicine, and theater and official protector of the actress Sophie Arnoult, who, one day, exasperated by her situation, drove into the court-yard in her coach and there set down on the *pavée* her gifts from the count: a coffret of jewels and, in a cradle, two babies. The countess adopted them, probably in the spirit of simple pragmatism that must have reigned among countesses at the time—and before and after.

By 1962, when we came there, no signs of former splendor remained. On the contrary, it was the same old transformational optimism that saw us struggle with basics like heating and bathrooms. Later, acquiring another space above it, we were able to relocate me from the miserable pad I had used as a studio up to then. With a big room, north-lit, on the rue de Lille, what more could I ask?

Meanwhile, another one of those Paris days, prismatic. A rendezvous with Max at the Café Flore. Arriving, he says, "There is an idol of yours at the café next door. Oppenheimer." A stunning announcement that suffuses me with something like embarrassment, the beginning of an impulse to pretend disinterest; oh, with Max I am always on the lookout for irony. But he is not smiling this time as he goes on, "Over there at the Deux Magots. He is sitting with a lady." Not to do something is for once unthinkable. Quite shamelessly, I want to see. Only to walk past. To glimpse the man from faraway Los Alamos; that place where the fate of the whole human race and everything else on this planet has been forever modified. To see this person who has changed the world and wishes he hadn't! Oh, I am certain he suffers regret: is baffled and chagrined by what he has made happen—he has said so. Let him stain the whole day, I rhapsodized inwardly. He will be an earthquake, a revolution, a northern lights. Seeing his blue eyes will . . .

He is over at the other café, blending in, just one of the tourists basking in the gentle embrace of this soft May afternoon on the boulevard Saint-Germain where the people, the aproned waiter, the table, marble with brass rim, all create a fabulous hazard that completes its picture with two little apéritifs for him and his companion. What is he thinking behind his prestigious forehead? What awful certainties are perhaps spoiling his Parisian afternoon? Can he even, just for one exotic moment, assuage his thought, forget his terrible burden?

Such are my fevered thoughts as Max, indulgent and perhaps feeling some of the excitement, walks with me through dappled shade and sun, where, as we approach, the man half rises from his chair behind the little table. "Max Ernst," he says, his beautiful face offered, half gesture, half smile.

It all comes together in one perfect minute. His invitation: "Please—have something with us . . . my wife . . . only a few minutes ago we saw a painting of yours in a gallery, just over there."

And Max: "In the rue de Rennes?"

By this time more chairs are drawn up and we, too, sit there. They talk. I listen. My awe amounts to anguish. Their easy conversation does not help. Instead my scrambled thoughts plunge on alone. Noticing, perhaps, my disarray, Oppenheimer addresses me: "What is that stone in your ring? It looks familiar."

"Oh, it's nothing," I disparage my ring. "It's fake, a bauble, junk. A friend gave it to me." He looks again.

"But I think you are wrong to call it junk," he says. "You see, when I was a little boy I collected minerals. And this, if I am not mistaken, is a kunzite. It is mined in southern California around San Diego. Yes, it's a real stone and even a very good one!"

As my hand writes of that day it wears the ring, the kunzite, and all kinds of reflections shaft out from the pink stone. I am remembering the evening when I first admired it, even the name of the restaurant (l'Escargot), and Hélène, taking it off of her finger and handing it to me—a rare kind of gesture, something like a butterfly alighting on my hand. I protest: "It's too . . ." And she: "No, no, I insist, you must have it," neither of us knowing anything about its name, its San Diego, only enjoying the give-and-take moment, the *pinkness*. So that for Robert Oppenheimer, "Father of the A-bomb" as he was called, to forget for a moment his place in the dreadful present and remember "when I was a little boy," a pink stone had to sparkle in the sun on the boulevard Saint-Germain.

CHAPTER EIGHT

*Provence
and a House*

THE SUPERSONIC blast that dislodged Madame Pihouée from her Huismes hovel but spared her bleak little life had also, as became apparent, dislodged us. For the farmer who owned the spot—it was not more than fifteen feet from us—almost immediately sold it to a pal of his who dealt in cement and who constructed on the spot a loading platform. Thereafter, beginning as early as five in the morning, we would be torn from sleep (our bedroom wall the only barrier between us and the trucks) as the cement business thundered triumphantly through the early-morning hours. A dispiriting change for two artists who had rather loved their sleepy lane, in a sleepy village, far from the wide-awake strife of cities. But perhaps a good reminder that sleepy villages in these times often wake up to the exigencies of modern life. We began to wonder. . . .

For several years the annual summer *randonnée* had included a stop at Seillans, in the Var, a Provençal village. Here were friends Patrick and Line Waldberg in her ancestral house on the village *place*. Here in Seillans everything moved slowly in a perpetual dream where past and present were the same thing and where the future was not really desirable—therefore inexistent. You went daily to the baker for bread like going for the Eucharist. You ate pasta and somebody's homegrown tomatoes. And in the afternoon, after the heat, you played boules under the old plane trees. When a house came up for sale while we were staying with our friends, we decided to live there. It was summer 1965. We left Touraine, left the tarny mists of Huismes that settled in Max's bones; left the green mold that hid in our shoes, more of it streaking up the bedroom walls, fast-growing pet of mother nature with roots under the tile floor.

Now we were *provençaux,* as sun-ripened as figs, and Seillans was our home, we thought, from then on. A square old house, a former sort of hostel with painted across its flank the wishful words "La Dolce Vita." It wanted only plumbing, soon installed, along with us: two beings trying (rather successfully, it must be said) to live up to its name.

One day four people walked in with the greeting "Hi!": Robert Penn Warren and Eleanor Clark with little son and daughter, enjoying a Provençal winter—his sabbatical from Yale—in a neighboring village called Magagnosc, just twenty-five kilometers away. Aside from the excitement of meeting these two jewels of American letters, it was the greeting that sent a shiver of recognition into my sleeping memory box. I had almost forgotten about things like "Hi!" I had been too far away and for too long to remember our American idiom, even that ubiquitous word.

Hi! To say that the Hi is what I remember of that day may appear to overlook the charm of the visit itself. But that magical word was only the beginning of a winter exchange between Seillans and Magagnosc that dressed up our meridional life in wonderfully colorful news from home. I soon realized that Eleanor's "Hi!" perfectly suited her razor-sharp, no-frills style. And no other word could have better prepared me for my eventual return home to the U.S.A.

They brought their pet goat next time. Goat, children, dogs (ours), nieces (ours), us, and them; we were complete. These days even included a stab at teaching painting to a little girl named Rosanna Warren, and I wish I could say that I gave her something to speed her on the way to becoming an artist. All it did was to decorate some of our afternoons and to prove, once again, that teaching was not in my powers. What's more, how could I regret the loss of a painter when I have gained a poet?—for I claim her, modestly.

During that winter we all told our most colorful stories. Max was especially happy at this, spooking everyone with his hexes: coincidences, omens, funny, freakish happenings, all cleaving a rather sinister zigzag behind him like the path of a tornado, dogging his step from one opening to another. Curious tricks played themselves out around his pictures, and brought him up each time, laughing and yet not laughing. Hearing them, I thought of those tales of headless ghosts on wild stormy nights that make one shiver while sipping cognac before the roaring grate in the trophy room of the old castle that your host, its sole heir, has idly decided to visit. Tales within tales.

The first exhibition of his paintings in New York at the intrepid Julien Levy's gallery. A good thing the artist was far away in Paris. For it opened in 1932 at the very moment of a nasty stock market dip. In Los Angeles, years later, another opening had hardly gotten under way when it began to snow. Amazing! All present rushed out in the street for the miraculous, never-before-seen snow-flakes. How could mere pictures compete? In Brühl (near Cologne), his birthplace, a retrospective exhibition was mounted despite the reservations of the city fathers, who smelled anarchy and sedition, and who cried I told you so when a stroke of lightning rent the MAX ERNST banner, strung across the main street, on the very noon of the opening. Prospective visitors to the exhibition hurried away to church.

Next there was the Hawaiian adventure. Summer 1952. By now I was there too. There was an exhibition (both of us, so help me) that contained a number of smoldering little paintings of volcanos (his) made over the past year. In the middle of the reception the news poured in: Kilauea, the volcano on the big island of Hawaii, had just entered into eruption after long years of playing possum. Who cared about painted volcanos?

One day in Paris we prepared to leave next morning for Stuttgart for a Max Ernst retrospective. This ill-fated date was January 24, 1970. About one in the morning, smelling smoke, Max found our kitchen in flames.

"Doro*tay*a!" he yelled three times. I finally stumbled out of sleep and through the flannel smoke to the phone.

"I'll call the firemen!"

"No, you will not. They ruin everything," he said, and with buckets of water he got the fire down, then said, "Now you can call them."

I must say here that they were on hand in four minutes. Visibly disappointed, however, at finding no pretext for the flooding treatment, they soon went away, grumpily deprived of water play, only carrying out the charred, smoking cabinets. Next morning, from up in his studio, Max called down to me.

"Doro*tay*a! I want to show you something." *Now* what? I went up trembling. Some awful damage surely. . . .

He pointed. There on the easel sat the picture he had made the day before. On a snowy white ground that could have been Finland or Siberia was a rectangular collage, made from magazine ads, slightly angled as was his way, and printed on it just three big letters: FEU (fire).

We made it to Stuttgart. The show was hung, all was ready. While I rested in the hotel he talked to his hosts at the museum. Then something very strange took place. From my bed I heard—was it the grinding rumble of a passing truck?—and everything churned, the armoire fell against a bedside table, I lurched to the window. Down below in the park a few people were running in zigzags. It was all over in a flash. What had happened? Had the hotel given way? When Max came in I learned. He had been telling about the fire at home, laughing as usual. The museum people laughed too. "All we need now is an earthquake," quipped someone. It was true.

The Warrens'departure in May coincided with my preparations for an exhibition to be held the next spring. In 1967 the Dorothea Tanning retrospective in Knokke-le-Zoute, Belgium's spa outside of Brussels, brought together not only most of my paintings but also a few friends: Marcel Duchamp—in a tuxedo—with wife, Teeny; Matta and Germana; also Magritte with his little dog, both in black with white plastrons. (An aside: In Paris later I showed Magritte his painting that art dealer Iolas had exchanged with Max for one of his. It was one of those big green apples occupying the whole canvas, and it said, in that careful Magritte script, *This is not an apple.* One day Max took it up to his studio and painted in the middle of the apple a little barred window with a bird behind the bars. Underneath he wrote in the same nice letters: *Ceci n'est pas un Magritte.* So when Magritte happened around one day and saw the picture where it hung in the study, my relief flowed free as he laughed gently and walked away. But he must have hated it. So I pondered: whose sense of humor was the more interesting one—Magritte's in denying his apple, or Max's in denying the denial's author? Maybe one of our most foolhardy impulses is to equate another's sense of humor with our own. Because there must be endless senses of humor, all but one's own unfunny.)

My first retrospective. It was a bracing event for me. At the dinner after the reception they had seated Maurice Chevalier on my right. I couldn't imagine what Maurice Chevalier was doing there, although it was summer and he was perhaps vacationing, He was a nice old man of seventy-nine but the aura of his past still clung to him. In any case he told me he was the person who had asked if he could buy one of the paintings in the show. "You are a collector?" I wanted to know. "But no, not at all." And I, "Then . . . ?" He smiled his famous smile. *"J'aime les chiens velus et les femmes nues"* ("I like furry dogs and nude women"). He had four years to live and left everything to a young friend when he died, including, of course, my painting, *Le Soir à Salonika.* I had occasion to deplore this circumstance when, for my retrospective in Paris seven years later, the loan of the painting was refused by its owner, who, having no idea what an exhibition was, decided it was some skulduggery scheme to divest her of her property.

Twenty years before, there was Capricorn Hill in Arizona. Now we had a new hill, older or perhaps not older. Olives instead of junipers, scrub oak instead of cactus. Viewed daily and with longing from the venerable windows of our village house, from behind tall cypresses imitating furled black umbrellas. No road, only the worn meanders of a rugged shepherd who actually brought his flock through the village to where—hop—they all swarmed off the road and up on the hill, his two busy dogs directing operations as smartly as any traffic cop.

We, with our covetous eyes, were the living symbols of encroaching modernity. For did we not act to dispossess the good shepherd (at least to spoil his afternoons); did we not run rough-shod over the innocent sheep, send them packing to graze elsewhere? We with our big ideas, standing on the hill with the village below, a burnished huddle of stones and rosy roofs whose geometries melted together like a benign puzzle presided over by the usual château (in this case a massive fortress reared against Saracens). Beyond the village stretched a ribbon of road winding between ever bluer distances leading to the sea, the entire panorama presenting a quite happy facsimile of those naive illuminations in ancient manuscripts. Later I would watch the ribbon anxiously when Max had gone off for errands in Draguignan or Vence.

It was easy to acquire the pretty hill. With Monsieur E., its part owner, we soon "came to terms," as the expression goes. Modernity was there before us, lurking in the desires of village descendants of Muslims and Romans, Phoenicians and Visigoths. Families of innumerable cousins who had not spoken to each other for years, inheriting the precious hillside from ancient grandfathers and grandmothers of grandfathers, desiring instead automobiles and television sets. They appeared at the lawyer's office in sullen silence, signed, collected, and left, never to be seen by us again.

Next day we stood up there looking down. It was ours now, henceforth our anchor and our view. So began The House.

For a year there was only the rumble of bulldozers on the hillside. They tore and gouged the gaping, gasping earth, its drowsy stones disturbed and dumped along with their paleodreams and dreamy names: Cambrian, Silurian, Devonian. Creation's hill had to be wrenched around, leveled, filled, sounded, reinforced where there had been nothing. All we wanted was a small place on the ground to receive the house, its *implantation*, as the geologist called it.

A kind of yellow sunshine is on hand, though it is winter 1967. A woman on leave from her canvas and paint bends instead over plans, a different sort of drawing, all straight and true, minutely measured, with logic of doorways and floors and stairway and stress. Most important of all would be two lofty ground-floor studios, with great north windows, in which to live our real lives. At the other end of the house, the stairway would lead to a "ballroom" (see above, "big ideas"—why lose sight of festivity?). The rest, all of it, to be on the ground. So that from his studio, a wide north-lit studio at last, smooth marble floors would lead Max across to everything our immiment domain would comprise: the columned arcades, the library, the wide hall, the keyhole pool, the garden terrace with its flagstones blooming with dendritic traceries that we all want to think are ancient ferns.

Looking deeper into our very own crystal ball, we see that cruel nature will soften her ways, provide us with green grass where there had been brown mud and sand, that the grass will receive a peach tree as fragile as spun glass, alive, at least, if not fruitful, and on another terrace will flourish the vegetables and forty chickens in splendid health, behind wire. (Indeed, they arrived when the time came—clownish barnyard creatures with their eternal pecking, strutting, dropping, mounting, egg-laying. Their glassy eyes as they sat there pushing out the eggs, the shocking voices of triumph that followed: long afternoon ruminations more terrifying than the roar of doom, expressions of their collective boredom sounding on the bucolic life we strove to believe in like inane reminders of eternity. Their presence made me wonder—along with some other bafflements, described below—if it was really what we wanted.)

A couple of details, therefore, should be noted before getting on with the building of the house. They are not overly significant but cautionary, the kind of warning that only crazy artists who think they can command a house to rise would need. Because no other sort of person would rule out the services of a professional architect, no one else would have the nerve to say: "Architect? I am the architect." Headlong, she rushes into pandemonium. Overweening, she draws plans that float overhead like soap bubbles and have to be explained at length. And as must happen in such an enterprise, she leans more and more humbly on the contractor, who, given the circumstance, is soon their chum. It may be said that no big-city entrepreneur, no dashing urban corporation head, no clutch of high-floor brokers, no wily lawyer is foxier in business know-how than the village builder. Ruddy cheeks testify to the great big out-of-doors, the bright grin is twinkly enough for Santa Claus. He wears the latest digital watch; his blue bomber jacket matches his eyes and his Porsche.

He tells stories in his picturesque accent. He waits at the door, the blue car's motor purring, and drives us up to the site. He is deferential with M'sieur Max, gallant with Madame. And at Christmas he brings a gift or two: an umbrella, a billfold, calendars, ashtrays. No wonder that with all his charm, all that *bonhomie,* we are soon on first-name terms.

He has invited us for dinner. In his home, which he calls his masterpiece, we cast about for a topic and come up with *la fête.* Just three weeks away, the annual four-day bash, stoically awaited during the other three hundred and sixty-one days of the year by the citizenry of Seillans.

Always the same, the festival is an arabesque embedded violently in a gloomy year, something to work for, to depend on, something open and noisy with clean, bright shirts moving in a small sea of bouffant blond coiffures (For, brunettes all, nearly every feminine head among them is certain that by changing the color of your hair you change your life and your potential.)

Behind old walls and dark doorways grow young girls who will hear the first notes of the dance and will float out to meet them, the heavenly rock strains of *Atomique Jazz et*

Ses Boys. Hours later, just out beyond the lights and the garlands, they will blissfully contend with eager youths who know a blonde when they see one, they think, and who think they know what to do with her as well.

Two days after this festival (this is July 1968) with its pastis flowing like water, its shooting gallery, its garlic, roulette, and bottle-smashing ninepins, the village square is once more quiet save for the click of boules in the late-afternoon shade. And up on our hill we lay the corner-stone of our house, a mini-ceremony attended by a dozen hungover workers as well as our own helpers, Olga and Albert. While the champagne spurts they all stand abashed, berets in hand. Then they cry: "Bravo, M'sieur Max! Bravo, Madame Max!"

Day after day sees me wave, call the dog, and climb the hill. If it is my house it has to be watched, like a nest of hatchlings, that no ill can come. A rectangular nest of stone sits upon my chest at night, its builder words securely mortared into my sleep. To this day, if I must describe the *portée d'un poutre,* there is only my precious Harrap's (French-English) to help me say "beam span"; the *doloire* that sounds so sad was only a shovel that chopped away at sand and *mortier de chaux* (lime mortar). *Limousinage* (stone masonry), *bétonnage* (concrete masonry), yes, and braces, lintels. Shall I always remember their hinges, their mor-tises, along with the smiles as I brought from my basket the bottle of wine, *le coup de rouge?* Sometimes Max waves from his window, down below.

Up there I am joshing, discussing the work, using

those words that I shall never in all my life use again. Knowledgeable perhaps. Freakish, unwomanly, I feel rather than see the house rise, feeding on me.

Biweekly lunch parties at the village hotel brought us together: the mason-contractor; the carpenter (nine generations of trade guild); the plumber, shirt-and-tie man of the world from Nice; the hometown electrician and tile setter. Our reunions were of the very merriest. I am not going to give descriptions of these people or comment upon them, their gestures, their tics, their indigenous words. They were like men of their calling anywhere, neither droll nor solemn, satanic nor adorable. It would be untrue, however, to maintain that lunching with all of them at one table in the village restaurant was anything but an ordeal. Max, of course, stayed safely at home, where I, too, might and should have remained, But I held tight to the conviction that the gods of our future hearth, gathered together at the Restaurant Clariond in concord and community of interest, would, without my presence and after a few glasses of Gigondas, forget their high purpose and fall into discord, perhaps even fisticuffs.

They began by seriously unfolding their lily napkins to protect the ties they had put on for the occasion. Orders were for all five courses—they all had lusty appetites and ate everything that was put before them. If I tried to keep up with them—as I did the first time, swilling the heavy wine and swallowing the *suprème de langouste, perdreau truffé, pissaladière, salade, baba*—there was certain to be a day in bed immediately following.

Instead, for two hours I would shamelessly carry on, with winks and laughter, a kind of jollity with these men; banter that I can only describe as grisly and that left me drained and gasping. Tottering home afterward, coming into the sweetly silent house—except for the faraway third-floor sounds of Max in his studio—was, I thought, the way a call girl must feel after her strenuous champagne gaiety, when she has thus earned the right to droop and sleep.

It was a period of bristling demands that provided me with a thousand needles of frustration. A two-sided medal marked the working days from those when the crew(s) didn't show up. More subtle were the calculations in numbers. Let's see, tomorrow a team of plumbers will begin to lay the underground pipe. Sure?

Puffing up the hill the next day and feeling exactly like one of those diminutive figures limned by talented monks in the margins of parchment manuscripts, I found a plumber, a taciturn fellow seated on the ground, idly fitting an elbow into a two-inch plastic pipe (it didn't fit).

"*Bonjour.*"

"*Jour.*"

"Where are all the others?" I asked.

He grunted, "*Il n'y a pas d'autres*" ("There aren't any others").

The grid, economical lines that had stifled the motley geometries of our imagined abode were themselves overlaid by a vicious schematic: the slanting rains, R, that made work impossible; delays of indispensable parts, P, tracing a glacial arc from faraway (Martian?) marts to us; dotted lines for long intervals of nothingness leading to X, that collapse of a xenolithic stone pile intended for drainage, occasioning a crushing back injury to our foreman; and diagonally back to Z, the zealous masons who managed to camouflage the lovely stones with gray cement; and Y, your favorite contractor madly misreading your careful dimensions of the pool and digging instead a perhaps secretly desired municipal-sized water hole. (His answer when confronted: "*Je m'excuse.*")

Yet everything moved toward dazzling completion; stones came together, oriels framed landscapes, and the house cast a marble shadow. Insanely euphoric by this time, I caused columns to be made in Touraine (remember Giles Chauvelin, our Huismes stonecutter?) and to be trucked all the way down to grace the loggia, Maxfield Parrish Doric, between which we would see in the stunning late-day light of rose and ineffable blue, the coral roofs of Seillans.

It was rumored around that such a house could only be dreamed up and built with posterity in mind, that it was surely destined to be a museum when we were gone. I believe this kind of museum or foundation (lovely unshakable word), devoted to the work of one artist, occupies in most minds a place something like that reserved for Jack's beanstalk, or better yet, the rainbow: a bridge, sprung from natural phenomena, to the supernatural and its glittering treasure. Its doors are open to all. Ten francs. Come in. Beauty reigns. Floors are scrubbed, windows sparkle, the pictures are straight and perfectly lit, the guardian smiles.

No dust dims the sculptures, there are no leaks in the roof, no menace of fire or thieves, no weeds in the drive. The lawn is mowed (at night, by brownies), there are no bugs in the trees, no rust anywhere. And no mutiny. With such a picture firmly in mind, several twentieth-century artists have gotten themselves consecrated. Believing in the possibility of their beanstalks, a few have used their own sudden success to build megalostructures with their names spanning the façades—chiseled as on tombstones, or blazing in lights, as on theater marquees. As for filling up the place, *ooh là-là,* a bumper crop of masterpieces waits in the studio.

Up in our Saint-Roc hills—almost inaccessible by any but sinewy-calved mountaineers, jeeps, and Land Rovers—we were clearly not preparing for posterity. In fact, Max hardly noticed the activity except to drag visitors up there to see the havoc, something that Dorothea was doing with the money people were bringing him. She sometimes asked what he wanted: dimensions of a room, for example, were decided as breezily as choices from a menu; he would always opt for the bigger one. This bounty was then something he could give her to play with, for she was in truth playing a game, conjuring out of stone and wood and glass a castle as magical as the one on Jack's beanstalk. Whence the confusion of motives.

On June 17, 1970, moving men struggled up the hill *on foot* between old house and new, their loaded truck having balked before the steep grade. Two weeks later the transfer—surely it would be the last (it was)—was complete.

Oh, we would live on our own veggies, we would keep

chickens. Not an outrageous plan, given the meager, and not always fresh, produce that found its way to the tiny Seillans grocery. But—also a given—local soil wasn't *soil*. As thin and poor and stony as faraway Sedona's terrain had been, it dared us to try. We asked around for manure. Ah, yes, Monsieur B. in the neighbor village of Bargemon had a horse, he could sell us manure. He did. Soon there were real lettuces and carrots and brussels sprouts and leeks in our paradise. Strawberries. Even artichokes. We will raise our own chickens without hormonic trash, we said. All we needed was some eggs, soon obtained from a neighboring farm. These produced, to our amazement, a family of tall, fierce-looking birds on high, bright yellow legs and eagle's toes, proving that the simple French farmer is as on to hormones as our American chicken factories.

Five years were lived in this massive haven (I almost wrote heaven) where nothing seemed to stem the flow of work and frolic, not even the harassment of the *fisc* (French equivalent of the IRS) in the person of a tight-lipped fellow in coat and vest whose reply, when Max confessed his ignorance of accounts, "You can keep books in the morning and paint in the afternoon," came too late

Though invariably appealing to women and some men, Max had never aroused the same affection in the New York art community as a whole. In fact, approbation was never quite his. (To this day he is remembered nervously, if not with alarm, by a group into which he never seemed to fit.) Odd attitudes, unpredictability, and the utter absence of *bon ton* assured final rejection with the same severity that apartment shareholders wield in passing on would-be occupants of their building.

When he chose me as his life partner I stepped up happily, took my bow, and arranged myself on his side. It would have been madness not to.

The following years, so warmly documented here, only confirmed my choice. His cloudy place in the American art landscape of today, somewhere off in the distance, is of no importance, considering that art endures only through artists and that the genuine among genuines prevails. With time, most of the rest is forgotten, above all the trainers and structurers of the "scene," all bouncing comfortably on the trampoline of past giants, all blending in with media stars, rock stars, food stars, movie stars, money stars, political stars, scandal stars. Besides, we judiciously mix our shows with great names, great ideas. We dip into history's trunk for disguises of worth. If they have to be altered and cut down to fit, no one will notice, for they do not know the source. We are heartily approved of on our island. What more can anyone ask?

There was about him something I came to recognize as time went on, and with trepidation. Now, to speak of it at all I must dig deep for words that, as they surface, turn brown and dry as clods, leaving me agonized, embarrassed, inadequate. The presence of this profound and absolutely impenetrable something, this incalculable distance—was he carrying some special burden of knowledge beyond the

things in books, a heavy arcanum?—removed him ever so
slightly from where he stood, so that his gentleness, his elegance, and the whole amalgam of his being spoke of apartness. Apart from the studio, from people; from even me, for
I saw it clearly and did not panic: why should I want to
plumb his very depths? Why bore behind the cool, faraway
gaze directed straight through my eyes?—for at times his
regard was of such distance that I was unsettled and had to
swallow a rising knot in my throat. Whatever one pictures
him doing or not doing, saying or not saying, it is well to
remember that deep-diving absence, hinting at a place one
could never hope to fathom. It sat upon him always, not
unkindly or yet sad. Save for those funny stories, he seemed
not to want to remember anything. The great bulging bag
of his past slumped unopened. Its charms and deceptions,
so easy for others to drag out and examine, and so hard for
him to notice, moldered dankly in their dark nowhere, lost,
unfound, and unclaimed.

What kind of artist is it who knows water sources and
courses, and weather signs as well as his favorite philosophers? He told me the names of trees, their leaves, their
roots, their rhythms. Flowers, too, collaborated with him.
He showed me everything from sunsets to beetles, which
he called "she." In fact, there were no "hes" in his natural
world except men.

We were two, artists as it happened, pursuing our separate obsessions. Conflict? Friction? Any weighing that
had to be done contended with jiggling scales heaped
with desiderata on both trays. Choosing was not, there-

fore, the word for what we did. It is a word for the shopper, for garments, dishes, details; uninvolved with the
heart—or even the mind.

If I had weighed my love, laid it like a pulsing heart-
shaped lump on the brass scales, with Advancement (star-
shaped) on the other tray, I would have been simply
contemptible. An artist? Indeed what artist could be anything but foolhardy even if, having done the weighing,
she decided to risk all for love? What is she risking? All
those rousing, honorific speeches, magazine-TV interviews, and power precepts were absurdly wide of the
mark, in my case. I couldn't find myself anywhere. It
seemed clear to me that I had better stay in my corner
where making art was allowed. And where I could be one
in a two-part rescue operation, reciprocal. There was no
consideration of options, no turning over of pros and
cons. They say that we are made of water. So maybe I was a
river crashing to the sea and merging with another stream
on the way, just naturally. How could I flow backwards or
sideways? Does the sharing of a direction deprive a female
of her imagination? Or her hands? Is it a hardship, is it
unfair to have to live in an enchanted space where striving
after approval by other not always distinguished human
beings is no more than a faraway rumor, frivolous as the
place cards at a distant dinner party?

To have been in a way a helpmate to so splendid and
mysterious a human being, while not a privilege (who
wants to be a helper, merely?), was in no way painful or
degrading. Instead, a strong emotion resembling sympathy

would grip me at certain times when he seemed to implore me to "take over," or at least to share his quiet disarray. But to share the fundamental wild truth that wrapped him close, ah, that was not for me. Why should it be? He could not share mine. And although our combined dream brought us together it was also the labyrinth that kept us blessedly separate. So here was a single desire growing in me to make him accessible for all those who found him abstruse, closed, arrogant, difficult, overweening. For this it is not enough to hold him at arm's length, squinting, with my head on one side. The only certainty was his presence and the fact that the "he" was mostly a "we."

Needless to say, these remarks, or rather gropings, apply to us only as a pair. But what of all the (previously referred-to) outsiders who must remain unnamed here? How to speak negatively of the outside without seeming ungracious, even barbaric? My peace stood firm before the long-drawn-out assault, evil as plague, that swooped down on the Artist. Disguised with names like Admiration and Understanding, vacuities and platitudes imperfectly covered intentions. They dripped like treacle under the wisteria bower in Touraine or, later, buzzed in the heat with the flies on the Provençal veranda.

Though only an artist, Max could be credited with a sizable real-estate boom. Seeing him, laughing with him, admiring him, and carrying off his works seemed to provoke in his visitors an imperious desire to live higher on the hog, starting of course with a new-old château, a country house, a new art gallery, or several of these, always larger and grander than what they had before. They fastened upon him as silkworms fasten upon mulberry leaves. There were all kinds of projects: a film festival needed a trophy sculpture; a town needed a fountain. A crackerjack inventor of multiples needed a painting.

His wife, also an artist, that's me, can be credited with having stimulated sales in Paris flea markets, perfumeries, stores, and boutiques of moderately priced jewelry. For the wheeler-dealers invariably brought her some trinket as if flinging a bone to the dog to keep it from barking.

The ruses were as obvious as Aesop's fabled deceits, and as successful. But sometimes Max opened his eyes wide, saw through the flimsy ploy, and rebelled. Or sometimes there just wasn't any more. Sculpture? Collages? Frottages? Then, in proportion to the shrinking of the booty, the bottles of perfume shrank too until the day when, the big deals having come to an end, there wasn't any perfume at all. It was amusing, when a gesture was in order, to offer a piece of her own making and to register the little squint of mirrored deception upon receiving one of hers instead of one of his. Politeness demanding, everyone smiled.

Perhaps the most outlandish were the two excited *messieurs* who wanted to make beds. Live wires, full of zeal, full of babble, full of ideas. Bouvard and Pécuchét. Or Laurel and Hardy. They came down from Paris with a cardboard box that one of them (Bouvard?) carried held out in front of him, a light but precious burden. Blown glass? A rare butterfly?

We all stood around our big table while it was unwrapped to reveal a shaky little bed, dollhouse-size, head and foot made of two sides of a Japanese birdcage, the kind Max used for his object-paintings. In fact, the picture, *Question Insecte,* that these two inventors hoped to "interpret" was at that very moment in his studio.

A bed for surrealist dreams, they said. It would have a moon and a giant spray of (plastic) fern leaves. It would have a coverlet of mink fur. Gimmicks were rampant— wispy end tables, lamps, veneers of the sort found in mail-order catalogs. All they wanted was his permission. Yes, yes. He would receive two beds for his signature! Yes, of course, yes.

This hideous object was actually realized in a number of copies, cardboard moon, plastic leaves, pitiful minks, and all. The visitors could barely contain their excitement. "Where will you put yours?" one of them asked me in gushing effusion. Our cellar folded its cobwebs over the thing upon its delivery. And after a flurry of embarrassing, pulpy publicity, the whole project fell apart. There were beds in Swiss warehouses, a bed in a Munich emporium, beds in the factory. We had only to palm off ours to forget the whole miserable fiasco.

Generous to the point of detachment, he gave. It never came to an end. Hardly a day passed after we left the safe haven of Arizona that did not see at least one drawing flutter from under his hand to perch in some acquaintance-tree. Rare portfolios, albums, frottages, etchings were passed out like cookies if there were any on the table. He never knew what happened with his sculptures. Always someone to tell him: "Money is being put away for you." Like a child.

Why didn't I do something? Would I, could I be one of those wives? Would I ever be one of those widows? *Les veuves abusives* (abusive widows) was his mocking term for them.

How can one piece together a cohesive history when so much connective material is hidden away in private caches on several continents? The answer is that one cannot. This may have been his intention.

Max did not welcome unannounced irruptions into his studio. Nor for that matter did I. Studio visits even between us were by invitation. At home, at peace, just us, a new picture was the occasion for: "Would you care to see . . . ?" Oh yes! You came, you gazed, you spoke your mind, sort of. If I said words like beautiful, luminous, magical, new, serene, challenging, vigorous, final, it was because I meant them. Once in a while a wrong note would rile the air: "That little yellow area," I might venture, "couldn't it be better green? I just wonder about that yellow bit. . . ." A bad moment. "You!" The brash critic is dismissed. Sad, sad evening. But the next day there is a visitor and I trail behind into Max's studio where I see that the yellow bit has changed to green. I am absurdly happy. In truth he would do almost anything for me, I think blissfully.

The same invitation, the same visit in reverse. My studio, my new picture. He comes, he gazes, he says,

"Wonderful."

"Do you really like it?"

"It's wonderful."

"But isn't there something? That form in the blue rectangle there, tell me, really . . ."

"But I *told* you—it's wonderful."

"But . . . you can say *something*. I won't be mad."

And he, losing patience now: "Listen. I said it was wonderful. What do you want? What can I say more?" Walking out in a huff.

The next day at lunch I make a little announcement: "Max, that picture I showed you yesterday . . . the new one with the blue *fond* . . ."

"Yes?"

"Well, I destroyed it."

He throws down his napkin, he glares, he thunders, "No!" And after a moment: "Well, it wasn't your best."

At times I felt a flush of resentment. A candid opinion, even a sketch of real judgment, perfectly severe, even brutal, was what I thought I wanted. Of course he was right. A criticism, even solicited, would have been as odious to him as, later, to me. An insult, an assassination. You have your own eye, your own heart, your own soul. What need of the teacher's foot in the bounteous garden of all that plenty?

"What is this mania for talking?" he would say. "What can you learn that eyes and mind can't teach you?"

"You can teach how to do," I said.

"You can't teach how to see," said he. And I:

"You can teach how to think. . . ."

"Not how to feel." He thus had the last word.

Sometimes I slightly wished he wasn't so right, hadn't done it so serenely. I would have liked to see a big crack so that I could jump in to help, to make of our twain the ultimate symmetry. "Indispensable Dorothea. She dolled up his life." Fragile dream. For anyone could see that he had always done it, always would do it, with or without an eager D. T. All of which had nothing to do with his very satisfying passion for me.

Well-defined loyalties were as alien to him as well-defined conventions. Open allegiance to any group, nation, party—even the surrealist movement had its hands full, with his often anarchic tangents, resulting in repeated exclusion and equally repeated blandishments—was somehow awkward. Dignitaries and celebrities were make-believe. Theater was on pages, not stages. He read avidly in Strindberg—too avidly, I thought—and Shakespeare—"Of course he wrote to be read." He went to the movies as all artists do: for pictures. Matta, another artist-addict of films, mentioned earlier, once said to me that there is no movie, no matter how abject, that will not give you one splendid moment.

Comment Je n'ai Pas Peint Certains de Mes Tableaux (How I Have Not Painted Certain of My Pictures): 43 days. 44 visits.

This is a notebook entry I wrote at the end of summer 1973, for which I may be pardoned, my notebook being a harmless steam vent seen only by me. The note is a slight deformation of Raymond Roussel's well-known treatise

Comment J'ai Ecrit Certains de Mes Livres, translating to
"How I Wrote Certain of My Books." It may serve, as well
as anything, to preface the following remarks.

I have spoken of my place in this world of visits. But
what I have not said, and must, is about my place as an
artist. Ah, there the delicate rapiers of almost constant
thrust—curiously unintentional in the main and as such
all the more offensive—have demanded of me all the
force of my patience and my pride to brush them off.

Has there ever in the world existed an artist (poet)
who has been for the greater part of adult life so relent-
lessly condemned to listen to, to read of, to watch at close
range—I almost said rage—the overwhelming attention
paid to a fellow poet? Can a poet (artist) be thus stifled
day after day, year after year, without prospect of change
and still survive? Has there ever been an artist who could
so drown without a call for help?

What had happened to my petulance? How had my
lifelong lordliness wound up in a tangle of maneuvers
having to do with woman rather than artist? From my earliest beginnings, every decision, every choice, had been
sparked by a sense of challenge, I learned French almost
belligerently. When I began life with this famous man I
was confident that I could continue as a separate, stony-
sided individual. Suddenly, from one moment to the
next—the time it takes to fall hopelessly in love (I did), or
face a firing squad—I was transferred from my unap-
proachable aerie to a nest on the ground. Solitary, I had
set my jaw a thousand times, had curled my lip, had been

sly, had been steady. Invincible? The world would answer that, would put things straight, would bring down all high fliers of the wrong gender. For, along with the relative, and much discussed, onuses of riches and poverty, I want to add here another one: that for a girl there is no greater handicap to creativity and self-fulfillment in the solitary arts than physical prettiness.

Pretty is a two-edged sword, not only because of the way the world sees you. Oh, no. More insidious is your own divided self. Divided because, like a muscle without exercise, you have become soft, you have diluted your dreams, and you have no one but yourself to accuse if you cannot deal with the resultant atrophy, if you cannot deflect the preferential treatment you get for the wrong reasons. Not to take advantage of your good looks, not even to *use* them, certainly not to let them lead you into gray areas or outright compromise; these are the mere starting points for a battle with an unlikely victory, in any case.

That I was a pretty girl seemed to be a consensus. Were they, all the others, seeing something illusory, even something wished for? And if so, by whom, me or them? So, although I was not all that pretty, something in me, not consciously willed, must have made me seem so as I watched, rather dreamily, and listened to those who took pretty for granted and treated me as only pretty girls are treated: kindly, then indulgently, tenderly. Oh, it was easy then, pleasant enough, but not quite right, not quite me. As time went on and I persisted in needing to be someone other than a pretty girl, a baffling frustration set in. It had always been convenient to be thought pretty. Now I was becoming impatient with the way it was getting in front of the artist I felt I had become. No matter what I did, I was always, first, the pretty girl who, indeed, would be foolish to imagine there was anything else reserved for her. I suffocated. I raged. Even growing older did not help. The label had adhered like a callus, unchanged except for the odious qualification of "formerly."

So to all girls who are born pretty I would say this: if creativity stirs within you, if it becomes your *raison d'être*, be prepared for a large dose of frustration, both from within and without. Even if you vanquish your own demons, even if you do not gaze long and approvingly into the mirror, even if you go into the wilderness where there are no mirrors, even if you produce good art, you may expect only the most uncertain notice, tinged with a touch of suspicion, at that. And then ask yourself if you will ever know what you really are.

Confusedly, in my case, it began with little drifts of surprise at the odd niche I seemed to occupy; all the time compromise seeping in unnoticed, mere smiles really, hardly to be confused with resignation. Over and over. Along with wifeliness, a tag that Max deplored as much as I, it leaked into those worlds where it did not belong. No matter, I was tempered steel. And still confident, for after all we were two to brave the many. I dwelt more and more in sublimation-land while the assault from without mounted in numbers and ferocity. He, my Max, stood helplessly by, incredulous and miserable. Sometimes he ignored the museum directors' requests just because of me. As if it helped! They bearded him, they positively lunged against our crystal. We were invincible. Yet, something was happening. My dedication was blurring, mingling with wifely occupations and colorful living, so that my vow was like a pile of empty picture frames stacked behind the door.

Two studios holding two artists; two easels, his and hers; the same clutter of tables, the sounds are similar. What are we? A school, a laboratory, a cottage industry? And the tardy thought: would it have been, perhaps, better to have two crafts instead of one? And better for whom? For that we would have had to take two different mates. No awkward hammering in unison, no identical turpentine clouds drifting from two doors, no mournful confusion of wall space in visiting minds.

From the very start, "they" were ready, eager, and determined to spot his *influence*. Never underestimate this word. It is everywhere, favorite nib of the poverty-stricken pen. Once, looking over a two-page article about my work, I counted the names of twenty-three artists (male) including Max. It was fun breaking this list down into centuries and finding that I was rather equally indebted to the nineteenth and the twentieth, to Italian, French, and Spanish (masters, of course), and that my work was, to say the least, feminine. Another time the art critic of a prestigious New York weekly, reviewing a mixed bag of paintings on view somewhere, saw fit to describe my *Birthday* as "hard, harsh and shallow, but effective."

Indeed, effective it must have been, for reappearing

in another show the following year it was mentioned by the same critic as being painted by a "talented new-comer." Was he losing his grip? Because when it was borrowed seven years later for one of those sweeping surveys called blockbusters that museums like to mount, the whole fabric of his intransigence had by that time apparently disintegrated, and the critic, reeling from his capitulation, called *Birthday* one of the "highlights" of the show. It was upon reading this last spasm of copy that the subject of art criticism gave me some moments of bemused reflection as well as a strong conviction that familiarity, far from breeding contempt, bringeth on pleasure and, if I may, understanding.

One moist Paris evening in 1969, in a mood of melancholy reflection, I sat in a concert at the Maison de la Radio, listening to a composer (Karlheintz Stockhausen) conduct his piece "Hymnen," a music that jolted me out of my negative thoughts and incredibly but clearly showed me what I had to do. Spinning among the unearthly sounds of "Hymnen" were the earthy, even organic shapes that I would make, had to make, out of cloth and wool; I saw them so clearly, living materials becoming living sculptures, their life span something like ours. Fugacious they would be, and fragile, to please me, their creator and survivor. I was suddenly content and powerful as I looked around. No one knew what was going on inside me. I had forgotten about "Hymnen," only noticing when it ended and everyone stood up, and I felt potent and seminal the way one does about works that have not yet happened.

This, then, was the genesis of what became five years of sculpture activity. Carried on in my studio in Seillans, the work did not involve familiar canvas or paint but carded wool and endless lengths of sensuous tweeds, the chopping up of which provided thrills of a kind very close to lust with its attendant peril.

Sometimes I remembered that musical evening where a risk had been taken and tamed. And where my melancholy had dissolved before the fact. An artist is the sum of his risks, I thought, the life-and-death kind. So, in league with my sewing machine, I pulled and stitched and stuffed the banal materials of human clothing in a transformational process where the most astonished witness was myself. Almost before I knew it I had an "oeuvre," a family of sculptures that were the avatars, three-dimensional ones, of my two-dimensional painted universe.

A retrospective (mine this time) at Le Centre National d'Art Contemporain—Paris's museum that three years later opened as Le Centre Pompidou—of paintings and sculptures. Indeed, I was now Painter and Sculptor. Aside from the satisfaction of receiving such consideration, there was a bonus: seeing again a number of my works long hidden in private collections; seeing it all together like the curtain call of some spectacle where everyone, even the prologuist, is onstage—a curtain call lasting eight weeks.

These sculptures will last about as long as a human

life—the life of someone "delicate." But it isn't a challenge, even though I find that being obsessed with the durability of a work doesn't appeal to me. In those 1970s, durability was still a valid prerequisite for a piece of art. I was often told, "What a pity your sculptures aren't more solid." They might as well have said "dead," or "paralyzed." After all, when you fall in love you don't ask the beloved, "How long are you going to live?" A fearsome question, too close to us.

Time blurs, and I now rarely blurt out Max mirrors: Max said . . . Max preferred . . . Max disdained . . . Max would always . . . Max never failed to . . . Max once told me . . . Max.

His do's and don'ts were often vehement and always colorful. The do's are all over this book. Here are some of the don'ts:

Don't regret the disappearance of horses. Just be thankful their martyrdom is over.

Don't eat health food. Don't put flour in the sauce. Don't say you love a shoe.

Don't take too long to buy something. Your time is worth more than your money.

Never wake anyone out of a sound sleep. (How he enjoyed telling of the court trial about a man who had murdered his wife for waking him—and was acquitted!)

Don't ever confess anything.

This last he scrupulously observed during our entire thirty-four years. Nor did he ever utter the words "I'm sorry" or "It was my fault."

To the above don'ts I must add one of my own: Never be persuaded to eat, drink, smoke, or insert anything you don't want (a summation of my driest and flimsiest wisdom in dry and flimsy categories—albeit categories that demand their due at some time or other in our bumpy lives).

Ten year in Seillans, five in each house. There is no way to end this sunny Provençal account without telling of the awful morning that saw Max fallen and surprised and helpless on the bathroom floor. There is no charm in the mournful business of ambulances and hospitals and a special plane to take him to Paris. No way to transform our disarray into something readable. No way at all.

CHAPTER NINE

*Plummeted
Bird*

1975. LOPLOP, Bird Superior, Max's self-bestowed alter ego, has plummeted, left wing forever still. The year is tense, eleven losing months on the number-clogged calendar. His bed is the axis; around it everything turns. The high white bed that narrowly holds his disgust, the bitterness lying in his eyes. On the next to the last day he asks his visitor, his old friend Robert:

"Tell me, Robert, what do you think of the letter?"

"The letter?"

Max insists: "Oh yes, you know what I mean. . . ."

Robert treads warily: "But . . ."

And Max, "The letter, the letter. Rimbaud's letter. *La lettre du voyant* ("The Seer's Letter").

This enigmatic letter that Rimbaud wrote to his friend and confidant Georges Izambard may not have any special significance for us, American readers of poetry, but it has intrigued French poets and philosophers, especially the surrealists, since it was made known. It seems to call into question (I am no philosopher; I am only reporting what I

have heard and read) some very basic ideas about poetry
or, rather, about being a poet. Specifically, to arrive at the
unknown there must be a deliberate "derangement of *all
the senses.*" This single phrase gave rise to lots of discussion,
and his "Morality is the brain's weakness" was echoed in
Breton's First Surrealist Manifesto: "without regard for
moral . . . considerations." (A grave mistake, said Max.)

As his final hours sift down, Max Ernst reveals his pon-
dering. Of all that he has seen, of all the spheres he has
negotiated, the towers he has thrown up, the prisons he
has escaped; of all that he has loved or honored or questioned, of all the words he has read in all his long life, it is
Rimbaud's letter that holds him now. There it is, locked
in the darkening corridors of his mind, its riddle intact.

He has not the slightest wish to know what, clinically,
has happened to him. The presence of the pretty nurses is
merely necessary; they do their work as he watches,
already quiet, his care and feeding with silent and sovereign detachment. His indifference to medicine is total.
The breathless doctor surges in *every day,* watches, doses,
juggles the drugs.

People come and go. Friend Patrick tells me, "Don't
despair, Dorothea. Georges B. lived for eight years in his
bed" (paralyzed). Is this supposed to give me hope? Shall
I be grateful for a horizontal Max, a fragile doll in the
high bed? Would Max be relieved knowing he could hang
on by such a thread? Would we both learn during those
endless days, watching the tiny dawns grow to ferocious
noons and then slowly, slowly to dark and perhaps sleep,

so that we might begin again next morning to make a bigger effort at learning hard to like the bubble; would we learn, he on the inside, me on the outside, unable even to hold hands? "Don't you touch that!" The still hand.

"Let us think of him now without being disorderly." Leaning to me, someone said it, and we as soon saw that it was not possible. Almost a whole year in that bed, knowing. He watched TV. Watched tumbling horses, the explosions. Watched the insects, gloriously enlarged and translucent, their intent, jerky movements so purposeful—no wonder they are stronger than we! Watching the cowboys' lined faces he might have thought of twangy Sedona, far away now; watching Bugs Bunny, international deity, with that laughing voice, not human, not rabbit, soon stifled on the dirty floor in the following commercial, where a zealous mop, having imbibed a detergent, swipes across the filth, revealing a bright rectangular swath that becomes a triumph for the housewife and a window in the blur of our woe.

Unshakable, removed. As he lay there it was stunningly clear that he would die. And that there would be no compromise, no revelation, nothing for me anywhere. He would die as a bird dies, wings closed and useless as painted tin; would die sloughing off those around him, the bossy nurses, the little cook in her tight jeans and loud clogs. My heart was so tangled with confused emotions that I clung to these girls as if Max's essence, his *élan vital*, had passed into their beings instead of where he lay in the high narrow bed in furious disgust—like a dying king who has no proper visible successor for his scepter. Certainly not the distraught wife, the burlesque doctor, the visitors. All strangers, all. Family, country, gods, all waited outside. He had plenty of time dying to capitulate, but did not.

There is the voice of Aragon who sits beside the bed: "Remember, Max?" Reminding, remembering the great days. Max half listens or not at all, his eyes on the television. Woody Woodpecker outwits the Fox. And Aragon, immense, carried away: "Remember, Max, the time when I hustled you out of that fracas at the Dôme, with dozens of cops swarming in? We were all Paris hometown brawlers, the rest of us, nothing to fear; but you, *pauvre bougre*, with your impossible German passport . . ."

Oh Max, turn your eyes to us. "Max, honey, Aragon says . . ." Woody winks, Max watches. "Mmmm," he says faintly.

Showing us the so obvious answer. But then he is sleepy and the answer can wait. Aragon will go, sad because his charming souvenirs must lie quietly in his memory and will not be shared by his old friend.

I cannot help noticing that he does not mention the rally of twelve years before when he had asked us to join him for a "ballet benefit." Of course. Arriving at the Palais d'Hiver we were ushered through dense crowds of humanity (matching Aragon's newspaper: *L'Humanité*) down to the front row, where, to my stupefaction, I found myself seated between Waldeck Rochet, French communism's then boss, and my poor Max, who, though trapped, bore the half-hour prelude of flashbulbs with tight-lipped fortitude.

At one point in this interminable evening (there is no ballet), Aragon, in his pretty black velvet suit, leapt with crisp energy onto the stage and read poetry from a sheaf of papers. By this time my brain was so glazed that his voice came to me as abstract sound and the subsequent wild applause as menace. I looked around. The immense space was packed with faces, all with the dreary look of controlled bitterness about pleasures they did not want; angular or round, dark or pale, they would, when commanded, sing lustily, cry hoarsely, trample thoroughly. I felt *surrounded*. It was clear that I had better sit tight. Every few minutes some photographer would snap around front to shoot us, Monsieur Rochet on my right, Max on my left. How should I look? Should I smile? Look stern? Preoccupied? Impossible to hide. I would steal glances at shaggy Monsieur Rochet. He was intense, tousled, his eyes were parked under shady trees. Needless to say, no words were exchanged between us. He probably thought of my chair as being unoccupied.

Although this was not the worst thing that ever happened to me, it was certainly one of the most grotesque. It had the same quasi comical scenario as those dreams in which you are, say, naked at the airport, racing a long walk for your clothes on the carousel. Was it really me, Dottie Tanning from Galesburg, the tender romantic, her fabric shot through with dreams of unearthly splendor, metamorphosis, sorcery, enchantment? Yes, sit tight.

When it was over we pushed out unnoticed, while

Aragon basked, surrounded and happy as he is here in this afternoon gloom, an altogether indomitable man. Goodbye, goodbye. . . .

Day pales to evening. TV girls, TV races and barking guns, a variety of sounds, the sounds are the targets. Undulating TV hair to prove something, to prove that everything is undulating, smoke, fire, fields, lava, water, worms, women under men. Now the lamps are lit and he is drugged to sleep. The evening is stony with its dead TV and its mocking teeth of hopeless white death sitting comfortably in the big soft round chair that Max cannot bear. It had been brought in for him, his favorite chair.

Here comes night to turn the room to blotch and sweep away our walls. What is the time? Is it something to laugh off? All the talk about how it doesn't exist. And here it is, taking charge, churning all, chastising bodies, bodies turning inside out, feeling cheap and jerry-built. Resentful bodies, forever dueling with minds. I am here, we are both here, it is midnight. Or is it? Early dawn is seeping in, a kind of blue dust on the dark. My lungs breathe worthless air that nobody wants, least of all Max.

Trying to bring him into focus, I am stingingly aware of my huge inadequacy. It resembles in a way the clumsy, wrong brushstrokes of picture restorers. I saw from the start that the tag "painter" would not place Max. It puts him with those who *can paint.* They are great painters, they did it well, better, best. Acrobats. But what do you call someone who invites you to step outside the rational world and to contend with the imponderables? Someone who does this without words but with signs, symbols, arcane intimations arranged on surfaces, slyly passing for paintings, where the very absences make their comment, where something you think you recognize, a wheel, a beetle, or a blaze has been put there as point, not paint. Unartistic. Serenely disrespectful of the craft.

Tonight, gray is the end color, the end result. Ash is the color of the sky, the lid of the town, the fur in the mouth. Time lives with space, unperturbed; Father Time, Mother Space. They are king and queen of the world and the universe and the whole bit. Invincible. They are the only ones.

There is no sound, his breath is feather-silent. A private event is taking place. Not to be disturbed by sorrowing faces, Loplop, Bird Superior, prepares in solitude, in the graceful space of his lofty aerie, his diminishing and his departure.

He is like a lake with an echo: I say Max, everyone says Max, the lake says Max, the echo says Max (far away), and Max is everywhere and part of my throat and the mote in the air.

I hold my screaming ears that no one but me can hear.

CHAPTER TEN

✒

A Time
Suspended

APRIL 1976. There is no light in the studio, nothing moves, and the colored jokes are fading fast. The disorder is grievous. (Is the heart condemned to break each day?)

June. Still in the studio. Everything is there at the bottom of my crazy brain. Everything. But it's stone-heavy and will not rise. Most of the time it's all dark down there. You can stumble around for hours without joy. My mind is a cave and its words are hidden in boxes and trunks with lost or rusty keys. If you find the keys they don't fit the locks. Or if they fit they don't turn. Or if they open the lock the lid does not rise the hinges are stiff. Even if, finally, the trunk is opened, most of its contents are ruined or moldy from their long wait and aren't worth the trouble of dragging into the light.

I went on painting, numbly, doggedly, somberly, something that when it was finished I called *Still in the Studio*. But it was as if the paints had curdled in their tubes. Colors that I had so loved stubbornly eluded my brushes

in this brokenhearted work that turned out to be a kind
of farewell to Paris and to France.

During this period, there wasn't a fiber of my being that
didn't long to be enfolded and consoled. It was as if my
wing feathers had been clipped and I could hop around but
not fly. Yet, this didn't seem to matter, a numb resignation
having taken over. Had my eleven-month vigil ended by
assuming a mask of indifference? The long enforced idle-
ness had so dulled my true feelings that I could carry on
frivolous conversations with whoever showed up with a
funny story to tell. My tumult hid under a slow boil, so far
from explosion that its force looked like a site for tourists,
little spurts of laughter imitating geysers. What is there to
tell that the watcher wants to hear? That at age thirty-two I
traded myself for someone else? An almost Faustian fate
awaited me: *there were no more doors* and I was not I.

Even now, when a summer and other seasons were
taking me and my valise far away from the rue de Lille: to
New York, to Senegal. . . .

Senegal. The river. The *Bou-el-Mogdad,* river-cruise vessel chartered by Sadruddin Aga Khan, cofounder of *The
Paris Review,* friend of poetry and of the people who make
it. Sadri and Katy, captain and hostess of thirty-five souls
(counting me: a listless waif still trying to get used to solitude). In the villages on the riverbanks, little boys with
smooth round heads like black grapes vie to hold my hand,
thus breaking my heart yet again. Podor, where, sitting on
the woven mats in a solemn circle, we drink camel's milk,
or pretend to, from the passed wooden bowl. And in this

amazing, blazing, crazy, hard-to-believe place (Dakar) on the edge of the Sahara, I meet Léopold Senghor, poet dear to Paris surrealists, now president of his country. He is receiving our party; it is my turn. Yes, he remembers his friend Max Ernst, and quotes him on the spot: "*A bas l'art. Vive la mode*" ("Down with Art. Long live fashion"), adding, with a dry smile, that it was premonitional, *non?* And this is Senegal!

There was the *mechoui* (lamb barbecue), under a relentless sun over our pitched Bedouin tent. And the closing evening costume party, for which I had devised a costume representing *The Story of O*, but that I do not attend, having collapsed from the heat, so that O's long chains will never be worn by me, and O's absurd story will remain safe and deadly serious with Jacques and Rosine, people to be met with here a little later.

Yet another spring, marking time in anticipation of nothing. "Morocco," said someone, deploring my inertia. "You will like it. Just two weeks. . . ." So Marrakech, and an old hotel from which visitors like me ventured daily into the souks, wandering like sleepwalkers in search of what the way out?—before getting safely back to the hotel lobby, the carpeted stairs, the burnoosed porters, the quiet room. Nothing there could tell me that this was Africa, the Africa of Flaubert, of Gide or Rimbaud, the Africa of wind and sand blowing its spell into their ears and eyes and nose. Nothing, that is, but the smell. It is what I shall always remember, that pervasive, heavy sweetness that hung like a dome over Marrakech.

Rather unbelievably, it was where I saw again, after twenty years, Dominique Eluard, who had been Paul's last wife, although I had known her only after Eluard was gone. And my mind leaping back to the one time I had met him, I saw again, and sharply, that Paris afternoon, in 1950-something, with the two men, Paul Eluard and Max Ernst, leaning together over Paul's old photo album. He was a great saver and enshriner of mementos, letters, photographs, objects, even, as I saw, a pressed something (flower)? Paul's fluttering hand turned the pages while I too leaned over these frozen images, markers of the adventures they had shared; today they were like any two old friends tenderly reviewing their past days. Poet and painter, who had both done plenty of living since those times. But that day it didn't seem to matter.

There in Marrakech, I experienced one of those rare, hallucinatory moments like the trancelike vision that can cloud the eyes in certain unfamiliar spaces. All my early fantasies of different worlds were suddenly for real in that candlelit Marrakech dining room where, against the opposite wall, sat the figure of a woman? man? in black. The inscrutable face, barely made out across the veiled candle-lit distance of little more than twenty feet, was a mask of deep intrigue that held me in thrall during the entire meal. Turbaned waiters moved around in silence on embroidered slippers; and something else, as if to complete the spell, a peculiar rhythmic whine, whether of love or lament, floated in the minty air. But then, all too soon, it was over and down to earth, as the person in black rose and came over to our low table (I was with a friend)—"*Bonjour, Dorothéa!*"—revealing in the closer light and with a smile that it was my old acquaintance, Dominique Eluard! Just Dominique. Not a man, not inscrutable at all in the candle glow that lit us and branded my feverish delusion as just another fancy.

We met several times after that. One blistering day we all looked at a house for sale in the very heart of the souk. A little door, a perfectly square courtyard, moorish tiles over all—what else?—and the calm fact of a central fountain (not working). I heard afterward that she had bought the house. Would she live there? To me, the very idea of life in a souk was not quite imaginable, even barely breathable; although it had seemed, once inside that magic postern door, that we were transferred to a hashish-dreamer's paradise of *volupté*, the sort of place one sees in those nineteenth-century pictures painted by frail European painters longing for bold lives.

A little book by Aldo Buzzi has stirred yet another memory and provoked a small mystery. Toward the end of the book he is at Lake Como, speaking of Pliny and the home he built, La Commoedia, on the lake opposite Bellagio. Having spent several intervals in a big, dreamy house, also called (Villa) la Commoedia, on that lake and, apparently, in the same area, I thrilled to the thought that it was on the same spot as the earlier one and that I might have trod the same coppices and water's edges as Pliny himself, centuries before. While there, and in friend Gretel's boat with its green canvas canopy that resembled a grown-up baby carriage, we sometimes floated across the velvety waft of languid water to Bellagio.

Bellagio: the quietest, the drowsiest, the most "retro" town I have ever seen, with its outmoded shops, its half-hearted kitsch for the occasional tourist, above all, its sovereign, almost audible melancholy. Sitting at the rickety table under exhausted-looking trees, I am almost surprised when the waiter actually brings our lemonades (a tiny piece of ice in mine) and a plate of wafers, lozenge-shaped and pale, like his own face and most of the other faces of miraculously preserved Bellagio. Then we comb the little shops—obeying the traveler's imperious need, when away from home, to buy something, anything that will encapsulate the day, snag it like a butterfly, to pin in a frame. And, in a shop where everything for sale is made of tortoise-shell—bookmarks, cigarette cases, the usual combs and hairbrushes and shoehorns—I buy a (tortoiseshell) hand mirror. Who knows? In it, one day, if I am good, I might see the face of Pliny looking back at me. (Would he smile?) I was never to know; in Paris, a few weeks later, the mirror exploded into a dozen pieces, refuting my outsized expectations.

And that was my Italy, the country I was not to know save for those earlier lightning visits: to Rome for a day so forgettable it didn't exist; to Naples, view of Etna, and as the veriest tourist, lunch with other people's friends. A *randonnée* with flash moments of ancientness and its marvels; all overlaid with a secret imagined scenario: I am sitting on the seedy verandah of a seedy hotel in Amalfi. The sea is directly below, a giddy one thousand meters. Tired morning-glory vines, moving shadows on the old marble table, on my coffee cup and my notebook. I must hold down the page that the breeze ruffles. I am alone. . . . Of course, all this was out of books, old books. But it didn't make the dream less mine.

Other displacements bridge my disarray. Sometimes it seemed I was destined to wander forever, not even able to die. Paints and brushes were more and more remote. Would I ever use them again? Perhaps in Seillans? I went, I tried. It sent me away foggier each time. Not at all sure about what now, I was hardly more than a diagram of anatomy, the stringy crimson-blue of nerves without epiderm.

Dove-gray Paris, most ineffable of cities, was still home base, where there were friends for advice: *"Dorothéa, il faut refaire ta vie"* ("You must remake your life"), meaning *with* someone. Provoking an inward shudder.

Spring 1978. A procession of pale afternoons sees me behind the graying curtains of our white rooms. No. I must learn to say "my." My rooms. In the rue de Lille. White all around, of walls and floors turning brownward gray, so mimetic to my mood. Downy goose gray, gentler than all that white. Now the real city is inside, a sift of black that I accept, all defenses down. So in my rooms, where I am polite to all. And where I am instructed as to my situation: not bad, really, if you know your place, do as you're told, do not ask questions, and remember that you are, well, a woman, a widow, and not very reliable. What am I doing here?

While some few talk of discourse, others of project, I am bubbling down into a swamp of silence far deeper than I would have thought possible. When I say "we" this and that, or "our," I am referring to what? A place, a tribe, a country? Do I identify with the human or do I just happen to be one? Happily they believe, the others who outwardly resemble me, that I am one hundred percent real. Lucky me, surrounded by them as I am, that they don't see straight through me or squash me, for it would be so easy. The social structure seems miraculously to keep chaos at bay. Most of the time we, they, don't harm each other. And if wits are sometimes sharpened on other people, all the better—I can more easily get by unnoticed.

Alone, you like to think you are on top of your situation, you now contain your loss without cracking up and you have arranged your space and your time; your wound has healed and now you will meet any exigency. But you can so easily become ridiculous; a breeze here, a gust there can topple you. Long years of trial in one column, error in the other, with small successes to spur you on in the pursuit of fearlessness. Not to mention a certain charming area of feeling that includes brief swaths of being kind to others, like holding your breath underwater.

Kindness, then, is the leitmotif of the following incident. Or is it? Reader, be the judge!

Youngest and favorite daughter of that same valiant

Yvette, our helper for eighteen years, was Rosine, fat wife and mother of three. She it was who had taken her mother's place in my house. Unlike her mama, she wore rubber gloves for dishwashing. When she pointed to a phone number or a torn collar seam her bevel-edged fingernail curved down to a yellowish-white tip of inordinate length, proving her complexity and gracing her smooth, plump hand.

For several months now she had had a lover, an older fellow whose name was Jacques. Pale blue eyes, strong, straw hair and orange beard. He would come to fetch her after she had finished pushing the vacuum around. He never failed to dart his pale blue stare about the rooms and to bow to me if I was there. *"Mes hommages, madame."*

I had smiled on their affair, even lent them a tiny attic room that belonged to the apartment. Why not, poor Rosine, so young and all that childbearing, a mule for a husband? Nothing but work since she was fourteen. Married at fifteen, with a big balloon already growing inside her, she was, as all of them in her milieu, eager to be a *madame*, never to have her ears boxed again. *Oui, madame.* To be mistress of a home as well as of the man in its bed. Such was their formula for escape, consolidated by the arrival of the infant. A second and a third followed in quick succession, along with certain cruel deceptions, mostly about the lack of money and the brutality of husbands. Hungry little mouths sent her back to work, to ride the subway at seven in the morning. Her handsomely painted eyes told her that the city was full of men.

It was on a Saturday afternoon that I answered the phone and heard a gruff voice:

"It's Jacques," and, as I hesitated: "Rosine's Jacques."

"But this is Saturday. Rosine is not here."

"Madame, I need to see you. It's about Rosine."

Oh dear. Good, foolish, faithless Rosine. Half a dozen guesses tumbled through me. Rosine is pregnant. Rosine is unmasked. Jacques is unmasked by his wife. Rosine is violent. Rosine is leaving him. . . . How to refuse? The phone was breathing from a padded booth where Jacques, Rosine's Jacques, appealed for help.

"What is wrong? She is ill. . . ."

"No, madame. I can't say it now. I need to see you."

So odd, in a way, and on a Saturday. Intrigued, then, I say three-thirty. I will listen, I will do what I can. No kindly employer would do less. And yet, sitting by the phone in a blurred, uneasy quiet, I gloomed over these alien pieces of life that, though so near, were terribly far from me.

On the stroke of three-thirty, there he was, Rosine's Jacques, leather bomber jacket, motorcycle helmet, pigskin gloves, which he removed. With obsequious mien, he inclined slightly before the weight of my kindliness. And I, to myself, dear God, am I being conspiratorial?

"Ah, Jacques, come in, come in." The understanding lady of the house showed him in. We sat at a table. "So you have problems." I am all sympathy. A short silence. He looks straight at me with his ice-blue eyes.

"No, madame. I have no problems. That is to say—"

"Then what is it with Rosine?" I am all ears, but careful.

At this he shifts in his chair; the straw beard, the blue stare crowding me oddly, and something else, a tic: the left eyebrow jumping up and down with his words. He is saying that something is "very difficult." Then:

"Rosine is not a woman." He lets this sink in. "You understand, madame. I must do it all."

Believe me, reader, I am really perplexed, and, registering my amazement, he goes on: "Oh, don't get me wrong. I adore Rosine. But she is not a woman."

"But what on earth is she then?" The certainty, as I asked, that he was referring to sexual matters did not deter me in this plunge toward an involvement that I believed to be kind and salutary. For whom? Selfless concern, an impulse to help Rosine, was losing its outline, turning into kinky ambiguity that I did nothing to banish. On the contrary, I added, "Oh I know she is not sophisticated . . ."

"Exactly," said Jacques, the eyebrow twitching faster. "And I have to change that. I have already made some progress. But I cannot do it alone." You would think he was building a bridge. "It's time for . . . well, it is very, very difficult, madame, to find , , , you see . . ." And here he leans forward with elbows on the table, and the pale eyes look hard into mine. "I want Rosine to make love with a woman."

Steady. "But why do you tell me that?" I brought out.

"I thought there might, perhaps, be someone in your circle. Oh, I would be present, of course." And as he murmured these words his gaze moved like a chess piece to the square on the wall above us where hung my painting *Family Portrait,* a handsome (I thought) drift of nudes. My circle? I thought of friend Roberto who spent afternoons in porno movie houses, later describing, to our amusement, the antics of these naked actors, as if he had been watching protozoa: the working, jerking, undulating, merging of connective tissue. He made us laugh. Spooky Roberto. No help there.

"My *circle!* This is indeed strange. You do not know anything about my friends, or even who they are. As for your special needs, there are *places* in Paris for these things." (I wasn't so dumb.) "You must know that."

He seemed not to want to hear. "It is very, very difficult," he repeated. Watching me again: "You wouldn't know of anyone?"

As he brought out his insane words I felt more and more removed from the table, the room—a slow reverse zoom that put odious Jacques way down at the end of a long corridor, though keeping him in dreadful focus. A funny torpor was washing over me; I could have been watching a show unfold its tinny plot.

According to Georges Bataille, the terrible needs of desire can confer extraordinary audacity. In fact, Max's old friend would have regarded the present dialogue as a glistening example of triumphant eroticism. He would not have completely disapproved of the situation, nor would he have considered the demands of my visitor unreasonable. He would certainly have deplored my naïveté. He would shake his head at my starchy remarks. Would he think to discover hypocrisy there, a secret attraction to the abject? So far, I had shown neither.

Still carried along by a bizarre sense of revelation while filling my role of confidante—because that is what I had now become—I told this man that I was sorry (can you imagine that? Sorry!) but: "I cannot help you."

The fellow was not ready to accept my gracious regrets. There was a mulish frown on his ginger-haired face. "Madame, if you will permit me . . . I had thought . . . well, Rosine told me . . ."

"What did Rosine tell you?"

"She said you were making a costume for a masquerade. She said you were going to wear a leather collar and a long chain."

Good God! It was true. I had asked Rosine to shop around for a weightless, probably plastic, chain. I would wear these foolish trappings to that costume party mentioned earlier. How could I know that Rosine would tell her paramour all about it, and that they would ponder it seriously? This time it was me who laughed.

"Oh, yes. Sure. I did make such a costume. A disguise."

"You were disguised as—?"

"It is of no importance. You wouldn't know. From a character in a book called *L'Histoire d'O.*"

"You see!"—a snort of exultation here. "I have been reading from it to Rosine every afternoon."

"No, no. You must understand. Not like that." The trap was narrowing, a closing elevator door, with us two in the cage. "Not seriously—it was a *costume*. For laughs." But it was no use. The facts were there: I had dressed as O. They were reading *The Story of O*. There was a stifling inference of concupiscence, we were all in this together, were we not—the wretched book a common bond?

My artist's vision spurted fuzzy images in kinetic profusion, none of them quite coming into focus, all of them hideous, hiding behind each other, far into the shadows and so shielding their ambiguous burdens. They say that when you are in mortal danger your whole life passes in review before your eyes. Indeed, I saw no real danger here. But something of the sort was happening. It almost made me laugh to see those momentous pictures of the past being jostled by Jacques's trashy merchandise of the future. Everything tumbled together. Past and possible ticked each other off like a lightning game of tic-tac-toe. It took only a fraction of a second. He was talking on. Inference was still impersonal but the air was charged. Proceed with caution.

"Of course," he was saying, as a doctor talks to his patient, "it is good to laugh. But *L'Histoire d'O*—"

"What made you come to me?" I cut in. "Was it the costume?"

"Only partly, madame. I have admired your paintings. It seemed to me that the author of such paintings . . ."

This was too much. Coldly at last, I repeated that I could do nothing for him and stood up.

"*Dommage*" was his sad rejoinder. But after a moment, he said, "Madame, there is something else I want to say to you."

Each of his revelations was offered as a precious object, well polished for the occasion, carefully unwrapped, set

down between us with ceremony. At my troubled nod he
went on: "Ever since the first day I saw you, when I came
for Rosine, and you were here, in your painting apron,
well, madame, ever since that day I have desired you."
That is what he said, *desired*, the French way.

The melancholy declaration faded as I sang my old
tune: "I cannot help you."

We both rose as he said *"Dommage"* once more, and
gathered up his helmet and gloves. I saw him to the door,
where he turned before going out, tucked the helmet
under his left arm, took my right hand in his, and planted
a deep, wet kiss upon it, saying, as he did so, that I was to
remember what he had offered, in case I should change
my mind, and, by the way, not to mention his visit to
Rosine, who might not understand.

You can't control the way people look at your paintings. You can't change their interpretive strategies. If they
wear Freudian-colored spectacles, for instance, they see
your picture stamped like a piece of tin to fit a couple of
crude categories. Right away, the gimlet eye is turned on
the artist to dig around in her psyche. And sure enough, a
telltale scrap of something—a stubbed toe at age ten, a
cross word from Dad at twelve—and there is enough
material to analyze you out of existence. But this time it
was the pictures that had betrayed me. They were all at
once suspect, false friends. I seemed to find in them intimations that I had never seen before. They had connived
with the insipid couple to make me ridiculous, their beautiful colors a thin skin hiding—what? One after the other

I gazed at them, asking questions to which I received only the cagiest answers. Before today they had been my testament, my profession of faith, my comments on life and death. Tonight I hated them.

There I was, alone with my tumult. The amused fascination I had felt during the interview gave way to an immense confusion. Had I been too kind? Was the man a ghoul or only a cheeky voluptuary lured to my door by his wrongheaded interpretation of my work and my life? The little widow, alone in her web. In the hour I had devoted to him nothing had been found, nothing solved. But if there was gain, was it not mine? For I had lived through one of those charged moments that bear remembering. . . . For such a one as Jacques, love was the Act with frills, no more. Indeed, what did it matter: fat or thin, young or old? So bleak it seemed to me that I suddenly felt sorry for them.

Incidentally, it may be said here that although I have never known erotic love with a woman, I think it might have been quite as rewarding as any other kind. To be enfolded by smooth round arms in that subtle sort of entwinement; to do anything else that would have defined our tender passion for each other; I might have liked that. We would have had celestial orgasms, profound quietudes, and perfect understanding. We would have known, without utterance, our common frailty and ferocity—so endless a treasure of potential. (One time, at a New Year's party, a pretty girl jumped into the ladies'-room stall with me and, kissing me rather fiercely, murmured, "You're mine, you're mine." Although I kissed back, I guess I wasn't hers, because I didn't keep the date I made with her for the next afternoon.)

Monday was as usual; of course I said nothing. Poor Rosine. Every time I watched her move about her small chores, a kind of distress would seize me; for, despite her dainty ways, so contrasted with the great, high hips and truly monumental breasts, she seemed more and more innocent and childlike with her little elegancies as she stepped across the carpets in perfect ignorance of my knowing what I now knew.

Rosine left soon afterward to live full-time with Jacques. A detail: when I went to the tiny abandoned attic I discovered a flesh-colored, high-pile wall-to-wall carpet laid down over the floor tiles. In such ways, exigencies are dealt with. Where would she be tomorrow? How long would Jacques content himself with her earnest efforts at originality in sex? One thing is certain: it is not often that one finds absolute obedience in another. So she would perhaps be treasured, smiling out from Jacques's slow-moving car in the Bois de Boulogne, where the evenings have always just begun.

Friends are near, of course. But I am a floating island. And Paris recedes a little more every day, leaving me to shift in the fluid of simple sorrow. Soon, even sorrow is arid.

Now it is a year later, 1979, and I am returning to New York (it takes time) as naturally as a pigeon; where I practice conformity, the finest freedom. You sit on chairs or stand in shoes, sometimes with something in your hand like a knife or, say, a glass of liquid that you don't spill or throw but bring precisely to your lips from time to time, taking small sips. You are presenting a pleasant facial expression—this of course when you are with them and, funnily enough, even sometimes when you are alone, taking the small sips exactly in the same way and standing, but without the tight shoes. Although this, too, is not sure, for the shoes are sometimes left on the feet, quite conveniently satisfying the need for small pain.

Ah yes, if I obey the laws, written and unwritten, official, stately, natural, or tribal, then I will not be harmed, my body will remain intact, will not be dismembered like the bodies of reckless grasshoppers who grew bold and let themselves be caught only to lose a big green leg and then how would I leap from place to place?

So, if now, at this late moment and pulling into the stretch, I take on the wiliest, trickiest, most daunting subject—the painting of a picture—the first question is: how. To imagine it, then to do it. All you need is courage and a space—here, there, wherever your heart and hands have taken you (in my case, to another land, another city: New York, where everything began long ago).

A fat mushroom cloud interposes its load of smog and no one wants to name the thing, the close-boned fundamental experience. It is big. An upheaval. It demands stamina; it involves a wrenching, exalted, pulverizing process that could be called making something out of nothing. Your heart beats fast—after all, you could fail—

you give everything you think you have—inside and out-side. It is a solitary business.

The beginning is uneasy. Only witness: the studio where an event is about to take place. Not proud, not humble, not at all certain of anything nor yet uncertain, you play with the light, although there is no need, so filled is your inner vision with promise, the kind that shifts behind your eyes in and out of focus.

There is confidence, too, in what would appear at first to be a gestural rite but soon reveals itself as a contempla-tion. With questions about the millions of ways it can hap-pen, yes, but withholding the answers you long for. Or do you? Perhaps you already have the answer you want to give. Because pride is there, too. How sure you are! How calm, even heedless!

To stand back and see what has been done, to know it is and will be unique, everyone wants it deep down, wants it more than anything. Not everyone will say so. Instead, on a studio visit, you are likely to be treated to a kind of professional modesty on the part of the artist, who, far from jumping up and down and beating himself on the chest, is silent and studious, something like a researcher in a science lab, complete with serious glasses on a chain, sneakers, spotty coveralls, mysterious beakers emanating formulae—stylish clichés ready for the TV.

One thing is certain: no one else could bring it off, your picture. How could anyone? The very smallest touch, the smudge called up from your own cache of smudges, the bold swath you will dare to trace across a rectangular surface, these are yours. They invite, they menace, they defy while you pause. You are a crowded closet piled with chaos, yet you know that just behind the door is an arrow pointing to the one splendid sweet line you think you need, the stroke that will take over and multiply until, the it having become a they, you have found a way out. Grasp it. It is your fingerprint, your whorled map. All unnoticed then comes choice, because, and here is where the unpredictable begins, you will choose. Not all at once, not one choice. But at every moment, every move, every thought and every fraction of thought, facet-flashing, swifter than swift. Such banquets of signs seen, never before seen, authentic all the same.

And the perils! Your hand may falter, misunderstand. A grubby stain, a wrong swath, and the humiliation of bowing, bending, taking it out. Or, having left it in, a looking away, and the certainty that all is lost, irrevocably. No, stop! This cannot happen.

Thus I have come one morning to the studio, into the litter and debris of last week and the day before. Tables hold fast under their load of tubes and brushes, cans and bottles interspersed with hair roller pins, that view of Delft, a stapler, a plastic tub of gypsum powder, a Polaroid of two dogs, green flashbulbs for eyes, a postcard picturing the retreating backs of six nudists on a eucalyptus-shaded path, a nibless pen, an episcope. On the floor or on the wall or on the easel, a new surface waits whitely.

Battle green, blood geranium, rubbed bloody black, drop of old rain. The canvas lies under my liquid hand. Explosia, a new planet invented with its name. That's what we paint for, invention. Unheard-of news, flowers, or flesh. "Not a procedure," I say to the room. "Nothing to do with twenty-four hours: just an admixture for all five senses, the sixth one to be dealt with separately."

Because this is only the beginning. A long flashed life, as they say, before dying. I am a fish swimming upstream. At the very top I deposit my pictures; then I die as they ripen and hatch and swim down, very playfully, because they are young and full of big ideas. Down and down and, finally, among the people who like to fish pictures, they are caught and devoured by millions of eyes.

In this artist's dream-plot there are only artist-scales, iridescent though they may be. And the rest? For thirty-five years, life was love, a second skin. Authoritative, instinctual love. Now life is life, sybaritic, an absolutely polished structure of skeletal simplicity. Uninvolved, uncommitted, underworn, deeply and evenly breathed. Its second plot, not life but art, unfolds painty wings each day to try the air, pushing out perhaps reluctant visions, uninvolved, yes, unaware of their public category.

It is one of those days and there is still time to reconsider. Time to turn inside out before the first gesture. You have drawn up a stool and sit gazing at the whiteness, feeling suddenly vulnerable and panic-stricken before your lighthearted intention. What has happened, where is the euphoria, the confidence of five minutes ago? Why is certainty receding like distance, eluding you, paling out to leave the whiteness as no more than a pitiless color? Is a canvas defiant, sullen? Something must be done.

Ambivalent feelings, then, for the blank rectangle. On one hand the innocent space, possibilities at your mercy, a conspiracy shaping up. You and the canvas are in this together. Or are you? For, seen the other way, there is something queerly hostile, a void as full of resistance as the trackless sky, as mocking as heat lightning. If it invites to conspiracy it also coldly challenges to battle.

Quite mechanically during these first moments—hours?—the little bowl has been filled with things like turpentine and varnish; tubes of color have been chosen, like jewels on a tray, and squeezed, snaky blobs, onto a paper palette. The beautiful colors give heart. Soon they will explode. A shaft of cobalt violet. With echoes from alizarin and titanium and purple—which is really red. There is orange from Mars, mars orange. The sound of their names, like planets: cerulean and earthshadow, raw or burnt; ultramarine out of the sea, barite and monacal and vermilion. Siren sounds of cochineal and dragon's blood, and gamboge and the lake from blackthorn berries that draw you after them; they sing in your ear, promising that merely to dip a brush in their suavities will produce a miracle.

What does it matter that more often than not the artist is dashed against the rocks and the miracle recedes, a dim phosphorescence? Something has remained: the picture that has taken possession of the cloth, the board, the wall. No longer a blind surface, it is an event, it will mark a day in a chaotic world and will become order. Calm in its commotion, clear in its purpose, voluptuous in its space.

Here it is, seduction taking the place of awe. After a quick decision—was it not planned in the middle of the night along with your subject and its thrust?—a thin brush is chosen, is dipped and dipped again—madder, violet, gold ocher. A last stare at the grim whiteness before taking the plunge, made at last with the abandon "of divers," said Henry James, speaking of birds, "not expecting to rise again." Now, after only seconds, blankness and nothingness are routed forever.

A hundred forms loom in charming mock dimensions to lure you from your subject, the one that demands to be painted; with each stroke (now there are five brushes in two hands) a thousand other pictures solicit permanence. Somewhere the buzzer buzzes faintly. Sounds from the street drift up, the drone of a plane drifts down. The phone may have rung. A loud his has here h loud came and went.

The beleaguered canvas is on the floor. Colors are merging. Cobalt and chrome bridge a gap with their knowing nuances. Where is the cadmium red-orange? The tubes are in disorder, their caps lost, their labels smeared with wrong colors.

Oh, where is the red-orange, for it is at this moment the only color in the world and Dionysus the only deity.

Now there is no light at all in the studio. The day is packing up, but who cares? With a voice of its own the canvas hums a tune for the twilight hour, half heard, half seen. Outlines dance; sonic eyes bid you watch out for surprises that break all the rules: white on black making blue; space that deepens with clutter; best of all, the fierce, ambivalent human contour that catches sound and sight and makes of me a slave. Ah, now the world will not be exactly as it was this morning! Intention has taken over and here in this room leans a picture that is at last in league with its painter, hostilities forgotten. For today.

As brushes are cleaned and windows opened to clear the turpentine air, the artist steals glances—*do not look too long*—at the living, breathing picture, for it is already a picture. Once again lighthearted, even lightheaded, the mood is vaporous. There are blessed long hours before tomorrow.

An evening may be full of silence or din, it is merely separate. Then a lamplit hour as I prepare for sleep, without braking even one out of all the flashing thoughts that cross my mind as fast as auto racers crossing the finish line, with always another one just behind to take its place. Did I attend that opening? Outlines of persons who occupied the event, whatever it was, clamor for attention. Jagged cutouts of people that I repair; I follow the slashed ribbons of their lives and of their possible lives, of what they did, do, and might do—to say nothing of what and who they were, wore, are and will be, may be. Remembering their chatter:

"Artists are mothers. If you don't admire their works they hate you."

"More like evangelists. Only instead of selling God we are selling ourselves. Remember: the idle painter winneth no fame."

"What an attitude! Better deal with that word *avant-garde!* There was such a thing, it came along with the century. They were breaking ground."

"You mean throwing everything."

"Even words. You would not believe their irreverence. The tone was boisterous. They risked plague and taboo but they said it was nothing."

"Ah, then you mean dada. Yes. It was called a movement—terrible word. An explosion spurting revolt like lava. A matter of six or seven years. Until the lava turned into cinder blocks."

It was to be expected. We look at *les Fauves* and wonder why the name. Such earnest, good work. . . . It was dada that rocked the boat, spawned surrealism while standing on its head: dada, art's fragmentation bomb. Who could have foreseen its present avatar as favorite game of postgraduates and artists in thrall to the instant immortality of found objects?

Movements have short shelf lives—ten, fifteen years. Then they dry or, worse, stiffen. But while they last there is no ceiling. Surrealism was a not-quite-spontaneous combustion. No flags waved, no slogans defiled its fabric, no cards were carried. No attentive scholars to monitor the madness. (That came later.) No museums, no art freaks would touch it. No PR—indeed, what could that be?

The only movement smashed by international war,

this quivering experiment in psychic discovery could not survive the storm. Minds were slaughtered or maimed along with bodies. Survivors climbed onto the raft outwardly safe, inwardly shattered.

Thus as we have seen, some of them got to New York. But surrealism was never the same. And to Breton's disbelief a few of its brightest lights stayed on to become Americans, while he, staunch captain of his sinking ship, returned to sit daily in the same café, surrounded by the young pedants who had replaced his banished (or simply vanished) fellow souls, wanting until the very end to believe they were as real. Indulgent, he listened. Their staccato pirouettes glanced like pebbles off the rock of his implacable intelligence. He waited, sad, polite.

In August 1949 we, too, are there with him. An epitome of desuetude, the café is deserted except for the surrealists. It is a dim dark-wood-and-mirror kind of place indistinguishable from thousands of other cafés across the city. There sit the surrealists, votaries all, typecast around the table. As Goethe in Weimar, Dante on that Florentine bridge, Freud in his Vienna, a tall blind house. Or there, on the place Blanche with André Breton. Before each one a grail of a sort: Ricard, Cinzano, Noilly Prat, even Coke— "*saleté chimique*" ("chemical filth"), pronounces Benjamin Peret, Breton's closest buddy—all iceless.

I spoke little French then. Imagine how I must have appeared, hunched against Max's shoulder for hours in that café where Breton reigned over a dozen excitable windbags strenuously imitating the pronouncements of their chief, my ears positively standing forth, my face arranged in what I hoped was a knowing expression! Then, like faithless groupies, we began playing hooky, Max and I, attending less and less often, finally not at all. Until, in 1954, the Venetian sin, the *primo premio* that brought Max's "exclusion" from the surrealist group. He seemed not to notice except for a snort of derision.

A few are still around to wonder aghast at the spectacle of drought that has replaced all that mad, luxuriant, explosive, howling weather that came to mean avant-garde. The vanguard. Adopted now like an orphan, its brash upheavals channeled, its cyclones harnessed. A tag word, appropriated, stripped, meaningless as the label in a shirt.

Have I slept? Once again before the daubed canvas, which is now upright in the harsh morning light. I am aghast. How could anyone have found it good, even a good start? Traitorous twilight, fostering those balloons of pride that had floated all over the studio! Yesterday ended in a festival, was positively buoyant. Syncopating with glances canvasward, brush cleaning drudgery was a breeze (a hellish task after a failed day). Now you are bound. The canvas is to be reckoned with. It breathes, however feebly. It whispers a satanic suggestion for the fast, easy solution. "Others have done it, do it, why not you?" How to explain? There is no fast and easy for me.

Daily depths of depression, as familiar as a limp is to

the war-wounded, are followed by momentary exaltations, sometimes quiet certainties: Yeah, that's it. . . . But if that is it, then the presence . . . on . . . the other side . . . all changed now, dark again. . . . Must wait for tomorrow. . . . Oh God. . . . How awful. . . .

It is not all joy as they would have us believe. The bearded fellow in his dungarees, his battered straw hat, his eyes full of stars and flowers and flesh, and the hand, his hand. . . . The good life holds him in its green rosy circle, in its sunny embrace; unheeded flies zoom about his head like tiny planes waiting their turn to land, and from the comfy kitchen of the rugged old house issues a blue-aproned someone bearing a cup of wine or is it milk (depending on the age of the artist)? The coffee-table books are full of them: The Artist in His Studio, the soaring sky-windowed studio which he has caused to be built, or the loft he has found, the barn he has remodeled, with north light; the photogenic studio that contains his past failures (over there in the closet) and his future triumphs; contains, too, his dedication and his optimism: bubbles in the perfect light that falls on the often empty canvas with a blinding crash of reproach.

Several days have left their gestural arabesques in the big room, adding up to clutter and despondency. Dust has been raised in the lens of the eye; intention has softened to vagary.

Then an idea in the night brings its baggage to the morning. Welcome! Go ahead. Stare at the canvas already occupied by wrong paint, hangdog. But not for long. Not this time. Because you dive—with an intake of breath you dive, deep into your forest, your desert, your dream.

Now the doors are all open, the air is mother-of-pearl, and you know the way to tame a tiger. It will not elude you today, for you have grabbed a brush, you have dipped it almost at random, so high is your rage, into the amalgam of color, formless on a docile palette.

As you drag lines like ropes across one brink of reality after another, annihilating the world you made yesterday and hated today, a new world heaves into sight. Again the event progresses without benefit of hours.

Before the emerging picture there is no longer panic to shake heart and hand, only a buzzing in your ears to mark rather unconvincingly the passage of time. You sit or stand, numb in either case, or step backward, bumping as often as not into forgotten objects dropped on the floor. You coax the picture out of its cage along with personae, essences, its fatidic suggestion, its insolence. Friend or enemy? Tinged with reference—alas, as outmoded these days as your easel—weighted as the drop of rain that slid on the window, it swims toward completion. Evening soaks in unnoticed until lengthening shadows have caressed every surface in the room, every hair on your head, and every shape in your painted picture.

The application of color to a support, something to talk about when it's all over, now holds you in thrall. The act is your accomplice. So are the tools, beakers, bottles, knives, glues, solubles, insolubles, tubes, plasters, cans; there is no end. . . .

Time to sit down. Time to clean the brushes, now become a kindly interlude. Time to gaze and gaze; you can't get enough of it because you are now on the outside looking in. You are merely the visitor, grandly invited: "Step in."

"Oh, I accept." Even though the twilight has faded to black and blur, making sooty phantoms of your new companions, you accept. Feeling rather than seeing, you share exuberance. You are surprised and uneasy when you seem to hear the rather conspiratorial reminder that it was, after all, your hand, your will, your turmoil that has produced it all, this brand-new event in a very old world.

Thus you may think: Have I brought a little order out of chaos? Or have I merely added to the general confusion? Either way a mutation has taken place. You have not painted in a vacuum. You have been bold, working for change. To overturn values. The whirling thought: change the world. It directs the artist's daily act. Yes, modesty forbids saying it. But say it secretly. You risk nothing.

This last additional touch with the light failing and when you thought you had done with it; you so believe what you have done when you have not done it at all: it has simply *pulled away*, detached itself from you like the ineffable division of a cell. You watch its final separation in the fading day with a nod of recognition, for you see that after all your *sixth sense* has been dealt with.

What is to be made of this, O analyzers? Is some help needed? Doesn't the paint say it all? What am I after? A long time ago I said that I want to seduce by means of imperceptible passages from one reality to another. The viewer is caught in a net from which there is no escape save by going through the whole picture until he comes to the exit. My wish: to make a trap (picture) with no exit at all either for you or for me.

Is this possible? Perhaps I must resign myself to failure in this. But in the long foregoing description of my states of being and working, I feel there is much that will be familiar to any painter (or poet?) whose vision includes leaving the door open to the subconscious, our other life. *Insomnias*, for example, the work that literally splintered away from those early paintings, was the first in a series of pure experiments where paint and perception are lost in each other. Twenty years and many pictures later, *Notes for an Apocalypse* appeared at first like a reference to the early work. A long table—was it the childhood Sunday table when the pastor came to dinner, the one that got covered with first a pad, and then the great gleaming white table-cloth shaken out and laid down, the folds smoothed out to make a gentle grid from end to end? Is the grid in my painting still trying to prove something, to reassure, to bring order out of confusion and to anchor its turbulent images? Once, years ago, a writer referring to an earlier work of mine (*Some Roses and Their Phantoms*, 1952) used the word "Eucharist." Wrong again, I thought then. But the Sunday tablecloth . . .

In my inquiring mind there was nothing to prevent a change of pace, of figuration, of territory, when a new white rectangle waited in front of me. Would it not, then and always, be my reflection and my world, with or without disguises? Would it serve any purpose to list here my visionary obsessions, their avatars, their shapes, their bid for communication? Could I even know myself why my evolving canvas contained a dog instead of a horse or a house and why the dog was howling? I could say that with each painting new discoveries in the process made me bolder in my dialogue with the medium. There was so much to try and to conquer.

Reference seems to be a dangerous word among today's artists, but an indispensable one for the art writers (I spare them the tag "critic") who must, like large-eared flying elephants, have something to hold on to. I have loved and venerated my references or influences. But to name them would take another book—not just an art book but a book as packed with images as the human brain. Besides, I believe that since Duchamp no one can say "first." Let us just be satisfied with, even grateful for, "latest"—latest in our never-ending hunt for revealment.

CHAPTER ELEVEN

*Unfinished
Picture*

Lying in bed too long can give rise to some very mediocre thinking, to untrustworthy feelings, even misapplied musings such as the kind of fractioned attention I have been giving in far too equal measure to the writing of this memoir and to my half-finished picture in the studio. Especially when recalling those violent hesitations, mountaintop, lake-bottom searches in the slippery psyche, when I opted for the life of a painter. You would think that had settled it. So it did. Like everyone, I balanced, chose: doctor-lawyer-merchant-chief, all lackluster titles it seemed then if you held them alongside artist-poet dancer actor orator acrobat. Although that too is a beggarly comparison, inaccurate. I want to suggest trembling youth with all the world waiting for you alone. No need to hide anymore behind strategic answers. No need to hesitate. God knows there are plenty of doors ajar for us all. Enter! Enter I did—the painter's door. Could I push the writer's door too? It always struck me as dangerous. It is still dangerous. Ah, this is where I should have put that tightrope, anachronism that it is, up there with just two ways to fall. Two siren songs. And this is noteworthy, central as the Great Divide: On one side I saw only voluptuous magic, constant explosion of possibility, stunning prodigies to be achieved in states of swoon and euphoria. On the other side was a labyrinth of wily, shifting, seductive, powerful, razzle-dazzle words that would either elude and mock me like a rank outsider or wrap me up in other people's *trouvailles,* as in a used mink coat from the thrift shop.

A vow was made to resist the lure of words, save for the blessed nightly entry into one's own burrow where thoughts rush in their trajectory from brain to beyond and scintillate giddily before they disappear forever. Unless, of course, they are snagged along the way, scratched onto paper, in the dark or not, as I am scratching now, to be considered in the morning when they will so often reveal themselves as husks of thoughts, crushingly insignificant. And was I not right, after all, to choose a path having little to do with erudition, of which I had, at twenty, virtually none? So pretentious, in a way, to try for something without it having been bestowed on one like a blessing. To have picked it up here and there, rather stealthily, yes, like snitching the towels in a good hotel. Or a spoon. The one you weren't born with.

Words were cutthroat, I thought back then. They pretended innocence, deviously danced and postured around me, but I wasn't so dumb. I knew they could bludgeon, and that they were often joyless. Paintings can fail but all is

not lost. Failed painters survive rather happily. They have
such a good time doing it, their friends love them, especially when having their portraits painted, and in the end,
if it doesn't pan out, can hide the thing in the closet
before the doorbell rings. Some of these creations blossom
in the street shows. "The beggars are displaying their
wounds," says my cruel friend Wes Strombeck.

My balancing act—writer? artist?—obviously never
quite came to an end. In the beginning, prevailing circumstances and my ready talent for drawing had as much
to do with the weighing scales as my bloated ambitions:
although the circumstances were bleak, the talent for
drawing was my open sesame to the cities and to their limitless promise. Spare time (Chicago) or full time (New
York and after), my creative activities were delightfully
double. Back in Galesburg one talked about something
called split personality. An affliction to be dealt with. How
many times one had worried about possibly having it, like
AIDS, and now how serenely you acknowledge it—why,
what luck to have two personalities instead of only one! In
order that your Hyde may rampage in brutal phrases your
Jekyll dutifully watches his syntax and never throws in a
word without first looking it up and stamping its passport
(A metaphor easily transferable to painting.)

Woman, I believe, is doted with two personalities, the
outside one and the inside one. She is the fire at the earth's
center. But for some that isn't enough. She would also like
to be a man. Or maybe replace him. In offices and board-
rooms; in uniforms and on garbage trucks. . . . Reading in

Nabokov that "nature expects any full-grown man to accept the two black voids, fore and aft, as stolidly as he accepts the extraordinary visions in between," I understand that I am "man" and I appreciate the phrase as being applied to myself. "We" created the word "man." We also created the word "brontosaurus." And "woman." A refinement? Double-talk? Or just a vagary of language?

Meanwhile the letters keep coming. A sea wave. The Movement washes over me, an unwary beachcomber; it pulls, drags, coerces, demands my solidarity, my *admission* of sisterhood. Looming large in my corner is the phenomenon of Women Painters. This category of endeavor, painting, has somehow captured the hearts of numerous champions of the cause. There seems to exist among them a belief that if women can paint they can do anything. People who never bothered with pictures before are now organizing woman exhibitions in every corner of the land as well as in foreign climes. They are feverish. They are scholarly. The exhibitions are documented and prefaced with five-pound catalogues on slick paper. Superbly undaunted by the shortage of quality material, they make up for it with long historico-analytical hyperbole about shadowy feminine painters of the shadowy past. ("In St. Médard des Prés, 1847, a tomb was found which contains the remains of a woman encaustic painter, surrounded by her materials and cauteria." From *The Artist's Handbook*, a manual.)

If I fail to answer their letters they write again. They love to argue. Some even get nasty and bawl me out in what I sense is a state of hysteria (thus proving their femininity). One of these organizers, writing from Italy, suggested that possibly my reluctance to participate in the exhibition was based on shame, that perhaps I didn't have anything good enough and that I need not be afraid to admit it.

I do admit that I have enjoyed answering some of these letters. They bring out the worst in me. "A medical exam," I said once, "should be a condition for inclusion—above all today when imposture is so rife that a woman exhibitor could turn out to be only a man." Things like that.

What is to be done short of revamping the whole human species? Oh, I've had a few ideas: shared possibility of pregnancy, for instance, to eliminate a lot of imbalance. Rape, for one, would disappear. Alas, useless musings. Not only useless, I am an enemy in absentia. Blacklisted by clique and claque. But there they are, these pictures that have no place in our biological morass, our mouse fate. Instead they are pirate maps, diagrams for mutiny. Compasses for farther regions. My never-never land? If you will.

Which brings me to Eros, the companion invariably assigned to me by the experts who are always ready with explanation, a kindness in a way, to tell me what I am painting, what is leaking out from under my fingers, all unconsciously. He, the god, is known to be blindfolded. We are both blindfolded, everyone is blindfolded, stumbling, groping, doomed. The fancy well-washed machine we call the body, its parts expected to mesh impeccably, *as is proper,* according to its powers and its limits; the machine admired, polished, enjoyed for its elegance, more or less loved. But heavy, watery, not a little absurd, running to keep up. There is wanton waste of hours to gain minutes. Perfect diagrams of rites having to do with skin, eyes, hair, secretions and excretions drawn up and scrupulously observed.

Oddest of all, the sad little procession of analyzers, trudging toward the altar of libido, singing their quavering hymns from the open books of people like Sigmund Sang Froid (Max's pun). For example, some paintings of mine that I had believed to be a testimony to the premise that we are waging a desperate battle with unknown forces are in reality dainty feminine fantasies bristling with sex symbols. Elsewhere, two rows of terrible teeth on one of my sculptures become, under these beady eyes, incredibly, a vulva. A statue that I thought was a moment of grace is the male member, this doubtless because it is standing up instead of lying down (O vanity). Death's face, which I fear, looks out at me from many of my pictures. But it is often mistaken by these hot-blooded writers for the face of lubricity. Though they can spot Eros every time, they see no one else. Who is hung up here, the artist or the viewer? Meanwhile there is the private daily amazement, which is still mine.

Another reason for shunning words—and this is not mere faintheartedness—was that I wasn't sure I wanted to reveal myself: crazy, sly, erratic, excessive, hopeless me, to give up the rag of reserve that, with careful ironing and frequent mending, had covered me so far. Writers are so transparent, I told myself. They tell it all. They become callous. There is not a corner of their soul where they don't rummage without mercy, snorkelers wrenching out private hunks of coral to serve up in some written context or other. A real self-rape. When they walk into a room you know *all* about them, the public persons, the transparent authors. You remember certain nuggets: fact or fiction? You think, ah, that one. Like identifying a species of gold-fish pushing around in its bowl with the others, gay little strings of syllables dangling from their bellies. The trouble is, I have now joined the swimmers.

Then there is the overwhelming final reason: emotivity. The fact is, a mere word can break my heart. So that a lot of them, dredged up from my own tender self, day after day, would destroy me. In a life defined by dearth, my ever-ready tears have provided opulence of a very superior kind. Whatever joys I may have longed for, surely none could have approached in conferment of sheer transport the shedding of tears. Abundant feeling, in fact, drenched the most acute delights as well as the cruellest privations. (Even iridescent, as I could conjure them when as a small child I was put to bed at night. Squinting through forced tears at the night light I could make long rainbows stretch out from the flame of the turned-down gas jet.) Over the years, knowing so many who could not weep, I have come to appreciate my sorrowing, or at least to view it with calm. Too, it has been the very true expression of my abiding, my utterly crushing sense of doom.

For a while I kept a diary, trying to put it all down, showing thereby some sort of resistance and even vaguely hoping that my pen would, in recording the components of the equation, penetrate its mystery. But it didn't do anything of the sort. A quite shattering experiment, it merely aggravated the sorrow and riled up the ooze at the bottom of my own familiar, beloved, impenetrable, shivering abyss. Along with abstract grief I battled with the conviction that nothing good ever happened to me that would not have to be paid for in some harsh way sooner or later. And that an inflexible unknown would calculate and collect my debts (except when I was with Max, who succeeded for a while in making me believe that this was not true).

My third spring in New York rolled around. Since returning from France I had been adjusting more or less to a condition that would be permanent: that of a solitary person. Brittle as glass and unshatterproof as an egg, I trod with caution. Don't look back if you don't want to be turned into something else. Because my selfhood seemed all I had left, and this, too, was shaky. For the other, strangely unreal inhabitants of my featureless high-rise rental, I was surely just as invisible.

You lay aside ardor, hope, and other impedimenta; you deliberately drift, never mad or sad or glad enough to spurn the mainstream. You wake early, think of yourself tenderly, more or less serene as you face the hoodlum parade of half hours laden with halfhearted minutes already wilting under their load of nothingness. Even so they tease you on, not into anything final—would I want it?—but only into the studio where those millions of choices lie. Grains of sand in the desert. Whirl of dust outside the window. Shaping up, imitating persons, tapping. Open the window. I knew you would come.

I knew you would come, milord—isn't that what they called you, Churlton, and dressed you up in velvet and plumes to camouflage your evil charm, your gashed mouth, your luxurious guilt? If you are here to tell me what I am, forget it. For you are nobody. Once you came, an urgent dream, swashing and trampling on my chest. You promised me the moon and the sun and gave neither. Now you are a scarecrow, an obscure monad, a smudge under my paintbrush which is the end of my hand. And I lift it away from the canvas in the nick of time to save your face from crumpling.

It is Sunday morning, Sunday quiet. A truce of noise down in the street floats up like noise itself. I have brought my tray to bed, an old habit. Soon from the other side of this wall come the screams and groans of my lovemaking neighbor. Full of energy and fury, they reach me and my tray just barely. Three years ago, the first time I heard her, and the second and the third, my ears fairly burned. I ate my toast slowly while listening to her in wonder and jumbled thoughts, realizing that I had never screamed like that and wondering if love was even more delicious *chez* my neighbor than what I had always known it to be. High silky screams in my own ears, making me guilty, willy-nilly, of voyeurism. Lying in my bed I am motionless, only my blood moves, doing its thing with discretion, keeping me warm and comfortable.

During the years that I have shared this wall with her and grown used to their punctuality (ten-thirty or eleven Sunday morning and sometimes Saturday, too), I have anticipated these strident, urgent sounds. They have even become a source of all's-right-with-the-world satisfaction to me until now, so accustomed am I, so hardened to the music of her transports that they are no more noticeable than a clock striking the stupid hour. Moreover, I will drop her soon in a change of abode. Goodbye Eros. Goodbye dear neighbor with your strenuous, thrashing, sweating screams, your hard-won ecstasy achieved in a city tower. I leave you on the dissecting table, a tidbit for the hordes of hungry analyzers while I pack up for the move to my next (and permanent) home.

On the way there, and never done with looking back to what was, I see myself, a small being age seven and then eleven sure that she could have it all. To be an artist—wasn't that a welcome command, even with what it implied of square-peg apartness, of wait, watch, work, wonder; of patience? Furnished with plenty of ardor, I saw no problems. It all went together so beautifully. If Lord Churlton did not come to Galesburg, the world would amply make up for him later. And I knew somehow that to replace my box of tinty watercolors, a multitude of means would pitch in to help realize the stirring imperative that possessed me.

My demon, or demons, were twins: though I left to become an artist, the act of going away from there made the command double, the need for physical distance (ah, that faraway dot on my perspective lesson!) being a way to see that should be mine. Go, I said, go forth. Find the round world. But, first, watercolors shared my eyes with maps, in those days of the 1930s a busy pastel geography where boundaries slithered and disappeared as fast as chess pieces in a whirlwind game: built-in obsolescence of nations, states, dukedoms, regions, with their tiny kings and tinier armies. If I was to see King Nicolas in Montenegro, "a mere chaos of mountains," area 3,255 square kilometers, or meet King Zog in Albania, I had better hurry before both vanished. (They did). How could I ever get to Hunza?

At least that one childhood resolve—I would be an artist and live in Paris, France—was realized. To what avail? Half a lifetime is hardly enough for such multifaceted discovery. Paris, a dazzling friend. I never really got to know her, years and years just always on the edge. Perhaps she wore too many pearls that added nothing, really nothing, to the ensemble and only brought out the pallor of her afternoons. The most beautiful city in the world, I said, and mine. Her arrogance, her garbage, her dead-end streets. But the arrogance was cautionary: Do not rock my secrets. If you must touch me don't probe.

My tunnels are locked, my byways lead backward, my slate roofs shelter French artists, poets, and phantoms. And now carbon monoxide is my hard heart.

There are still times when the thought of distant and various unknown places cannot be contemplated without a clot of suffocation. The certainty that I will leave one day, having known so little of place, so few campsites; the unbearable thought that I may have been in the wrong rooms, that another front door, back wood, side street held revelations I never dreamed of. Even as I ride on a train or bus with houses streaming past, it never fails to possess me, this queer longing: how would it be to live behind those two windows, with someone coming home at night? It is essential to know this, how it would be, how I would be.

Not that my familiar spaces are unfurnished. Consider the eventful mirrors, the talking phone, the cozy materials of my craft, the microcosm involving my own tool drawer with its tangled string and orphaned keys. I muse on the roof garden opposite where apologetic little wisps of "trees" sit in rationed earth and concrete tubs, bending to city wind. Who is not charmed by trees on a roof? Knowing that their days are rationed, too. They will not grow great and old but will live briefly as those pale doomed girls lying on sofas, barely able to lift a transparent finger in the whispered gesture of farewell.

An artist is still a Giotto hermit alone in the desert. Removed from the world as he is, the bustle in the distant town (visible in the background), all the splintered spectacle of collective turbulence affects him not at all, he confidently believes with all his heart and soul that it doesn't count, that his desert suffices when inhabited by his own dedicated self. Then of a sudden the sky lights up to flare its message: the world does count, some. We leave enigmas lying around, signs to be read ranging from knife edge to nebula—pleas for guesses. Having posed our riddle we hide behind a tree or a gallery wall and wait for a sign. Even a firefly radiance. We have time enough but we wait rather anxiously for a pair of eyes, any eyes, to flash contact, or a mind, any mind that will take us on with our visual propositions. Meanwhile we plan, tomorrow and next year and next summer. Late reflections ripen, late leaves redden, and uptown a lecturer will speak on "Finding Worth in Human Beings." Of course he will find it. He would not have chosen us otherwise. Assessed, interpreted, pigeonholed, our riddles are in truth consigned to the cold star of solitude—the painter's oldest pal. You have gotten used to it like an infirmity, an extra toe, a jagged scar, a smashed ear. You cover it up, and after a while you can even forget about it for long periods, that is, if you have had your share of shouting and dancing naked

Ardent ringer of doorbells, hungry for other people's memories, an interviewer will eat up my afternoon. What can I say that will end on an upbeat? He thaws me, he draws me out. But why tell him that at twenty-four, choosing a life full of mentors, I rarely ever again shared thought or deed with anyone of my own generation, much less of my very own age? It was like skipping grades Everything around me was colored by attitudes of seriousness based on the weight of experience and erudition. I persuaded myself to adopt them. It was a privilege: benefiting from the already tried, from superior knowledge. Safe from storms. Wanted, too, and needed, cared for. There was room to turn around, room to dance when no one was looking, room to do, to paint, to play, and no limit on solitary thoughts. It seemed enough, it *was* enough.

Only, excitement slowed as the years went by. Quieted. My poets no longer raised their voices in dithyramb and diatribe but sat at copious lunch tables with uncrumpled napkins on their laps, reminiscing about their pasts and deploring the present (ennobled elsewhere) in comfortable voices. Nostalgic they were and not unsatisfied with their violent histories. But all had become ordered, the lunch table swam in harmony, we were splendid.

It could have gone on; it should have gone on if they had not begun to disappear, imperceptibly—the nimble flash of the trapdoor. Or like one of those motley processions in a Fellini movie—poets, actors, musicians, painters, party-goers, waving goodbye, or not waving, certainly not dying conventionally on embroidered pillows, surrounded by grieving family. They departed like phantoms, for the most part. One heard later a whisper to tell you, each time, that you are a little more alone. Gone were Tzara and Arp; then Marcel Duchamp. And Lee Miller, Roland Penrose,

Caresse Crosby; Man Ray, Picasso. And Yves Tanguy, Kay Sage, Julien Levy. My poor Rosine, by the way, shot down at close range one evening, along with lover Jacques, by her deserted husband.

Even the suicides were only half-noticed. At first it grieved me. A betrayal, shocking, a *supercherie.* How unimaginative to retire from combat, to hide, to disintegrate, to take leave of one's senses; above all, to die and leave me in accumulating dust. So that I fled, left the cruel absences to come home to America, where life still breathed. Not clever enough to know that absence is everywhere, and that the same procession thunders along in another movie, the one I am always watching.

Here with the interviewer who has become a shape merely, a dubious presence, I am teased by unspoken questions, and chastened by answers that I try on like glass slippers that don't fit. There is no use telling him about my hours at the computer. It would only confuse. And I would have to say that as these pages piled up it became clearer and clearer to me that I had undertaken something impossible; that no matter how intensely certain moments came back to me as annunciations as memories, they were still only moments. I would never manage to make them represent one life, much less two, even by multiplying them a hundred, a thousand times. And the more I try for some defining picture of my absolutely incomparable life, with its passages from ignorance to revealment, its opposite poles, its complexities, banalities, terrors, euphorias, the more I see that I am not going to bring any order out of its confusions or identify its wavering pictures.

A wedge of late-day sunshine lies on the floorboards between our two chairs. Yellow ocher bright as paint, so far from the faded hues of Tzara's rainbow carpet, far from pearly Paris, far from all those gardens in diverse climes, spaces, soils. Twenty-four Parma violets, planted in red earth, in Sedona, and neatly eaten by morning. Tall corn cross-pollinates with lustful frenzy in Touraine. And Seillans is infested by homeless cats that feed on our chickens, unfazed and amused by their flapping human pursuer.

You can laugh at the past, you cannot laugh at the future, I think. So I look out at that tree in a tub, waving on its roof.

CHAPTER TWELVE

✧

Veils and
Verities

T HERE WASN'T much point in waving back. That tree could not see me behind my curtains, and would be even less likely to now, fifteen years later. My window garden has grown in direct proportion to the little tree's diminishment. For lo!—just as I thought: it isn't there anymore.

The map of milieus must surely change for everyone just as the map of countries must be redrawn—more and more frequently. Here, in this memoir, I have pored over old maps, but how can I draw a present one? Any evocation of a living friend or acquaintance would bring either offense or nausea. Candid camera? One would never dare, on the other hand, even real information would translate to ucuik. Could I mention poet Richard Howard's happy red shoes and the way they leapt onto the platform at the Morgan Library with the same élan as Leonor's taffetas swishing through the Marché de Buci? Wouldn't the reader prefer to hear a word or two about Richard rather than about his shoes? As for Harry Mathews, poet too, who but me would cry when he, with

349

his wine expertise, condemned my preciously saved (too long) Château Margaux to the kitchen sink? Would anyone want to hear, from a profane source, some groping words about avant-garde music as written, sung, and played by Bob Ashley? Or can I put some people in this book just because they're mine?

For there they are, each of them doing what they do, just like me. It has always seemed a real bonus, this way that what we do has of showing, far more nakedly than those long-ago porno photographers in Chicago could dream of, what we are. Our transparence, whether writer or artist, is our prism, our color, our music. So that anyone coming to me comes to someone they know already, having seen X-rays, you might say, of my thought and its bones, all laid out in the pictures, sixty years of them. Until now, when a few words have been made to fill in the lamentable gaps between my English and my hard-won French.

Coming back to my country in 1979 and 1980 after those twenty-eight years in France and resuming my American speech was an event in itself. I had been "away" in the truest sense: living in another country and in its language. For, unlike most Americans abroad, I made my life, while there, with French people, their preoccupations, their lifestyles, their artistic attitudes, and, above all, their language, which had always sounded in my ears like music of a peculiarly sensuous charm—the women's voices, especially, having a fluted roundness, like murmurous birds. Trading *bons mots* and colloquialisms and even ideas in a foreign language was not only fun but most nourishing to my sense of universality. Why, I could live anywhere! I thought, feeling worldly and dynamic. But, as the years drifted by, my fatuity faded. For as the writer Wilhelm Busch said of language, "In order to understand its facial expressions, one needs to have been born and brought up in it." (Not a quote with appeal for the translator. . . .)

Did this word-consciousness prepare me for the return to New York? Were my antennae more receptive when suddenly American words again revealed themselves to me for what they were—or could be? Coming back . . . how intoxicating it all was in this greatest of cities—the turquoise sky, the smell of near seawater, the tall streets! Even the screams of sirens (oh, if only they were!) in the city night, telling me, "We are watching over you. We are your guardian angels. We keep chaos at bay," were like a lullaby.

Floods of words issue from loudspeaking cars, from TVs and radios behind open windows. And my mind leaps back to square one or two, our Galesburg radio station to which I listened with breathless over my ears thin scratch ety pops and buzzes; and, through it all, ah, the voice of my Aunt Lucy, its most reliable Galesburg performer, singing, time and again, "I am the master of my fate, I am the captain of my soul." So that now, when on a heavy summer night, lying in the dark, windows open, I hear New York Harbor's foghorns moaning "My soul, my soul, my soul," it is Aunt Lucy out there in the Atlantic ocean, piloting her fate through shoals of static, superbly unfazed by bergs of watery time.

There is the drugstore I knew, still there. The lunch counter, coffee machine, (different) counterman. I climb onto a stool and order an old favorite:

"I'll have a BT on, with lettuce and mayo."

He looks at me with scorn. "We don't say that any more. It's a BLT."

Humbly, I stand corrected. But these are not the only words that have changed, I soon realize. Clearly, my native language is not made of stone, and if I had problems with *Beowulf* as a hopeless student, I am going to have more of them now with other teachers, other words.

Not problems but delights, as it turned out. Beginning with the BLT a never-ending procession, or rather rap session, of signs and sounds stamped themselves on my days, and helped me to fit into them without attracting too much notice as a has-been. (French teenagers call us oldies *son et lumière*. For them we typify the floodlit châteaux and other architectural monuments and monstrosities of the decrepit past, music added for the tourist.)

What, of course, I had to consider, here and now, was who was doing the talking. And just how much of the BLT world I would need to steer my solitary way through the redoubtable tangle of New York discourse. For even in the geographical areas I would inhabit, between midtown and downtown, there were, are, as many strata of speech as leaves in a croissant. Far from being discouraged, however, or ignoring most of the leaves as tasteless, I found it all exciting and even stimulating. It had always been fun to play with jazzy—I mean cool—language. Mix and match. That sort of thing.

And its sources were everywhere. Street-sign language, taxi language, computer language, the language *out there,* all skeined up with the suffocating dust-storm of media, to which you either succumb or, like a true New Yorker, tolerate, the same way you tolerate pollution, firearms, and politics. You do not rail against this sea of human exaggeration, for you know it would be like spitting into the wind. Besides, there are such marvels to be found, chiefly among the ads, those invitations thinly hiding their menace—indispensable items, presented in unopenable plastic, to nourish, to enrich, and generally to gear up your life with ease and beauty in all things: "Turn your armpits into charmpits."

From where I am, rooted in the city like a tree beside the highway, I wonder at the lure of constant travel, now become a need as urgent as the addict's needle. Higher up I watch the ever-moving stream of clouds that hovers over me, over the purposeful cars. If the clouds collide they leak electricity; when cars collide their passengers leak red blood. "There is no more ignominious way to die," said Max. (For those who are spared it is never too late: "Now enjoy brilliant college courses in your car.")

Sluices open now to negative thought (always at night), I try vainly to stem the tide—of regret? pity? Even frustration can rub off on me in the dark, though it is mostly feeling sorry, so sorry for someone, someones, for

lonely anguish seen in public places, in an airport wash-
room, someone bending over a bowl and whispering in
another language. At John Cage's concert it happened
after the performance was well under way: a swinging
door broke the hush, a woman sidled elaborately into the
theater. A minor irritation. But after several minutes she
was still there tiptoeing up and down the three little steps
that led to her seat. She was, it soon became clear, elsewhere; in all her movements she was totally alone, alone
somewhere hearing the astral sounds called forth by John.

So, each of us there was utterly alone and tumbling in
a siren space away from earthly fundamentals. Only,
instead of leaving emotions behind with other flotsam
such as gravity and disorder, I found myself rolling on a
sea of strong feeling, hopelessly involved with my planet;
sorry for every rent in every fabric, for tormentor and tormented, for lost dogs (cult animal sacrifice in a Brooklyn
garage. The policeman: "They kill babies, too"). Elephants
assassinated in the savannahs, swarmed by flies. Bulls made
fools of by strutting humans. Clubbed snakes, oil-soaked
birds, bears in traps, steel jaws biting through their man-
gled paws . . . and our own hopeless pride and prideful
hope, ingredients in a utopian formula.

Ah, but art—art is pure, art is positive. Wishing to
catch up on the local art scene, I read what comes my way.
Interviews in glossy magazines: "What's great about art
here in New York is you have collectors." Or "You have to
emerge. I hang out with several other emerging artists; we
talk about everything—how to get a show, finding a stu-

dio, or comparing prices." It must be admitted that this preoccupation with economic stability is a commendable wrinkle when remembering the sloggy bohemian head-in-the-clouds painter whose studio had no air-conditioning, and who, often enough, did not even gain enough money to help out the government at tax time.

So much for medial surface, imposing its daily power, and quite fitting in with poet William Merwin's comment "Nothing is real until it can be sold." Yet, it was soon enough clear and reassuring to me that, in its sober moments, there was the language, the one thing that could still be depended on to map the nuances of my interior life as well as the inner one that picked up the mail or the menu. Right now, it is helping me to tap out my souvenirs of yore; to convey this account of wonders (like Max) and woes (like his absence) without too much fretting over its thousand omissions. After all, memory is a habitable word. But it's a down-at-the-heel one if, like me, you see how in a last chapter you have made your rather dramatic and overwrought farewells, and must now admit that you are still hanging around and feel, furthermore, obliged to justify the fact. You think so much has happened in these last fifteen years and yet so quietly has it all occurred that you are not sure it wants to be noted at all.

All you are sure of is that certain beings have disappeared from the earth and that new ones have taken over. There are so many of these, with formulas for everything from birth to death; for our towering sexuality or heartbreaking lack of it, our out-of-body states, and our myriad substitutes for the natural world, so much of nothing and so little of everything—that anyone born in the first years of the twentieth century is as odd and inconsequential as a buttonhook.

However, as any in the foregoing time-spans, these years have brought me their own load of events, of emotions, and especially of people. There are those whose role in life is to be best friends. Not the Boswells, so respectful of their mentors; not the writers of memoirs either. No, these anonymous beings are too far from that. They are best friends. Many are still with me along with the others, too near to be transformed into commentary, too vigorously occupied. They were and are my life, such as it is, here in a New York apartment, where I sit and wait with spidery patience for wingy bits of affection to crash into my web where I immediately swallow them—always still hungry.

Indeed, without the warm glow of certain refound interests that have sustained me, and that may be said to have shown me how to hang on with pleasure, such equanimity might have been elusive. One of these, poetry, has turned out to be for me a vast and enchanting world, a land that has been there all the time, like the stile in the fairy tale that Blunder did not recognize as the wishing gate he had sought all day. To say that this enchanted place is not the world of visual art may seem self-defeating, coming as it does from someone who has spent her life as a painter. Does she now, and in print, relegate that life to a secondary position?

Not at all. For if these late years have brought me closer to poetry—written and spoken poetry—they have also shown me the luxury of an artist's perspective of the crucible where these arts meet and mate to produce plenty of reasons for staying with them. I think again of those long ago years when, hesitating, I had waded into visual art. While my aptitude for drawing was earning my living there was little time left over to pine for poetry. (What's more, the poetry we had been encouraged to read and to admire in my school—those bombastic drum-beat middle-west voices—hardly threatened to lure me away from my paints. They were easy to forget as I moved further and further from that place and that time, so utterly lacking as it was in painted veils and verities.)

Having fled the cruel phenomena of death and disappearance in France, I have since seen the folly of thinking to leave them there, like empty paint tubes. Was the Atlantic ocean going to be big enough to distance us? Did I imagine that a solitary life in America would confer some serene immunity from sorrow? And that my chest would never again tighten at news of another lost friend? Oh no. Oh yes. Because New York is Samarra, appointments have been kept, and though I have not yet been contacted by the odious reaper, he (she?) has been more than punctual in taking away my friends. Johnny Myers, Sylvia Marlowe, Bobby Fizdale, Denise Hare, John Cage, Teeny Duchamp, Vittorio Rieti, Balanchine, Xenia Cage,

Octavio Paz, and Dominique de Menil, so recently. And James Merrill. . . .

Jimmy Merrill. We first met long ago at some lunch, in a late October, after which he walked with me to Park Avenue looking for a taxi. There was a raw wind trying all too successfully to blow away whatever was left of the afternoon and we were glad when our taxis showed up. Then, handing me into the car with the graceful air that I was to know and love later on, he said, "Have a nice Christmas."

But I was still living in Paris and our friendship only began several years later, when I had returned to New York. One evening he read some of his poems before a group of rapt listeners. Including me. That evening brought me up to *now;* it filled my rather arid life with affirmation, the affirmation that only poetry could give to it. Of course, I had known poets, in France and in French. Several of them even wrote poems about my paintings. But what is that, if you can't really read them? Because for all my assiduities in their language, my ears were not ready for the music. For all my comfy belief that I knew French deeply, I was far from total immersion. Here, on home ground, I was now looking at the two faces of language and seeing how they were somehow related, like distant cousins, each of them rather wary of the other yet unable—and unwilling—to deny the kinship. Getting to know Jimmy Merrill I saw the delight that vernacular words gave him, saw how one chosen word from the street would illumine a poem of his as perfectly as the brushwork of William Blake distinguished his manuscripts.

James Merrill knew all about our BLTs and how to play with them, make them appetizing! Listening to him that evening I heard the English language's "facial expressions," along with its music. How dim now seemed that far-off day in Chicago when I walked into Oscar Williams's lamp-lit world!

Jimmy *was* poetry—the palpable, unsparing embodiment of poetry. And he did something more, something that I see reflected in the words and ways of his friends: he made himself available. Far from showing off his erudition, he was delightedly playing with it, just as he played with the world he lived in and felt so splendidly a part of. If a beggar had asked him to take his place with the tin cup while he went for a coffee, Jimmy would have obliged with grace. He just fundamentally loved, and knew how to be loved back. It worried me that he had said in a poem that painting is not one of the highest arts, not way up there with music and poetry. And do you know? I half-believed him, he must be right . . . so under his spell I was! Then the thought: I would change his mind. I would prove . . . But there wasn't time. And, finally, my fragile good luck just couldn't last, any more than the fragile, irreplaceable James Merrill.

I was also finding other kinds of poetry, in other places and other arts.

One Sunday, when I was spending winter weeks in Key West, I sat in a room with an unusually thick carpet and a grand piano. These were in a house perched on thin wooden legs like a wading bird and set on a little-known Florida key with water all around. Open on the piano was a sheet of music: John Cage, *Sonatas and Interludes.* Amazing! A John Cage score on a not-quite-desert island! It was a dream, it could only be. . . . Before the windows and out in the ocean lay several tinier islands sprouting mangroves. I thought then, how would it be if the sonatas, or the interludes, were played simultaneously on all those little islands and beamed to us in the middle? It was an idea John would have had, a "chance operation" to delight his avant-garde heart. John? . . . I miss our chess games, the funny stories that had to do with amazement, the macrobiotic dinners and John's own baked bread. This bread, incidentally, became famous when the *New York Times* published his recipe, remarkable for the inclusion of some moldy vegetables, which, of course, provided the necessary yeast. But oh my! The great *Times* could never bring itself to print something *moldy,* and discreetly edited out the nasty stuff. Result: a flurry of baffled if not downright furious calls to the *Times* from the many ladies whose John Cage breads were pancake-flat. Was this another avant-garde joke? they demanded to know. John laughed, softly. It had nothing to do with him. Nothing to do with his music, his mesostics, his chess moves, his prepared instruments. I can feel him out there now, in some cosmological garden, wrapping his astral piano around heaven's sounds and silences, preparing our next music, so far away from New York City, so far from us all.

"But I am still here!" one cries triumphantly. (An inadvertent reaction to obituaries.) In truth, the triumph is dubious. Mocking. Freakish. Because the question looms: Why am I? Why *still* here? Is there yet some essence to extrude, something I must deliver myself of, a definitive brushstroke—or turn up my eyes and beg for? I, the child of a mother and a father, not the widow of a man, am asking for simple answers, not assurances. Of course, these questions are to be kept to myself. I have met no other person who will accept reflections of this kind. The mere subject of disappearance, of *cessation,* insults the dialogue like a blasphemy. Poets can write of dying, and do so rather often, to the throat-tightening appreciation of their readers. The rest of us are not permitted to even hint at death, much less mention its imminence—as tasteless a subject as bodily needs. Embarrassment, denial.

In this sedate apartment that in 1981 became my home I was fired with positivity. The place had to be immediately "bombed out," torn up and converted. To make up for lost time. Here on these walls I tacked my (by now) lily canvases; here I painted—and paint—what my mind and heart tell me my art should be. And, like everyone, I need more time, another life. More time even to wind these ruminations down to a tight ball of a book—even if made of disjointed fragments like my unperforming bones that caused the broken arms legs ankles and elbows scattered

through my years; like the phantoms of my little dogs who
occupied such a big place in them; and like my secret
friends who, in order to be secret, must remain back
there in their secret places.

Yet all the time the sieve is leaking, filtering me out: fantasies diluting facts. Creeping into bed, I push and pull
parts of myself around until I'm in the position I think I
want. But it's the moment when the light is turned off
that counts. It's dark then. I am quite alone. What am I
waiting for? Do I really want to sleep? Hibernate? I roll
over with eyes shut, as if it mattered. Why shut them?
What is going to happen? Why don't I just *stay up?* All the
time rummaging away, dragging my life all out like *bro-*
cante, or frayed vintage clothing once glorious, but who
would know that, to look at it now? How can I be sure
here in the dark about what to throw away? All the time
knowing that it won't make any difference, that my decid-
ing is clumsy and vain. All trains do not stop in Galesburg
as they once did. Or did they? The Chicago gangster has
joined the movie myths if he ever was there. I can still see
washboard roads in Sedona . . . if only they will stop shimmering in the heat. New-agers negotiate them now, and,
indeed, why not? Let them deal with the developers and
the tarantulas. If they have not sat among junipers, or
heard the dust's whisper, they have at least felt the land's
agelessness. Let the rue des Saints-Pères choke brown
with carbon fumes, a silted stream carrying debris. Others

turn pale there now. Let the sound barrier shatter our innocent Touraine countryside as another saint topples from cathedral spire, gentle victim of war games and dominion. What is a stone saint, after all, when rivers and sewers everywhere run red with sacrifice—to what? The black space around my bed is laden with collapse, hazy now, losing outline.

Meanwhile, minutes fly by like pollen. A dry gust from the window cups me like a seed and I take root, far away, in some dreamy constellation, until the first gray of four a.m. brings me home. Finally morning, and then afternoon. They are both undeniably seductive: green light strikes through the grape ivy and the euphorbia in the window, to prove there is still a green world, the one we have forgotten and will surely find again; and, of course, there is the promise. Just that: the promise. By evening the pall has lifted. Everything waits, radiant. Life is okay.

L'avenir

Acknowledgments

MY GRATITUDE goes first to the poetry world that I found on my return to New York after many years in France. My great good luck was to know James Merrill and through him to meet the many other poets who all together and all unknowingly sparked my wish to write this book.

Of these Richard Howard has my warmest thanks for his constant support. His reading of my various efforts, his always incontrovertible suggestions, and his recommendations on my behalf have been, and are, invaluable.

I thank you most especially, Jill Bialosky, for your enthusiasm and belief in this work; for securing it, and watching over it like a devoted and gifted gardener all the way to its eclosion. May it prove worthy.

My sincere thanks to Drake Bennett, the editor of these pages, who with his unerring sang froid has managed to tame some of their wilder extravagances, thus tacitly reminding me that poetic license is for poets and not for memoirists.

I thank painter Sam Francis, even though he is gone, who published some of these chapters fifteen years ago in a book we called *Birthday*.

To Adrienne Rich for her close reading of that book and her perceptive comments for this one, my grateful thanks.

And to Mimi Johnson, my niece, go my fondest thanks for her ever-ready help in getting much of my scribbling in readable typed form, for helping to remember shared events, and for her patience in guiding me through the thickets of computerland.

Above all, I thank everyone mentioned in this book—except the obvious villains—for existing.

Index